1

2

Isa's Daughter

Catherine M Byrne

Fireflash Publishing
Bagend, Standstill, Watten
Caithness

Cover design by http://www.selfpubbookcovers.com/

Acknowledgements

I wish to thank the following people for their help in getting this book ready for publication.

For pre-reading, commenting and giving editorial and constructive criticism where necessary.

Margaret MacKay, Margaret Wood and Sheona Campbell.

Chapter One

'You can't get married to the minister.' A horrified Annie Reid faced her mother.

Isa wiped rough, red hands on her apron. 'Why not?' Her brown eyes, so like Annie's own, grew darker as she stared at her daughter.

Annie knew that look, the look that said no amount of argument would change Isa's mind. That knowledge, however, did nothing to deter Annie. 'How could you put another man in Dad's place?'

'I'll never forget your father, but he's gone. I've been lonely. In any case it's hard enough for Bel to feed herself let alone us as well.'

'So we're leaving Scartongarth? Dad might have been heir to the farm. Why should Bel have it?' Annie set her hand against the lime-washed wall which held the faded framed photograph of her grandparents on their wedding day.

Isa gave a pained sigh. 'Look, Annie, there was no will. I imagine it should have been your cousin Jimmy's, but he doesn't want it. His sister does.'

'But you said we might have a claim…'

Isa held up her hand. 'I said it was a possibility only. I didn't know then how Bel felt about the place and I won't fight her for it. She's worked hard to keep it going with the war and all.'

'Then why did we come back? Was it for him, the Reverend Charleston?'

'Of course not. There was nothing left for us in Canada. You know that.'

The arguments died on Annie's lips. She, too, had been captivated by Bel's gentle charm and had no real desire to take the croft from her. However, as far as her mother's plans were concerned, she had to use all the ammunition she could think of. 'So we'll be moving into the manse? You who never had time for religion.'

Isa sighed. 'It's a fine big house and Donald has his stipend. We'll be comfortable.'

'Is that why you're getting wed, so we won't starve?'

'No. I like Donald a lot and he's a good man. You'll be welcome until you decide your future. You're clever, Annie, you could go back to school, maybe get a job in an office.'

Annie considered this for a minute. Perhaps her mother marrying the minister wasn't such a bad idea after all. 'Would he pay for me to go to college?'

'You're *my* daughter. I wouldn't expect him to even if he could afford it.' Two pink dots appeared on Isa's cheeks, a sign that her patience was wearing thin.

Annie cocked her head. 'Then how will I ever get a better education?'

Isa took an inward rush of breath. 'It'll not be with Donald's money, I'll tell you that now.' She turned her back and, grabbing a duster from the rod across the mantelpiece, began to rub at the range with small, quick movements.

Annie pursed her mouth and stared at the floor where the flagstones shone with Isa's regular polishing.

'Maybe, maybe if I had a word with Mr Dick...' Isa twisted around to face her daughter.

'Mr Dick – the schoolteacher?'

'He could give you some learning at nights. I could do a bit of washing, a bit of cleaning for him. If you want an education we'll find a way to make it happen.' Isa spoke with the grim determination that had taken them through all the hardships of their lives.

Annie's mood lifted. Perhaps, after all, there was a chance of her doing better than ending up a herring gutter or a servant or worse still, having to marry to keep food on the table and become like the island women she saw around her, producing bairns and slaving from dawn to dusk in order to live another week.

'I still won't live with you and the minister,' she muttered.

'Bel would never turn you out, but see how you get on with Mr Dick. Right now I want you to go to Lottie's shop. I need to make some bere scones for tea.'

Annie snorted. 'I'd best go get my coat then.' She moved sideways around the table in the middle of the floor. To go anywhere in this room she had to move sideways. Against one wall sat a pinewood dresser which held the crockery, on another was a bed in a recess with a door on either side, one leading to the passageway, the other to a steep staircase. On the third wall was the window with a sideboard in front, on the fourth was an iron stove and a mantelpiece with a rod for drying clothes. It was all so different from the roomy space where they had lived in Canada until a few weeks ago.

Annie climbed up to her room beneath the rafters, sat down on her makeshift bed with the large sack of chaff for a mattress that Bel called a caff seck and put her head in her hands. In spite of her words, she liked Donald Charleston and he would be good to her mother. She had seen how quickly the rounded curves of Isa's body had turned to angles and the strands of white had streaked her coal-black hair after the Great War took her

9

husband. Then the drought had devastated the land. Over the years, Annie watched her mother's beauty fade as they struggled against poverty. Annie Reid hungered for more. She had thought something better would be waiting for them in the place her parents referred to as 'home,' but the war had devastated Britain, nowhere more than the islands. Without an education, a woman had few options.

From beneath her pillow she pulled out the magazines she had bought to pass the long hours on the journey to Scotland. In the meagre slice of day entering through the skylight, she studied the photos of grand ladies, fine carriages and city streets. 'One day,' she said, and slapped the magazine closed.

Annie knew she was beautiful. Even if the pock-marked mirror on the passage wall hadn't told her, the way men's eyes followed her did. No, she was not going to settle for becoming a mere crofter-fisherman's wife or a skivvy for some rich family.

She didn't want lessons from Mr Dick with his big belly and bulbous nose and the veins that stood out on the backs of his hands like fat worms. The young teacher, the one who taught the first year pupils, he was a different matter. Even his name had an exotic ring to it. Alexander Garcia's black hair was short and he shaved most days, not like the young men of the island who, it appeared, only shaved once a week. But it was his eyes that really got her: dark, intense, burning with a fire that matched her own. From the first time she'd seen him, she'd been wondering how to get his attention. Unwittingly, her mother had given her the excuse.

'Where are you, lass?' Isa's voice came from below.

'Coming, Ma.' Annie stood up and lifted the coat which doubled as a blanket. She was taller than the average woman and could only stand upright where the beams met in the middle to form the roof.

Downstairs her eyes fell on the big pot on the range. Her stomach clawed for a good feed. She lifted the lid. 'Is there anything to eat other than porridge?' She had never been fond of the grey, gooey sludge and since it had become their staple diet she detested it.

'There's a crust of bread in the larder and some cheese.' Isa went to the jar on the mantel and took out some copper coins. 'See if Lottie's got any flour, then go and collect the eggs.'

Outside, a sharp breeze blew in from the Pentland Firth lifting the strands of hair that flew round her face. She never tied her hair in a knot or plaited it the way the local women did.

Sucking in the sea-salt air, she looked around. After the big, bright skies and miles of prairie she had grown up with, it would take time to get used to the flat expanse of Raumsey with its one-storeyed, stone-built cottages, miles of ocean beyond, and a sky that was seldom free of clouds.

Sloping down from the shingle path, behind the hummocks of waving grass, the pebbles on the beach rattled as angry breakers smashed over them. For seventeen years she had grown up in Alberta and had never seen the ocean. Now she embraced its wildness; it was the one thing that fascinated her about this island. If only her dad were with them now, he would have built a boat for the fishing and turned Scartongarth back into the success it once was. Her brother Dan, who had remained in Canada, would come to help them run it, she would go to university, and her mam would not be marrying the minister.

Chapter Two

In order to explore the island and not being allowed to ride the work horse, Annie opted to use a rusting bicycle which she found at the back of the barn. She hitched up her skirts and jolted up the track which led to the metalled road. Bel's collie dog, Poppy, ran after her, barking and snapping at the wheels. 'Give it up, ya silly mutt,' she shouted, laughing at his antics. Half way along the road he gave up, but stood with his ruff raised, watching her.

Lottie's shop was situated at the crossroads among the small clutch of houses known as 'the village' The school and schoolhouse sat at one end of the road, at the other, the manse and kirk.

A bell jangled above Annie's head as she entered. She was met by a blast of stale air, scented by the dried fish hanging along one wall and something even less pleasant. Her eyes were drawn downwards. A black and white dog with clouded eyes and matted hair lay on a folded blanket by the door. He lifted his head to give a hoarse bark.

Annie bent to fondle his ears. 'Poor old boy,' she whispered. Milky eyes turned towards her. The tail thumped a few times.

In the window, a bluebottle, which had managed to avoid a sticky flypaper dotted with the corpses of its mates, buzzed and threw itself persistently against the salt-encrusted pane.

Middle-aged and thin with springy red hair, bad teeth and pale, sad eyes, the woman behind the counter nodded at her. 'Annie is it not? What can I get ye?'

Annie straightened up and looked around. On the back wall next to an empty shelf was a faded poster declaring that 2lbs of sugar a month was allowed per person. Although there were only a handful of women carrying shopping bags or baskets in the shop, the space seemed crowded. All eyes were turned towards her. On her short time on the island, she had already met many of the population, and even those she hadn't, knew who she was. 'They were here before me.' She indicated the others.

'Ach, don't mind them. They only come in for a blether,' said the woman with the red hair. She held out her hand. 'I'm Constance. Lottie's my mother. She's no so fit now. Hardly ever gets out of bed.'

'How are ye settling down?' The speaker was dressed similarly to most of the island women, a roughly-woven square of cloth on her head and tied under her chin, an apron made of sackcloth over her clothes, and work boots on her feet. 'Raumsey'll be a big change after Canada.'

There was a communal murmur of 'ayes' and nodding heads. 'Tell Isa we're fair glad she's back. But she'll find the island a much sadder place than when she left. As well as them that was lost in the war, the young yins are leaving to work wi' the herring an' they're no coming back.'

'Ah, but I aye say,' another interrupted her. 'There'll come a day when the island'll thrive again. New hearts'll beat in old houses. But I'll no be around to see it.'

13

'Aye, I'll tell my mam.' Obviously the news of her mother's hasty decision to marry had not yet reached the ears of the population. 'My mam wants a poke o' flour.' Annie held out a ha'penny.

'I'm sorry, lass. I'm out of flour. It's still hard to get supplies, although things are starting to be a wee bit better. I got a box of tea in yesterday. Would ye like some tea?'

'I think we've enough tea.' The bell above the door tinkled. Annie turned and the breath stuck in her throat. Before her stood Alexander Garcia.

'Good morning ladies.' He smiled at the assembled company. Then his eyes fell on her and lit up. 'Annie, isn't it?' He raised his eyebrows and his smile broadened.

'Yes.' Her blood grew hot and she tore her gaze away. 'I'm in a hurry.' She dropped her head, marched past him and out of the door, mounted her bike and pedalled, her feet pumping, dust and small stones from the road spraying from beneath the wheels. She passed wide-eyed, island women who shook their heads and tutted in disapproval.

'Faigs, that lassie'll cause a calamity yet, mark my words,' said one, loud enough for her to hear. Annie smirked to herself as she turned the bike down the road towards home. Poppy raced towards her and snapped at the wheels narrowly missing her ankles.

She laid the bike down on the grass, left Poppy attacking the still spinning wheels and went to the side of the cottage to the stone seat her father had described so well. What was wrong with her? Why did that young man affect her this way?

'There was a couple of rabbits in the trap.' A sudden voice made her jump. She had not heard her cousin approach.

14

Bel, pale hair hanging in two thin pleats that almost reached her waist, held up a lumpy sack.

'Thank goodness.' Annie was sick of the taste of fish and sicker still of bread, soaked in milk or mashed with potatoes.

Bel wiped her brow with her free hand, lowered herself onto the seat, leaned back and closed her eyes. 'Since Jimmy left, there's no enough hours in the day.'

Annie felt a stab of guilt. She knew she could do more to help. Her mother had been right. It was Bel Reid who kept this place going.

'Are you happy, Bel? Running Scartongarth on your own?' Annie asked.

Bel gave a short laugh. 'What else is there for me? Things'll get better now the war is over, but I need to marry. It takes a man to fish and do the heavy field work.'

'Have you got your eye on a lad?'

Bel turned slightly pink. 'Nick Sinclair. Ye *have* met him.'

'Ah.' Annie remembered the bonny lad with the corn coloured hair and cleft in his chin. It had been no more than a quick introduction, but Bel had gone all coy.

'Don't you want something better from life?' asked Annie.

'Aunt Chrissie wants me to come over, live with her, but life is no easier on the mainland. I'd need to be a herring gutter or go into service, but I love the land. Anyway, I could never leave Scartongarth. It's where my mam and dad lived and died, and I feel they're still here.' Her pale eyes took on a faraway look. 'If I went, it would be like leaving them behind.'

Annie thought that was daft, but didn't say so. 'Did you know my mam's getting married?'

Bel's head snapped around, her eyes opened wide, her lip twitched. 'To the minister? They've been right

15

friendly sure enough. Who'd have believed it?' She sounded pleased which irritated Annie. She had expected at least a modicum of outrage.

'But it's so sudden. We've only been back a few weeks.'

'Aye, well, they kent each other before, so I'm told, and money's tight. He'll be able to support the both of ye.'

'Do you think that's it? That's why she's doing it?' Maybe Isa didn't love the minister after all. Annie hated the idea of her mother marrying in haste because of their situation. 'Maybe if I got a job on the mainland, I could send you money, you and Mam, then she wouldn't need to marry.' She said this half-heartedly. The idea of going to college had taken hold; it was what she wanted even if it meant giving Isa her blessing, which she was loathe to do.

Bel shook her head. 'There's no point dreaming, Annie. There's no enough jobs for the men who came back from the war. What hope does a lassie from the islands have? Anyway, with yer looks ye'll be married soon yerself, then yer job'll be bringing up the bairns and helping yer man. Auntie Isa would likely marry the minister anyway, she seems right fond of him and she's a bonny woman.'

Annie gave a snort. '*I'll* no be getting married, not unless he's as rich as a lord, lives in a mansion and has servants.' But as she spoke, her thoughts flew to Alexander Garcia and her words carried no conviction at all.

Bel gave a small smile. 'Yer head's in the clouds, Annie. Ach I've sat here long enough. I need to get on. Are ye coming?'

'I'll be in a while. Tell Ma there's no flour.'

Annie watched the other girl rise, watched her thin form unfold itself and marvelled at how gracefully her

16

cousin moved, even dressed in work clothes with her feet bare. She could imagine Bel wearing a fine gown with her hair cut in a fashionable bob. She could see her on the arm of a city gent with Brylcreemed hair and a waistcoat, but strange as it seemed to Annie, Bel had no such aspirations.

Then her thoughts spun back to Alexander Garcia, how her heart had raced at the sight of him. What had Bel said about Isa being right fond of the minister? Surely her mother couldn't have similar feelings at her age? It was improper. But Annie, too, had seen the way Isa's eyes lit up when the Reverend Charleston came into the room, seen the way *his* face softened and his fingers tightened on the brim of his hat, but she had not understood the implications until now.

Above her seabirds yelped and from the rocks seals cried like lost souls. In the distance the herring fleet ploughed its way northwards, and a heavy barge-like vessel sailing south passed them by. Looking around the fields and the heather-clad moor dotted with cottages and outhouses, Annie stretched, easing the kinks out of her back. Once more she thought about her father sitting here on this same seat, enjoying this same view, longing for it again, but never managing the journey back home.

Suddenly islanders appeared in their doorways, women in the fields stood upright, even the children came out of school and hung over schoolyard wall, all attention riveted on the sea. The herring fleet had gone, but the larger vessel was sailing towards the island.

'It's *The Endeavour*.' Bel was beside her once again, her voice high with excitement.

'What?' Annie asked.

'Part of the fleet of shops from Kirkwall. We didn't expect them for a while; they can't get the supplies since the war.' She ran into the house yelling, '*The Endeavour*... Auntie Isa, *The Endeavour*'s coming.'

17

Isa appeared holding a glass jar, coins rattling inside. 'Oh, it's been so long. Do we have any eggs to sell? I'll run and check the nests. Is there herring to spare?' Isa's eyes shone. She turned to her daughter. 'Remember I told you about the floating shops? How I used to work in the warehouses back in Kirkwall? They stopped because of the war, but they've come back – they've actually come back.'

'There's still some herring in this firkin.' Bel lifted the lid and looked into the small barrel. 'We can maybe change some for a piece of meat. I've a couple of hanks of wool spun and ready.' She raced into the house to return with a bag of wool.

Already the islanders were pouring past Scartongarth towards the harbour, baskets on their arms, sacks slung over their shoulders.

'Come on Annie.' Bel grabbed the other girl's hand. 'They've got all sorts of stuff. Hurry.'

The three women joined the crowd already gathering on the beach where the atmosphere was charged with a sense of excitement. A tall thin girl with straggly, colourless hair joined them and slipped her arm through Bel's.

'Tess, hello.' Bel turned to Annie. 'My best friend, Tess. Tess, this is my cousin Annie from Canada.'

'Aye, I heard about ye.' Tess was not a pretty girl. Her nose was too big and her eyes too close together. When she smiled her teeth looked enormous, but she oozed affability and Annie liked her immediately.

'Isn't it grand? Things are getting back to normal after that awful war.' Her eyes met Annie's. 'My brother was badly hurt, but at least we have him home.'

Her smiling mouth became serious, but only for a minute. 'My, I can hardly believe the shops are back!' A tear trickled down her cheek and she dashed it away.

The large vessel anchored in the bay and a small boat was lowered into the water. After a few moments it sailed towards the shore.

'Doesn't the shop come right in?' Annie asked, eager to be on board.

'The water's too shallow.' Tess nudged Bel. 'There's Nick.'

'Where?' Annie looked around. Several men were pulling their boats into the water.

As she spoke a young man turned, caught sight of them and beckoned. 'Come away,' he shouted. 'I'll take ye out.'

Bel's face turned pink. 'That's Nick,' she whispered.

Isa laughed. 'He's a bonny man.' And the four women made their way over the sandy beach.

'Bel, how are ye?' Nick held his hand towards her as they neared, then his eyes slid to Annie. 'Ye're the cousin from Canada. I'm right glad to meet ye again.' His full lips parted to show white, even teeth, not yet stained by the ravages of smoking and chewing tobacco. Eyes the colour of polished steel met hers. He grasped her hand and held it too tightly for too long. Then he indicated the boat with his head. 'I'll help ye aboard, ladies.' When he turned, his navy gansey stretched over the ripple of muscle.

'There'll no be the wealth of goods we had before the war,' said Bel as they were helped aboard the larger vessel, but Annie didn't care. To her this was a novelty, another experience to be enjoyed. Isa followed them up the rope ladder, looking flushed and happy.

Once aboard the large vessel, Isa immediately started a conversation with the boatman, asking about people from Kirkwall, giving gasps as she digested news about long-ago friends.

'Come on,' said Tess grabbing Annie's arm, 'Leave yer ma to her blethering and I'll show ye the rest of the boat.'

With Bel leading, the girls followed in single file down the centre aisle past the bulkheads and the shelves of scant groceries. She steadied herself against the swell by holding on to the bars of wood nailed along the shelf fronts to stop the goods tumbling off in heavy seas. It was over-warm inside the shop and the smell of old wood, tar, dried fish and oatmeal permeated the air.

Mid-ship they edged their way around a large weighing machine and sacks of flour, oatmeal, bran, and corn which were built up along the sides.

At last they reached the stern and the drapery. Shoes, boots, rolls of waxed cloth, oilskins, overalls and other items of clothing sat out on a bench, as well as on barred shelves and hanging on lines overhead.

Bel fingered a pale piece of material. 'This would make a bonny frock,' she said, her voice almost a whisper.

'Did ye know,' said Tess, 'there's a dance tomorrow night, the first one since the war?'

'I heard.' Bel clasped her hands. 'I need something new. My clothes are tight and too small. But ye've got some bonny things, Annie.'

At that moment Isa joined them. She fingered a piece of brocade, gazing at it for too long.

'It would make a fine wedding dress,' said Bel, almost as if it were a thought inadvertently spoken aloud. Her face immediately flushed.

'Aye, it would,' said Isa.

'Wedding dress? Are ye getting wed, Mrs Reid?' Tess's small eyes became circles of surprise. 'I heard ye were friendly with the minister. *Surely* it's no him.'

'And why shouldn't it be him?' asked Isa.

Tess wrinkled her nose. 'He's a *minister*. Can't imagine him being wed. Sorry Mrs Reid.'

20

Annoyed, Annie sighed. The news would be all over the island by tomorrow.

'Everyone will know soon enough,' said Isa, as if reading her daughter's thoughts. 'But there'll be no wedding dress. It'll be a quiet affair.' She looked at the coppers in her hand. 'I need a pair of boots. Mine are letting in.'

Bel ran her fingers over the material she liked. 'Aye. I'll make do as well.'

'We can make something of mine down for you,' said Annie, 'Although I've little fit for a dance.'

'Dance?' Isa asked.

'Aye,' said Tess. 'Saturday night.'

'In that case, Bel, you must have a new dress.' Isa held the coppers towards her niece.

'But your boots?' said Annie.

'They'll do a season yet. I mind how it was to be young and bonny and no have a thing to wear. Go on take it.'

Bel looked at Annie as if seeking approval. Annie nodded. She would have loved a bit of material herself, but she'd seen how scant Bel's wardrobe was and doubted the lass had had anything other than cast-offs for many a year. If anyone deserved it, it was Bel. 'Take it, please.'

With their meagre purchases clutched in their hands, Bel, Isa, Tess and Annie sat in the small ferry boat heading back to Raumsey. Once they approached the shore, Nick laid down the oars and leapt over the side, expertly catching an incoming wave and running with the yole up onto the beach. As the wave retreated and the boat settled on the sand, he held out his hand to help Isa with her shopping.

'Thank you, Nick,' she said, as he turned his attention to Annie.

'Come with Bel to the dance tomorrow night.' His fingers closed over hers, a little too tightly and he pulled her

21

close so that she had to lean against him before jumping onto the sand.

Tess had already leapt out without help. Annie wondered if she was imagining it, but she could sense a distinct coolness between her and Nick.

Last of all, he helped Bel. 'We did want to have a box social, but, ye know...' He shrugged his shoulders.

Annie was immediately interested. 'A box social?'

'Aye, the girls make up a box of baking and handcrafts to prove what a good wife they'll make, then the lads bid for them. If a lad wins the bid, that lass is his partner for the night,' explained Isa. 'They were such good fun.'

'Since a few of the lads didn't make it through the war, we thought it wouldn't be fitting,' said Tess.

'You're maybe right,' agreed Isa. 'But I'm glad you're having the dance.'

'He's a good looking lad,' whispered Annie as they walked back towards the cottage. 'And you want to marry him?'

'Aye, I do.' Bel gave a little skip as she spoke.

'I'll have to get home,' said Tess quickly. 'It was nice meeting ye, Annie and Mrs Reid.'

Annie remembered the way Nick's eyes had trapped hers, remembered his coolness towards Tess, and made a note to ask Tess about it at a later time.

As they walked back to the croft, Isa said, 'Bel, what do you think of me getting wed again? Do you think it's too soon?'

Bel shook her head. 'The manse is a fine house. All these big rooms are wasted on one man. I mean, it's no as if ye'll be sharing a bed. It'll just be for the security and a bit of company like.'

Isa lifted her dark brown eyes, still as bright as a young girl's, and a little smile flirted with the corners of her mouth.

Chapter Three

Tess trailed up the road. The cottage where she lived with her father and brother stood before her, but held little welcome. She heard the raised voices before she reached the door.

'Bloody useless that's what ye are. I've slaved all my life for what? A pair of imbeciles. Daughter with a face like a horse and a son who can hardly lift a hand to help. And me crippled. In my prime I wouldn't see the pair of ye in my way!'

The door opened and her brother burst out as fast as his damaged leg would let him. He was about to push his way past Tess when she caught his arm. 'Don't let him get to ye, Magnus.'

Magnus shook his head. 'I didn't sleep well last night. It's no my fault if the dreams won't leave me in peace.'

'Of course it's no.' She looked at the cottage. It was as if a cold dark shadow hung about the place, had done ever since her mother died. 'I'll go in and take all his girning.'

Something about her very appearance seemed to anger her father further. Rubbing his painful hands together, he looked up when she entered. 'Where the hell have you been?' he thundered.

'Am I no allowed some time off from *you*,' she snapped. 'I tell you, Father, if I get word of a job I'll be out of here and who's going to be your skivvy then?'

'Skivvy?' His eyes bulged and his twisted hands pushed down on the arms of his chair. 'For all the work you do round here, ye might as well be gone. Get out of my sight.'

Ignoring him, Tess cut three slices of ham from the smoked haunch hanging from the rafters above the stove, slapped them on a plate and, along with bread and lard, set it on the table. She went to the door and called for her brother, then poured out cups of milk.

'What's this rubbish?' said her father.

'Eat it or leave it,' replied Tess, cutting his ham into small pieces. 'It's all one to me. How my poor mother put up with ye all those years I'll never know.'

'Don't bring yer mother's name into yer foul mouth.' He painfully took his seat at the table and glared at her. 'By, if I was fit I'd lash yer sorry backside.'

Neither of his children answered him as he began to shovel the food into his mouth, using the fork like a spoon.

The following day was Saturday and Annie was wakened as usual by the rooster greeting the morning. Outside the cow bellowed, the dog barked, chickens clucked and the day had begun. Annie eased her arms from under the covers and stretched. She rose, shivered slightly in the morning chill, pulled her shawl around her shoulders and went downstairs, her bare feet padding carefully on the wooden stairs. The kitchen was already muggy with heat from the iron stove.

Isa, fully dressed, her hair loose around her shoulders, her eyes still heavy from sleep, turned from stirring the porridge. The box-bed where Bel spent her nights lay empty and unmade. The curtain that hid it from view was pulled to one side.

'*She's* at the milking.' Isa turned back to the stove and her stirring and the words hung in the air like an accusation.

25

'You should have called me.' Annie took down the tea-caddy, spooned three teaspoons of the black leaves into the pot and checked the kettle. It was hot enough. She poured the water on the tea leaves.

'I don't want porridge,' she said.

'There's a heel of bread left.' Isa continued her stirring. 'And some lard. Then go and meet the boats, could you, love? Maybe someone will be kind enough to give us a fry of fish.'

Annie smiled at her mother's words. Of course she would return with fish. The fishermen were always ready to share the catch with women living alone, especially the young men, eager to impress the lassies with their skill. It had always been so and the fiercely proud Isa had never seen it as charity. She, in return, was willing to wash, sew or cook for any man if his wife was ill or confined.

The door opened and Bel came in with a bucket full of frothy milk and the warm smell spread through the kitchen. Isa scooped some porridge into two bowls and poured the rest into a drawer lined with greased paper, where it was left to cool and set. Bel filled a jug from the milk bucket on the floor, filled a cup and placed it before Annie. 'Milk's still warm. Dip yer bread in that. Won't taste so stale then.' Three cats and the dog had followed her in and now sat expectantly around the table, a small puddle of drool already forming beneath Poppy's nose.

Annie smiled her thanks. 'I'll do a baking later,' she promised, warmed by the love that surrounded her in that small room.

Dressed and washed with her hair brushed and falling around her shoulder in soft waves, Annie cycled to the harbour. It was a fine day with an unusual warmth in the air for the time of year. She took her time and waved to anyone she passed, those working in the fields or strolling up the road, and they waved in return. The air was full of promise.

Two women, shawls covering their heads and shoulders and wearing sackcloth aprons and heavy work boots, were thinning turnips in the field to her right. They looked up and rested their hoes in the ground as she passed.

'Hear yer mam's marryan' the meenister,' one shouted.

So the news was out.

'Yes, she is,' Annie called back to them.

The women looked knowingly at each other, and Annie guessed that Isa and the Reverend Donald Charleston were hot on the lips of the residents of Raumsey Island.

It was still early and only a few yoles dotted the distance. She checked the position of the sun. The fishermen would not return for some time yet.

She left the bike and walked along the cliff edge to where she knew there was a secluded bay, seldom visited by the locals. Her booted feet crunched on broken shells dropped by birds. Straggly heather scratched her ankles. Whenever she could manage, she liked to sit at the shore in the quiet and listen to the seals and the birds and the calming, rushing sound of the waves. This was her time of reflection, her time to think about her father and imagine him here beside her, telling her legends of the sea and of the struggles of her forefathers.

Finally she reached Laries Goe and half walked half slid down the steep grassy path to the beach. She found a suitable boulder on which to sit and removed her boots. Pushing her feet into the warm sand, she wriggled her toes and rubbed her chaffed ankles. She would perhaps be better going barefoot while weather permitted. as did most of the young islanders, she thought.

Slightly irritated, she realised someone else was already here, standing a little way off, his head bent as he baited the hook on his fishing rod. He took a few steps nearer the sea and, as if sensing her eyes upon him, he turned.

Alexander Garcia. Annie's heart leapt and raced.

A smile spread across his face and he changed direction, walking up to stand directly in front of her. His shadow fell across her, blocking the sun.

'Hello, Annie,' he said in his deep voice. 'What brings you down here?'

'Sometimes I just like to sit at the shore.' She gave him her best smile. 'Makes me feel close to my dad. He loved Raumsey. He always wanted to come back.' She bit her lip and her eyes turned to where she was poking the sand with her bare foot.

'He was killed in the war wasn't he? I was in France for a while myself.' He gave a bitter laugh. 'I was one of the lucky ones. Do you miss Canada?'

She shrugged. 'In a way. I never saw the sea, but I like it. It's as if it was waiting for me here.' She raised her eyes, trapping his, and was warmed by the compassion in them. Up close, Alexander was even more handsome than she thought. But older too. Small lines radiated from the edges of his eyes and the beginning of grey peppered his temples.

'My mother's marrying the minister, did you know?' Why did she say that? It had burst out without conscious thought.

'So I heard. He's a fine man. He'll be good to her.'

Annie wrinkled her nose. 'I know they'll be happy and she deserves it… it's just…' her voice faded away.

Alexander set his hand on her shoulder and squeezed gently.

She felt the weight of it, the warmth. He smelt of soap. Not the harsh carbolic the islanders used, but something softer, more fragrant. Tears filled her eyes and she did nothing to hide them.

'I don't know what'll become of me. I don't want to be a herring gutter or go into service. I was good at my lessons. I finished the basics, but I wanted to go further. It was hard in Canada. We were miles from school and we were often cut off in winter. I think I could have worked in an office or been a teacher. I help Bel run the croft for now, but when she gets married, she'll not want me around.' She stopped when she realised she was babbling and she trapped her lip between her teeth, suddenly wishing he would go away and stop her feeling things she did not understand.

'Couldn't you go to college in Scotland, then?'

'We don't have the money. We've nothing.' Suddenly, as if her body had developed a mind of its own, she reached out and grasped his hand. 'You could teach me, you could teach me to do accounts and type.'

'I wish I could. I'm a teacher not an accountant, and I don't even have a typewriter.'

What was she doing? What was she saying? Her rebellious voice carried on. 'But you could teach me to be a school teacher.'

'I could teach you all I know, but I can't give you a qualification.'

'I'm sorry. I shouldn't have asked you.' Letting go of his hand, she lowered her head. Her wriggling toes had found their way below the sand. She pulled her foot out, then dug down again.

'I can teach you what I know,' he repeated. 'Then if you ever do get a chance, you'll be ahead of the other applicants or at least on a level.'

The blood rushed up her neck. 'Really?' She grasped at the possibility.

29

Rising to her feet, she suppressed a sudden desire to fling her arms around his neck and clasped her hands together instead. 'That's…kind of you.'

He nodded at his fishing rod. 'I'd better go and catch something for my tea. Come and see me at the schoolhouse tomorrow evening. We'll talk about it.'

'Thank you. I will.' Annie watched him for a while as he walked away and settled on a shelf of rock before casting his line into the sea. She was not going to fall in love with him, she told her racing heart. She was not going to fall in love with any man. Much as she loved this island, she would not, could not spend her life here. Then why did she feel as if an invisible cord was pulling her towards Alexander Garcia? Already nervous about the following evening, she stood up with a force of will and walked up the hill towards the pier to await the returning boats.

Chapter Four

Annie cycled along the rise with a pair of cod strung over the handlebars. Almost at the croft, the soft strains of Bel's voice singing a sad lament about a girl whose sweetheart had gone to war drifted towards her. The song sounded strangely poignant in an air where the mist was floating in like ribbons of smoke from the sea.

Bel sat in the doorway, a sheep's fleece at one side, a basket of the fine, unknotted wool at the other. She stroked one wooden carder over the other, the sharp teeth teasing out the knots in the wool. Without ceasing the process, she looked up as her cousin dismounted and leaned the cycle against the wall.

Annie dropped on her knees in front of the other girl. 'I'm going to the schoolhouse tomorrow night. Alexander Garcia asked me.'

'Alexander Garcia?' Bel looked surprised. 'Why?'

'It was Mam's idea. I want to go on with my learning.'

Bel set the carders on the ground and laughed. 'Is he coming to the dance tonight? I'm going with Nick.'

'I don't know. I'm looking forward to it anyway. I think I'll love dancing.'

'Ye like the teacher?'

'He's handsome and he's clever and he's going to teach me what he knows.' She giggled and Bel giggled with her.

'He's a bit older than ye. I hope it's only lessons he'll be teaching.'

'Oh, Bel, what a thing to say.'

31

Bel lifted a hand and stroked the hair back from Annie's brow. 'Ye look all flushed.'

'I told you I'll only marry a millionaire! A teacher's wife is not the life for me.' But at the same time she thought she rather liked the idea.

'So ye'll just play with his heart for a while?'

Annie grabbed her cousin's hands and bent forward until their foreheads touched and they giggled in unison.

'Come and get your food.' Isa's voice drifted from the kitchen.'

Still smiling, Bel stood up and tidied the wool away.

Annie jumped to her feet and ran into the house, into an air permeated with the scent of rabbit stew. She set the cod in the basin, wiped her hands on a towel, grabbed her mother's arms and twirled her around the kitchen.

'You're in a better mood. How did you get on with Mr Dick?' Isa asked, getting her breath back.

'Fine. I'm going up to the schoolhouse tomorrow afternoon. But it'll be Mr Garcia who's teaching me.'

'Ah,' Isa nodded, 'Now I see what's put you in such fine fettle. I'd best speak with him myself.'

'No, Mam, let me.'

'You like him, don't you? Be careful. He must be well in his twenties. You're barely seventeen.'

'I'm not a child. Many girls my age are already married. But don't worry, I'm not interested in him like that.'

Isa studied her daughter. Finally she nodded. 'Sit down while the food's hot.'

'You'd better say grace, Mam,' said Annie. 'You'll need to be good at it if you're to marry the minister.'

'Don't be impudent.'

Bel and Annie looked at each other and grinned. Isa had never been one for religion since her sister died when they were very young. Bel, however, stuck with the age-old practice of saying grace and reading a passage from the bible every night after tea.

'Are ye hearing Dolly?' said Bel, as she gathered the plates after the meal. The cow was bellowing from the byre, something she only did when her udder was full and uncomfortable.

Isa glanced at the clock. 'Goodness. The cow knows the time better than I do.' She wiped her hands on her apron.

Dolly let out another mournful roar. 'I'll do it, Mam. I'll milk her.' Touched by guilt at having wasted so much of the morning, Annie ran into the back porch for the bucket. Milking a cow was a chore she didn't mind and it was best to get out there before her mother asked her to wash the plates.

Inside the byre, Annie sat with her head against the cow's belly enjoying the steady rise and fall of the beast's breathing and the warm animal smell. The milk flowed freely, hitting the bucket with a tinny resonance. Three farm cats sat around her. Every so often Annie twisted a teat upwards, squirting some milk straight into a cat's mouth. All the time she fought to keep Alexander Garcia out of her daydreams.

'Mind save some for the calf.' Bel appeared at the doorway, her shadow falling across the dusty floor.

Annie laughed, twisted a teat and sent a stream of milk at Bel. It hit her apron and she gasped.

'I'll aim higher next time,' said Annie.

'Now I'll have to wash my overall or it'll be stinking by morning.' Bel's mock serious retort held more than a trace of merriment.

'Might as well be hung for a sheep as a lamb,' said Annie as she squirted Bel again. This time the liquid hit her lips and dripped from her chin. Bel gasped and wiped at her face.

33

'Here, feed the calf.' Annie exchanged the pail for the one in which the family's milk was kept.

Bel lifted the full bucket, scooped up a handful of milk and threw it into Annie's face.

'Oh, ye hussy!' Open mouthed, Annie wiped at the froth.

'Aye, well, they say it's good for the complexion.' Bel giggled. Then both girls laughed together, loud and hearty.

'I'll go and take in the washing,' said Bel. 'Ye'll manage to feed the calf, now?'

'I've been feeding calves all my life,' replied Annie, wiping her hand on the side of her dress.

Bel was still smiling as she left.

Annie lifted the calf's milk bucket and took it into the stall where the young bull waited. She opened the stall door and gave him her fingers to suck. She lowered her hand into the milk and soon the calf was drinking confidently on his own. Standing up, Annie brushed a few stray stalks of straw from her skirt and started as a shadow fell across the shaft of weak sunlight streaming in the door. 'You back again?' Thinking Bel had returned, Annie lifted her head and gasped.

Nick Sinclair stood in the opening.

'Bel's up at the house,' said Annie.

Nick came all the way in until he was standing directly in front of her.

Uncomfortable, she turned away from his direct gaze and walked around him and towards the entrance.

'I've been watching ye ever since ye first came to the island. Don't say ye haven't noticed.' His glittering eyes followed her.

'No, I've not noticed. Anyway you're Bel's lad.'

'I've no made her any promises. I like ye, Annie.' Nick stepped in front of her once more and put one hand on the door jamb, barring her way. 'When ye took my

34

hand yesterday, I knew. If ye were interested at all, I'd leave Bel in an instant.'

Annie's scalp grew hot. 'Get out of my way. Bel deserves better. When I tell her what you said...' She pushed him hard on the shoulder, but he was as solid and immovable as the hind end of a horse.

His face darkened. 'I like ye better, what's wrong wi that? I had to give ye a chance. I'm right fond o' Bel and all, mind.'

Annie glowered at him. 'Aye, you'd be well set up with the croft too.' Trying hard not to show fear, she lowered her voice. 'Get out of my way.'

He didn't move. 'But ye'll have a share in the croft...won't ye? And I'm a good worker. We could be a team. Ye'll no get a better catch than myself. Come here, I'll show ye what ye're missing.' He lurched towards her, his intent showing in his steely eyes, in his ragged breathing.

Annie stepped backwards and grabbed a graip from where it leaned against the wall. She raised it and pointed the tines at him. 'I have no interest in you and I think Bel deserves better than a man who would leave her so easily.' Gripping the handle of the graip tightly, she backed away until she was up against the wall of the stall.

'Am I not good enough for ye, is that it? Look, if ye'd only give me a chance. Come on, put that thing away, ye know ye're not going to use it.' He started towards her again, one hand reaching for the handle of the graip.

With a strength born of anger she stabbed at him. The tines scraped his hand and came in contact with his stomach. His work clothes protected him from the sharp points, but still the blow winded him.

He yelled and clutched his bloodied hand, fury replacing the desire in his eyes. 'Look what you've done, you crazy bitch. Ye're lucky the fork didn't get through my clothes or I'd have ye for attempted murder!'

Annie threatened him with the graip again. 'Then I'd better make a good job of it.'

He stepped back. 'I didn't touch ye.'

'Just stay away from me.' Annie hoped he didn't realise how scared she was. Graip or not, if he wanted, he could easily overpower her.

He stepped back with his forearm pressed against his stomach. 'Look, don't tell Bel what I said. I'll just deny it. I'll say ye came onto me. Ye wouldn't be the first.'

'Do you think she'd believe *you*?' Annie glowered at him. 'Don't you ever come near me again.'

Nick blew out a puff of air. 'I wouldn't come near ye again, not if ye begged me. But what are ye going to do? Are ye going to make trouble, like? Because if ye are, I warn ye, ye'll be the one that's sorry.'

'I'm not afraid of you. I won't tell Bel if that's what you mean, but for her sake not yours. But if you ever hurt her…'

He seemed suddenly deflated and ran his good hand over his head. 'I won't, I promise. I made a mistake. I'll no bother ye again.' He gave an awkward laugh, 'Ye're a might feisty for me anyway.' But she could still feel his eyes boring into her back as she left the byre.

Chapter Five

Alexander lifted the newspaper, almost a week old but just delivered that morning. He regularly kept in touch with the situation in Europe and agreed with his mentor Mr Dick, that the Great War had not been the war to end all wars.

William Dick sat in the chair directly across from him, stuffing tobacco into the bowl of his pipe with a yellowed thumb.

'That girl, the one who came from Canada with her mother, wants to continue her education. She asked me to teach her and I agreed.' Alexander did not look up as he spoke.

William Dick placed the stem of his pipe in his mouth, applied a light to the bowl and gave several puffs until the smoke swirled up past his face. He shook his hand to extinguish the match and threw it into the fireplace.

'Teach her what?' he asked.

'Apparently her education was scanty in Canada. She seems bright enough, and keen. I can't blame her for wanting to better herself.'

'Where, in class?'

'No. I can't imagine her sitting in a classroom with a bunch of children. I thought here in the evening.'

Mr Dick gave a pah and removed the pipe from his mouth. 'Waste of time educating girls. You'd raise her hopes for nothing. She'd be better accepting her lot.' He narrowed his eyes. 'You're a fine looking young man with a good future. I'd lay bets it's more than learning she's after.'

'She's at least a decade younger than me and anyway, there is a girl back in Aberdeen who my parents want me to marry. I probably will someday, I am rather fond of her, but in truth, getting married is the last thing on my mind.' Alexander folded his newspaper and set it down. He decided to change the subject. 'There are riots in the streets of Glasgow. How can the government turn its back on the men who gave their health for their country?'

'We're all suffering the effects of the war. It'll take time to recover.'

Alexander shook his head. 'Men were willing to cut their own working hours to give the ex-service men jobs, and the government comes at them with tanks. There's something far wrong with this world.'

'I'll not argue with you there. When's the girl coming?' asked William.

'Tomorrow evening.'

'You know I'll be up at the manse?'

'I thought it better if we're alone. Of course we could go into the study when you're here, but that would mean lighting two fires.'

'I hope you know what you're doing.' William Dick reached for his own newspaper and snapped it open, disapproval in the tight lines of his face.

'Of course I do.' Alexander fingered the plain gold cross he wore round his neck.

William Dick pointed at him with the stem of his pipe. 'And hide that cross. You know it matters little to me what a man's beliefs are, but there are those on this island so steeped in Presbyterianism that they wouldn't have their bairns taught by a papist.'

Dick had made it quite clear on their first meeting, and reminded him many times since, that he was to keep his persuasion a secret. Alexander surmised that it had more to do with Dick's own beliefs than those of the islanders, most of which he found to be a tolerant lot.

He dropped his cross back down the neck of his gansey. 'Don't worry, I am well aware of the prejudice of some of the islanders.' And your prejudice, he wanted to add. He knew that the only reason Dick tolerated a Catholic schoolteacher was because there were no other candidates willing to spend their initial year in such an isolated position.

William Dick read for a minute, then peered over the top of his glasses. 'I believe there's a dance in the Main's loft tonight.'

'We should go,' Alexander said.

'I'm a bit long in the tooth. I'll leave all that to the young.' He returned his eyes to the paper and drew deeply on his pipe. 'But it's good the island is getting back to normal.'

Alexander's thoughts took him back to the girl he had met by the shore. Attractive, young and headstrong, she wanted to make the most of her life and he applauded that. He had noticed her before; any man with eyes in his head would notice her. Remembering the way she gazed at him with something like adoration, the way her mouth turned up at the corners when she smiled, he wondered if William Dick was perhaps right, that it wasn't just bookwork she wanted. To his bemusement, he had discovered very quickly that most of the unmarried island girls had a crush on him, but he had learned to handle them without causing offence. It would do no harm to see Annie Reid again.

He glanced at the clock. There a stack of paperwork he had promised himself to complete tonight, but he should be able to make the dance before the evening ended.

Chapter Six

'It's the latest fashion,' Annie said.

'Is it no a bit...daring for Raumsey?' Bel screwed up her face at the dress Annie showed her in the magazine she'd brought from Canada.

'Ye'll be the best dressed lassie there!'

'I doubt it. Anyway, I'd more probably be a laughing stock.'

'I'm going to remodel one of my own, so you'd better make up your mind.'

'Oh my, are ye sure it'll be alright?' Bel put her hand over her mouth. She had never imagined herself in something so bonny.

'Definitely.' Annie pointed to a dress with a low waistline. 'That'll not take long with the machine.'

'Ye cut it and I'll sew it.' Bel no longer felt any doubt.

'You look lovely, Bel,' said Annie, standing back to admire her handiwork once the dress was finished. 'Doesn't she, Mam?'

Excitement danced in Bel's grey eyes, her normally pale cheeks were flushed making her look pretty.

'A picture. You look so like your mother.' A slight catch halted Isa's words, she blinked several times and her eyes shone with sudden tears.

Eager to avoid any sadness spoiling the coming night, Annie undid one of Bel's pleats and the hair slipped like silk through her fingers. 'Now we'll have to do something about this. I can give you a bob.' She grabbed the scissors and brandished them.

'No, ye'll no cut my hair.' Bel warded Annie off.

'Well, I'm cutting mine.' Annie handed the scissors to her mother. 'I've shortened my best dress and I want to look modern. Go on, Mam, make me look like this.' She nodded at the model in the magazine.

'No I won't cut your bonny hair.' Isa took a step backwards.

'Then I'll do it myself.' Annie grabbed a chunk of hair and sliced through it. Wavy locks of coal black fell to the ground.

Isa gave a little howl of distress. 'Oh, Annie, your bonny hair; you'll make a fine mess of it.' With a deep sigh, she took the scissors. 'I suppose it's not the worst thing you could do.'

'Thank you, Mother.' Annie pulled out a kitchen chair and sat down.

Isa trimmed the hair so it sat just below Annie's ears. 'It's the best I can do.' Regret was heavy in her voice.

'Now,' Annie said, admiring herself in the speckled mirror. 'What do you think, Bel? Shall we do yours?'

'It looks bonny on ye, but no.' Bel shook her head.

'Then leave it out of these silly pleats, they make you look like a wee lassie. Sit down.' She ran the brush through Bel's hair until it fell in loose waves around her shoulders. 'What do you think?'

Bel smiled at her reflection. Her eyes shone. 'I love it.' Suddenly a tear glinted at the corner of one eye and she rubbed it away. 'I wish my mam could see me.'

Isa came up behind her. 'I'm sure she can, Bel. You and Annie, you both look lovely.' She glanced at her daughter. 'Though I still think you shouldn't have cut your hair.'

'Everyone has it short in the cities,' said Annie with a laugh, 'let me do yours. Take off your apron.'

'I'm comfortable the way I am, thank you.' Isa wore a white-collared, brown dress tied at the neck with a cameo brooch, a gift from her own mother. Her hair was twisted into a sausage shape around her head. Annie decided she looked like a minister's wife already.

The hay loft of the Mains had been swept out and a couple of lads who were good with the music, tuned up on an accordion, a fiddle and a mouth organ. Storm lanterns hung from the beams at various intervals, the flames flickering from the draught below. Slipperine had been dusted on the floor, and the bairns slid around on the white powder, shrieking and laughing. It seemed as if every able-bodied occupant of the island had turned out for the first big dance since the Great War.

Amid it all a few hardy chickens which had escaped the efforts to dislodge them, slept on the rafters, heads tucked under their wings. They looked like balls of feathers. Occasionally one would object to the noise and, squawking, would flap down among the revellers causing a few minutes disruption before the offending fowl was caught and thrown out the door.

When Isa and the two girls entered, all eyes were drawn to them. Bel shrunk behind her aunt and cousin. 'I thought this might not be a good idea,' she whispered. 'I feel as if I look … fast!' Most of the young lassies had made do with worn skirts and blouses.

Annie slipped her arm through her cousin's. 'Not at all.' She waved to Tess who immediately bounded over, her heavy feet thudding on the boards. 'My heavens, don't ye two look grand! Why didn't ye tell me ye were shortening yer clothes? Look at me – such a frump. The morn, ye,' she pointed at Annie, 'are going to cut my hair like that.'

The band struck up a lively tune. Music filled the loft, bounced off the walls and swelled to push the men to their feet and, like a wave, they surged towards the lassies. Within a matter of minutes the floor vibrated with thumping boots and the air with swirling bodies and laughter.

Nick elbowed his way across the floor and grabbed Bel's arm. 'Ye look right bonny. Come away and dance.'

Clean shaven, his curling hair catching the light from the oil lamps, he wore a checked shirt, black trousers and real shoes, not boots, on his feet. Apart from the bandage on his hand, being attacked by a two pronged fork did not seem to have done him any harm. He didn't as much as glance at either Annie or Tess. A glow lit up Bel's face as she followed Nick across the floor.

At Annie's insistence, Bel had applied a wee bit rouge, although Annie thought she hardly needed it; her face would soon be as red as a boiled lobster the way Nick was birling her around the floor.

'She seems taken with Nick,' said Annie, still doubting the wisdom of keeping silent about what happened in the byre. But she'd never seen Bel so happy, and maybe he would be good to her after all. She was about to question Tess, when a lad she'd barely met grabbed her arm and dragged her onto the floor.

From then on Annie was whisked away for a dance by every available young man on the island, or so it seemed. She had hardly time to draw breath before another would-be-suitor was at her shoulder. And all the while, her eyes searched the crowd for Alexander Garcia, emptiness filling her when she realised he wasn't there.

'C..could I have this dance?'

Annie turned around to see a thin-faced lad with faded hair and sad eyes standing before her.

For a moment she searched her mind. She had met so many islanders since her arrival, it was difficult to keep track. 'Magnus?' she said at last. 'Of course.'

'Tess's my sister. She said she'd met ye.'

Isa had heard talk about Magnus, the young man who had come home from the war with a ruined stomach, a constant twitch and a damaged leg and had never slept a wink since. 'Badly affected,' was how Isa had described him. He slipped an arm around her and they moved hesitantly onto the floor.

Annie tried to make conversation, but was quickly aware Magnus' attention was riveted on Bel. 'She's too good for him, ye know,' he said.

'I agree. What do you know about him?' asked Annie.

'He's a man for the girls.'

'Was there ever anything between him and Tess?'

'I don't think so, but I've been away for three years. Nick somehow managed to dodge the call up. Claimed he was the only person to run his father's croft, his father being unable. It was all lies. His father's as fit as any man. Nick's a coward. Always was at school. A bully and a coward. Do you know what he loved to do? Catch flies and set them free just beneath a spider's web. He thought it funny, especially if it was a bluebottle or a bumble bee and it was a little spider.'

'Have you tried to warn Bel?'

Magnus shrugged his thin shoulders. 'She would only think me jealous. She knows I like her, but what can I give her? I can barely work and I've no money.'

The dance ended and Magnus walked her back to the girls' side of the room. 'Thank ye for dancing with me.' He turned and limped away.

By the time the fiddlers and accordionist slowed the tempo from merry jigs to waltzes, Annie had danced with almost every lad in the room. But her eyes constantly found the door, waiting for the only face she hoped to see.

'Are you having a good time?' She turned to see Donald Charleston and her mother at her elbow. Isa's face was flushed, her eyes shining, making the years slip away and, in the dim light from the paraffin lamps, she appeared no older than her daughter. Annie found the thought faintly unnerving.

'Mrs Reid?' She heard the deep voice at her shoulder and spun around. Alexander Garcia was introducing himself to her mother. 'I believe you know I will be tutoring your daughter.'

'Of course.' Isa took the proffered hand. 'It's good of you. We will have to discuss payment of some kind.'

'If she does well that's all the payment I need.' Alexander turned to Annie. 'Would you like to dance?'

She nodded and forgot everything else.

As the strains of the last dance drifted round the room, Alexander waltzed her over the floor. He knew all the steps, making Annie feel clumsy and she tripped more than once. His strong arms supported her and they laughed every time.

'You'll have to teach me to dance as well,' she said with a giggle. 'I haven't had much chance in the past.' Her face grew hot. What must he think of her? A gauche country girl and him a gentleman.

'That could be arranged.' He smiled and escorted her back to her mother. 'I'll see you tomorrow night, then?' With that, he was gone, swallowed by the crowd. Everyone, it seemed, wanted to talk to him, especially the unmarried lassies. A knot twisted in her gut as she watched him smile and pay heed to their fawning.

'My, but it's been a grand night.' Isa slipped her arm through Annie's. 'I've never had such a night since we left Raumsey for Canada. It's good to be home.' Her face was flushed and a few tendrils of hair had escaped. She looked around. 'We'd better find Bel.'

'Yes, aye.' Annie stretched her neck pretending to look too, but really looking for Alexander. In the short time she'd turned away, he had disappeared. 'I can't see her.'

'She's maybe gone home afore us,' said Isa. 'She was with that Nick.'

By the disapproval in her voice, Annie realised Isa, too, had her doubts about the match.

'Isn't it grand to hear folk laugh again,' whispered Isa, as they crossed the fields, their way lit by a misshapen moon.

'I think I like dancing,' said Annie.

Isa stopped and looked up at the star-studded navy dome above them. 'The first time I danced was with your dad on a night like this, There was a moon then too, and music drifting over the fields.'

They walked on in silence. Annie imagined her parents, not much older than herself, dancing under that same moon and she thought of the wistfulness in her mother's voice. Perhaps the minister would never take her father's place after all.

Apart from the dog and a sleepy cat, they found Scartongarth empty.

Isa sat down, took off a shoe and rubbed her foot. 'It was a grand night. I've not danced for so long.' Then a shadow crossed her face. 'There was always dancing, in the Mains loft. Your dad was a good dancer.'

'Do you still miss him?' asked Annie, remembering the way Isa looked at the minister.

'Part of me always will.' Isa gave a slow smile. 'But I believe he led me back here and has given Donald and me his blessing.' When she looked up her eyes shimmered in the pale light. 'Do you mind waiting up for Bel? I'm a bit worried about her and I need my bed. I tire more easily than I did as a lassie.'

'Away you go, Mam.' Annie was too wound up to sleep anyway. She settled in the arm chair before the stove and opened the door allowing a welcome heat to

46

flow around her cold ankles. Her eyes closed and she relived the feel of Alexander's arms around her, the way his body felt against hers when she stumbled. Thinking of his lips, she wondered what they would be like to kiss. The outside door eased open. Annie started, suddenly awake.

'Ye didn't have to wait up.' Bel took the opposite chair, leaned forward and clasped her hands. 'Nick said he wanted to marry me.' She kept her eyes downcast and fiddled with the material of her skirt.

'And what did you say?' Annie sat upright hoping the answer was no.

'I suddenly don't know. He kissed me but he was rough and I didn't like it. It wasn't what I imagined.'

She raised a shaking hand to her forehead. For the first time Annie noticed how very pale she looked.

'My God, Bel, you didn't let him have his way with you?'

'No, no, of course not. He wanted to though and I felt... frightened. I didn't get any of the feelings ye read about in books. Maybe that's all there is. Maybe I'm just as hopeless a dreamer as you are.' She removed her shoes and held her feet up to the warmth.

'Then he's not the one for you.' Hope flared in Annie's heart. Hope that the relationship would die a natural death.

'How did you get on with the school teacher?' asked Bel.

'We had a dance. He's going to teach me. But there is no romance so watch where you go with your thinking.' Alexander had not kissed her, yet, in her imagination, she had experienced all the feelings Bel had not.

'That's a shame,' said Bel.

'It's the best way.' Annie dropped her eyes and studied her fingernail. 'Bel, are you sure it's Nick

Sinclair you want? There must be other lads who want a good wife and a croft.'

'He's a good worker, strong as anything, the best looking lad on the island and he's after *me*.'

'That lad, Magnus, he was worried about you. I think he likes you.'

'I like him and all, but not like that.'

'Please be sure.'

'Ach, Nick's just a bit rough, but he's got a good heart in him.'

'Do you love him?'

Bel shrugged. 'I think so. There's no another lad who's taken my fancy.'

'Bel, there's something…' Annie began, and then her voice faltered as she doubted the wisdom of what she wanted to say. She stopped. Maybe she shouldn't shatter Bel's confidence by repeating Nick's words. Instead she said, 'Don't marry for less than love. You don't have to. Between us we can run the croft. Think on it, please.'

'I will.' Bel still stared at the flames, a faraway look in her eyes.

'I'm away to my bed now.' Annie rose and climbed the stairs, the need for sleep taking precedence over anything else.

Chapter Seven

Her blood ran hot, her stomach fluttered. She waited, each minute unbearably long. The footsteps sounded from beyond the door, nearer, nearer. The schoolhouse door swung open and she was confronted by the rotund figure of Mr Dick. The gold-rimmed spectacles sat on the bulbous nose and disapproving eyes met hers. Annie released a suspended breath and it rushed out with a little pah as she fought to stop the disappointment from showing on her face.

'Ah,' Mr Dick said. 'Alex told me you wanted some tuition. Come in, come in.' Standing aside, he allowed her to enter.

He led her into a room with deep mushroom-coloured walls and red curtains at the window. A brown leather couch sat before a fire which was almost out.

'It's getting dark.' He walked over to an ornate table holding a writing pad, an inkwell a couple of pens and a paraffin lamp. After removing the globe and funnel from the lamp, he pumped the small handle at the side up and down a few times. Then he applied a match to the fragile white mantle at the same time turning a knob to allow the fuel to hiss upward. A blue flame flared, changing to yellow when he replaced the funnel and the soft light spread through the room.

Dick cleared his throat.

Annie glanced around. Against one wall was a bookcase lined with books. Black, deep red, deep blue spines, some faded, others fresh and new-looking.

'Have a seat.' William Dick indicated a rocking chair with ears, also in brown leather and, pulling a peat from the basket at one side, threw it on the fire. At the other side of the fireplace sat a matching chair and beside it, a small table piled high with newspapers and magazines. The uppermost paper was in a foreign language.

There was a bareness about the room, no ornaments, no cushions, no flowers. Apart from a clock, only a pipe, an ashtray and a tobacco pouch sat on the mantelpiece. Mr Dick reached up, took the pipe and the tobacco and pushed them into his pocket. 'I'm sorry I will have to leave you for a few hours. I have my discussion group. I believe Alexander has been working out some lessons for you.'

'That's all right,' Annie said too quickly. She ignored Mr Dick's disapproving frown. There was nothing she could do to stop her relief from reflecting on her face.

The door behind her opened. Footsteps whispered on the wooden floor and Mr Dick said goodbye to someone. She lifted her head and returned the welcoming smile of Alexander Garcia.

'Where's he going?' she asked of Mr. Dick.

'Up to the manse. He and the minister and a few others like to discuss the state of the world. Once they get started, they'll be all night.' He was so close to her now she could breathe in the pleasant, slightly masculine smell of him.

Alexander moved away and pulled out a couple of chairs from the table. 'We'll sit here,' he said. 'What level of education have you had?'

'I can read and write and do sums. My father and grandfather didn't think education was important for a girl. I suppose if I stayed in Canada and married a farmer it wouldn't have been except for the accounts, I'd have to do them.' She stopped as her voice almost ran away with her.

His eyes crinkled and lips lifted slightly at one corner. 'And you have no wish to marry a farmer in Scotland?'

Conscious of the rough skin and broken nails, she took her hands from the table top and hid them on her lap, lowering her eyes as her face grew hot. 'If I fell in love, maybe. But I've not met anyone and I will have to make my own way in life.'

Alexander cleared his throat and rearranged the papers on the table. 'So what would you like to learn about?'

'History. I want to know more about ... everything.' She leaned towards him. 'Where do you come from?'

'Aberdeen. I did my degree there. My father is a factor on an estate outside Buckie. '

'No, I mean,' she bit her lip ... your name, Garcia, it's not Scottish.'

He gave a brief laugh. 'I'm half Spanish. More than half.'

'*I've* always been interested in Spain. I probably have Spanish blood too. My father told me how some of the Spanish Armada was wrecked on this very island and the sailors stayed. They couldn't get home really, not back then.'

'So that's where your looks come from.' He had a twinkle in his eye.

'Why did *your* father come to Scotland? Oh, I'm sorry, I'm being nosey.'

No, it's all right. My ancestor escaped to Britain during the Spanish Inquisition. My father was always interested in his Spanish roots. He returned to Spain one summer and met my mother, but Scotland has always been his home.'

Annie listened intently. She had never heard of the Spanish Inquisition, but she wouldn't admit that. 'The newspapers,' she nodded towards the small table, 'Are they Spanish?'

'I get a Spanish newspaper once in a blue moon. But most are in English.'

'Tell me about Spain.'

The flickering flames from the fire lit up one side of his face illuminating the strong jaw, the high cheekbone, the sweep of his eyelashes. 'Are you really interested?'

'Of course I am. I want to learn about everything.' She wanted to find out all there was to know about Alexander Garcia. If his father was a factor, maybe he was fairly well off.

He smiled and folded his hands on the table. 'Although I've never been there, my mother described the Spain of her childhood so well I can see it in my head.'

That, Annie could understand. 'My father was the same about Raumsey. I knew it before I came. I saw it in my dreams.'

He rubbed his hands together. 'But enough of this. You came here to learn and learn you shall.'

She loved the sound of his voice and could have listened to it forever. 'Then tell me about the war. I want to know why it happened, why my dad was killed.'

He studied her for a moment, rose, went to the shelf and removed a book which he handed to her. 'You can borrow this,' he said. 'But take great care of it.'

'Thank you.' She read the title. *Serbia and Europe*.

Alexander removed a newspaper from the pile on the small table. 'You should read this as well.' His face was serious. 'Europe is rumbling. The political situation is far from settled.'

'You're so clever,' she whispered. 'I thought it was over. Wasn't that the war to end all wars?' She had heard that somewhere and quoting it, she believed, made her sound knowledgeable.

52

He snorted. 'Far from it. If you're interested, I'll pass the newspapers on to you when I'm finished. I'll tell you what I think, no, what I know. But read the paper first, then we can discuss the situation in more detail.'

'Thank you. Have you been on Raumsey a while?'

'I arrived not long before you.'

'Will you stay here, on this island?'

'No. I have a sweetheart. We planned to be married by the end of the year. She doesn't want to leave the city so I suppose it'll be next year now. I came here for the experience. The children here are great, biddable.'

As if he had slapped her, Annie fell back against the chair, eyes dropping to her lap. She heard nothing after the word, 'sweetheart'.

'Are you all right, Annie?'

She quickly recovered herself. 'Yes, a little too warm. So, do you think I'll be able to get a qualification some day?'

'Of course. You're bright. You'll make an excellent student. I'll have to make enquiries though, as to how we should proceed.'

She gave him her brightest smile. 'Thank you, Mr Garcia. I'll not let you down.' Inside she seethed. A sweetheart indeed. She would see about that, aye she would.

'European history then it is, at least for now.' He handed her an exercise book and a pen. 'I'll give you the important facts. Then you can take away some books to read and we'll see what you've made of it on your next visit.' He pushed a sheet of paper and a pencil across the table towards her.

Much later, when the clock struck ten, the door opened and Mr Dick entered, bringing with him the chill of the night.

'Miss Reid, still here I see.' He removed his tobacco pouch from his pocket and, along with his pipe, laid it on the mantelpiece.

Annie stood up and smoothed her skirt. 'We've been discussing the situation in Europe,' she said in her most no-nonsense voice.

Mr Dick raised his eyebrows as if in surprise. 'And *you* are interested in politics?'

'Yes I am.' Annie bristled. His tone indicated such an interest was beneath all womankind and her especially. 'I always have been,' she lied. 'My dad was killed in the Great War and I want to know why it happened.'

'And when you learn all that, will you change the world?'

His condescending tone angered Annie further.

She pulled herself up to her full height. 'I might not be able to change things, Mr. Dick, any more than you and your friends can with your long discussions, but I'm young and with an education, I can try.'

'You sound like one of those damn suffragettes.' His face reddened, his heavy eyebrows met in the middle then shot apart.

Annie had heard a little about the suffragettes from newspapers and snatches of conversation. Now she wished she had paid more attention. 'If I had the chance I would join them.' She glanced at Alexander who was watching her, a bright gleam in his eyes. She warmed to recognise admiration in them. Strengthened by his support, she carried on. 'Why should women not have the same rights as men if they have the ability?' Tears burned behind her eyes and she blinked them away. She realised she should not get into an argument about something of which she knew little. 'I have to go now. Goodnight, Mr. Dick, Mr. Garcia.' Her eyes met Alexander's and he winked. A warmth spread through her and calmed her indignation. No man or boy had ever winked at her before.

'It's getting late. I'd better walk you home.' Alexander reached for her jacket and held it out for her to slip on. Another gesture unfamiliar to her. He was indeed a gentleman.

'Thank you,' she murmured. 'Goodnight, Mr Dick.'

With a slight nod, William Dick puffed at his pipe.

Alexander took a storm lantern from a shelf and lit it.

They walked along the road to the accompaniment of low moans from the fog horns around the coast, each island a different tone. The mist was thick now and prickled her skin. A hazy moon fought to be recognised, and the meagre light from the cottage windows glimmered along the road, a row of faded stars. As they neared Scartongarth, Poppy, the sheepdog, barked crazily then ran to greet them, circling their legs, almost knocking Annie off her balance. Alexander caught her and for a moment, she felt the heat from his body, the strength from his arms, the beat of his heart.

With an embarrassed laugh, he righted her and in silence, with one arm still around her shoulders, they approached Scartongarth.

At the end of the house they stopped. 'I'll bid you goodnight,' said Alexander, removing his arm. He offered her his hand. She shook it, feeling the strength, the warmth.

'I'll bid *you* goodnight,' she whispered, lifting her face, wishing he would kiss her. When he released her hand she slipped it into her pocket, wanting to hold the warmth there.

'Goodnight,' he said again, his voice low. 'Can you come tomorrow?'

'If I can, I will.'

55

He nodded and backed away before turning. She watched as the lantern light bobbed in the darkness until it was all that was left of him.

The muggy air hit her the moment she opened the door.

'How did you get on?' asked Isa from her chair by the stove. She'd been darning socks which she now set to one side.

'I enjoyed it.' Annie pushed the tendrils of her hair back from her damp skin. 'But I don't like Mr. Dick. I could be as good as him if I had the chance.'

Her mother sighed. 'Don't fall out with him. You're there to learn and this life's hard enough so don't get all uppity with your grand ideas.'

'Mam, what do you know about the suffragettes?'

'Suffragettes? It's been a long time since I've heard of them. They were very active before the war. If I'd been born in a different place I would have been marching with them, not that women getting the vote has made any difference to the likes of us. Why do you ask?'

Annie ignored the question. 'Can we vote now? Can you vote?'

'Only women householders over thirty are allowed to vote. And…' Her voice rose. 'If a woman wants an education and be, like, a teacher or a lawyer or something professional, they will have to give it up if they wish to marry.'

'So if I became a teacher…'

'You could not marry and remain in work.' Isa finished the sentence for her.

'But that's not fair.' It seemed no one should be forced to make such a decision. A woman's lot was indeed a sorry one.

56

'Many man-made laws are unfair. But we're stuck in a situation we can do nothing about. Best not concern yourself with it.' Two red dots appeared on Isa's cheeks. Annie looked at her mother in surprise. It had been a while since she'd heard her so animated. This was a different mother than the one who baked scones and scrubbed floors and spoke of lamb prices and told her what she should and shouldn't do.'

'How do you know all this?' She lowered herself down on the opposite chair.

'I do read the papers. And then there's Donald. We discuss things.' The dots on her cheeks spread. 'He had a sister who died fighting for the suffragettes' cause.'

In a matter of seconds the minister turned from a solemn middle-aged man in a black coat, who spoke of God and righteousness, to someone far more interesting, someone who might actually have a life beyond the pulpit. 'Is he in favour of their movement?' If his sister had been a suffragette and he discussed politics with Mr Dick, maybe she should get to know him better. He was to be her stepfather after all. New ideas began to form in her head, so many she felt dizzy.

'How do he and Mr Dick get on?'

Isa laughed. 'They discuss and they argue. I don't think they share the same ideas at all.'

'In that case I think I like your minister.'

Isa looked at her daughter as she might look at an equal, not an errant child. 'A lot of men supported the suffragettes, still think they were not treated fairly. We work as hard as men, we should have a say in who runs the country. I didn't give it much thought before I came back here, but Donald likes to discuss things like that. He's different from any man I've known and I'm interested, just to *know*.'

'Alexander's like that.'

57

'Alexander?' Isa's brows shot up and Annie was her child again. 'So it's Alexander now?'

'We... we talked...' Annie's voice faltered. 'Maybe I should ask Donald about ... stuff. Mam, I want to find out more.'

'He'd be happy to talk to you I'm sure.' Isa shook her head. 'But to go anywhere, even buy books, you need money. Fight to get an education and a good job, then you'll have the funds to follow your dreams. I'm sorry I can't help you more, lass.' She paused for a breath. 'I am proud of you, but the young teacher, just be careful.'

'I will. Where's Bel?'

'She's away out with Nick Sinclair.' Isa leaned forward, opened the range door and held her hands to the heat. 'I'm glad I've got you on your own. As you know, Donald and me, we're planning to get wed soon. We've set the date for the end of next week.'

Annie gasped. 'But... so soon? Mam...'

Isa held up her hand. 'We have to leave Scartongarth anyway. Nick Sinclair's aiming to get his boots under the table and you and I will no longer be welcome here.'

The fire spat and the light in the paraffin lamp flickered as if in an unseen draught. Annie shivered as something cold crept up her spine.

The wedding was a quiet affair. Isa and the minister with Bel and Annie as witnesses went to the mainland for a quick ceremony in Canisbay Kirk. The celebration was a respectful tea party in the manse, with one tot of whisky per male visitor.

Annie watched her mother move around the guests. In the soft lamplight, dressed in her sensible brown dress, Isa glowed in a way Annie had not seen before. It was as if she was born for this, the perfect wife of the manse. Her life would certainly be easier than it had ever been. Yet Annie felt a stab of sorrow. Since her father died, her mother had been hers alone and now the minister would share her affections. As she watched the telling exchange of smiles between the newly married couple, Annie felt like an intruder and was glad she had chosen to stay with Bel for the time being.

'She needs help on the croft,' Annie had explained to her mother. 'Once she marries, I'll move to the manse.' Then she had a quick vision of her future self, saw herself married to Alexander Garcia and living in the schoolhouse. Would that be so bad? They wouldn't stay there forever. Alexander would eventually be the headmaster of a grand school in the city. She had not thought as far as how to dispose of the fiancée. In her dreams that obstacle did not exist.

The next few months passed quickly. Without her mother, Annie found there was much more work to do both indoors and out, but she bent to the work willingly. She enjoyed sharing confidences with Bel and she lived for her evenings at the schoolhouse. Alexander was never anything less than a gentleman, yet Annie sensed they were growing closer, as if there was an invisible thread drawing them together. These evenings lifted her spirits and fed her thirst for knowledge. But Sunday was always out of bounds.

'It's my day of rest,' he told her. 'There'll be no learning done on the Sabbath.'

Isa had not been a strict churchgoer, and had not brought her family up that way, but even in her household, the Sabbath had been honoured.

On the nights when she did not go to the schoolhouse, Annie seldom joined the other young folk at the shore or the shop for the banter or a singsong, preferring to stay at home with her nose in a book. Isa still helped with the mending and washing, but she was spending more and more time on parish matters. She

59

organised a knitting circle for the women and home-making classes for young girls. She had never looked happier.

Bel, however became quieter as time went on, as if the weight of rain clouds was slowly descending about her shoulders.

Chapter Eight

It was about three months after Isa's wedding. Bel threw the door to Scartongarth open and stumbled inside. The house lay empty and she thanked God in her heart. She was not ready to talk to anyone, even Annie. Pressing her fists on the surface of the kitchen table she began to cry, great silent sobs, which shook her body. The dog came up to her and pushed himself against her legs with a sympathetic whine. She fell to her knees and wrapped her arms around his neck, dampening his fur with her tears.

Finally, she struggled to her feet and stood trembling in the soft wind from the open door. With a deep sigh, she moved herself into action once more. From the rainwater barrel outside, she filled a basin, brought it into the kitchen and added warm water from the kettle. After stripping off her clothes, she washed herself with a flannel and carbolic soap paying special attention to the painful area between her thighs. By the time she donned her underclothes, her teeth were chattering, yet she no longer felt the cold. She pulled on her nightgown, lay on the bed and stared, dry-eyed, at the shadows on the wall.

Meanwhile, Tess and Annie sat at the top of the rise. The evening was mild, but the mist hung heavy in the distance like a great rolling blanket threatening to cover the island before morning. Tess seemed to be able to get her hands on cigarettes easily and she passed one to Annie. 'The smoke keeps the midgies away,' she said.

Annie's hands and face were stinging with minute insect bites and that seemed as good a reason to smoke as any. She reached for the cigarette, drew deeply and took a fit of coughing.

Tess laughed. 'If the minister could see ye now!'

'What pleasure do you get from that?' Annie said between coughs.

Down on the beach several lads were skimming stones across the water. Tess stood up and waved to them. A couple waved back.

'I'm worried about Bel.' Annie recovered and passed the cigarette back to her friend. 'I don't trust Nick Sinclair.'

'She won't listen. If only she liked our Magnus. He's in love with her, ye know. Has been ever since school. Hangs around her like a puppy dog. Or he used to.'

'Nick tried it on with me.'

'Really?' Tess gave a snort and sat down again. 'I'm not surprised. Don't be flattered. He's tried it on with every girl on the island. There's some that's taken him up on it and had their hearts broken. Bel now, she's different. He'll hang in there. She's got a croft.'

This news made Annie more sure than ever. Bel should not be marrying Nick. 'You?' she asked.

Tess rubbed her forehead. 'I was young, no more than thirteen. Nowadays I wouldn't be so foolish.' A guarded bitterness lay behind her words and Annie felt it better to ask no more.

'Should I tell Bel?'

Tess shook her head. 'It'll only upset her, but she'll marry him anyway. She's been obsessed with him for years.'

'Then it's best to keep quiet?'

'Least said soonest mended, so my mother used to say.'

The girls sat in silence for a while. As the day died, the mist came in and chilled the air.

'I'm leaving,' said Tess. 'The island, I mean.'

This startled Annie. She had become very fond of Tess in the short time she'd known her. 'Where are you going?'

'Service. I worked there a while before, when I was fourteen. The work was hard, but we had a laugh. I had to come home when my ma took ill. There's no room at the same place, more's the pity, but the Missis has recommended me to one of her friends.'

'And is your ma better now?'

'She died.'

'Oh, I'm sorry.'

Tess shrugged. 'We can't change what life throws at us. I'll be glad to get to the mainland again, but I'll miss ye and Bel.'

'I'll miss you too. You will say goodbye before you go?'

Tess laughed. 'I'll come to see ye all when it's definite. And I'll try to get a wee bit whisky to go with the fags.'

The night closed in and the lights of passing ships shimmered like fallen stars behind a curtain of gauze. The lighthouse beam slowly swept the firth, the foghorn moaned and cottage windows glowed faintly as lamps were lit. And in the bay, the nightly dirge of sad-voiced seals drifted in with the fog.

Back home, Annie found Bel already in bed lying in a foetal position, arms clutched around her stomach and her back turned to the room. She did not move as Annie entered. Annie lowered herself down on the bed and put a hand on Bel's shoulder.

'Why are you in bed? Are you sick?'

Bel didn't respond.

A trickle of ice ran down Annie's spine. 'Bel, Bel, for any sake talk to me.'

Bel slowly turned so she lay on her back. Her face was streaked with dried tears. 'He forced me.' Her voice came as a monotone.

'What? Who, Nick? Oh, Bel.'

Bel twisted her face all the way round. An ugly bruise decorated one cheek and one side of her lip was swollen. 'He said I was teasing him. Said I'd been teasing him for weeks.' She took a deep shuddering breath. 'He hurt me so bad.'

Annie stroked Bel's hair with a trembling hand. Oh God, why didn't she tell her about Nick? 'The brute. When we tell your brother…'

Bel pushed herself upright. 'No, no, ye mustn't tell Jimmy. Ye mustn't tell anybody. Promise me ye won't ever tell.' She grabbed Annie's wrist, her thin fingers cold and vice-like.

'It's alright. Hush, I won't tell.' Annie pulled Bel into her arms. 'But he has to pay for hurting you.'

Bel's body shook with silent sobs. Eventually she spoke. 'No. It was my own fault. I didn't know how lads could get…I should have never gone to the barn with him, but he kept on at me. I told him I wanted to wait till it was proper, like, married and he promised he wouldn't do anything I didn't want, but … he lied.'

The ice in Annie's body melted with the fire of anger. 'You can't marry him now.'

Bel shook her head. 'I hated it. I hate him. I'll never marry him or any man. How do women bear it?'

Annie said nothing. She rose and marched to the window, looked over the rigs towards the sea and laid her head against the cool glass, her angry breath steaming up the pane. 'He'd better come nowhere near Scartongarth again.'

'I don't want to see him, but don't say anything and don't tell Auntie Isa, please. If word gets out, I'll look the bad one.'

Annie drew a deep breath through quivering nostrils. It was true what Bel said. If she made public accusations, Bel would be the one to suffer. Yet anger fuelled her energy. She warmed some milk, added a tot of whisky and pressed the mug into Bel's cold hand. Bel sipped slowly and when it was finished she lay down, her eyes wide open staring at the ceiling. Annie heated water and filled the stone water bottle, then tucked it in beside her friend. 'You're as cold as ice.' She stroked Bel's head.

'Stay with me, Annie,' Bel whispered. 'I don't want to be alone this night.'

Annie quickly changed into her nightclothes, pulled back the quilt and climbed in beside her cousin and they lay like that, each girl drawing comfort from the other.

After several hours, in which she lay awake listening to Bel's frequent quiet sobs, Annie finally slipped into the dark well of oblivion.

When she next awoke, Bel was already up and shivering before a struggling fire. Annie rose and pulled the kettle over the flames. Once it boiled she made tea and handed a cup to Bel who still crouched before the fire. 'Drink this,' she said. 'Then go back to bed. I'll do the chores today.'

All morning Annie worked with an energy born of anger and guilt, because she had not spoken up. From time to time she returned to the kitchen to check on Bel who had refused to stay in bed and insisted in doing tasks around the house: baking, washing, preparing vegetables; her hand shaking, her face white and listless.

When the sun was high, Annie checked the clock and began to remove her apron. The men went to sea at first light, and they would be coming home about now.

'Where are you going?' The panic was back in Bel's voice.

'To check the animals.' Yes, she thought, one animal in particular. 'I won't be long.'

She stood at the top of the brae and waited until the men had hauled the boats. The murmur of voices and their occasional laughter drifted up towards her. She hoped Nick was not making jokes at Bel's expense.

When he saw her he lifted his arm in a wave, picked up a couple of cod from the bottom of his boat and walked towards her, an innocent smile on his face. 'Tell Bel I'll be to see her the night. Here's a couple of fish for yer table.' He held them towards her as if nothing had happened.

Annie glared at him and made no move to take the fish.

He stepped back as if struck by the ferocity of her eyes. 'What is it?'

'Don't ever come near Scartongarth again.' Annie spat the words out.

'Why, what have I done?'

'I don't have to tell you that. Bel doesn't want to see you again and we don't need your fish.'

'Ah, ye're on yer high horse because I gave her a wee slap. I didn't mean to hit her so hard. I'll make it up to her.'

'She does not want to see you again.'

His face whitened. 'We're getting married. Why are ye interfering?'

'She will never marry you. Forcing yourself on a girl. You're worse than an animal.'

'Hey, come on. I did not force her. Everybody knows she's been after me for months.' He stepped closer and pointed his finger in Annie's face. 'Ye make trouble for me and see where it gets ye, and her. Now take the fish and we'll say no more about it.'

Annie took the fish from his hand, breathed in deeply and, with all the strength of her anger, drew her arm back and swung the fish at his face. There was a wet smack as they connected with the side of his head. Nick yelled as he tried to catch hold of her flailing arm. She continued to belt him with the cod until he managed to grab her wrist and twist her arm back forcing her to drop her weapons and cry out in pain. When he released her, she stumbled forward and fell to her knees on the sand.

The other fishermen, watching from where they were securing the boats, obviously found it amusing

Annie turned her furious eyes on them. 'If you knew what he'd done...'

Another guffaw of laughter. 'Aye, Nick, lad, ye've been annoying the lassies again.'

Annie stood up and dusted the sand from her skirt. Even if they knew the truth, chances were that it would still be a big joke and Bel's reputation would be in tatters. Nick glared at her, his face red, his lips pursed, silvery fish scales clinging to his skin. His hands tightened into fists and she knew, had they not had an audience, he would strike her as quickly as he struck Bel the night before.

'Just don't come near Scartongarth,' she hissed, and turned on her heel.

'I'll get ye for this, ye hard-nosed bitch,' he shouted after her.

Back home, Bel was peeling potatoes. 'I'll be alright,' she said to Annie's concerned questions. 'I don't ever want to speak of this again.'

'You don't need him. I'll stay with you and help you run the croft for as long as you want me to,' promised Annie.

'Ye don't want to stay on the island. Ye've said it many a time,' Bel replied. 'There are other women here who live alone and survive. I'm just sorry I'll no be able to bring Scartongarth back to the way it was. I'll like as not have to rent out some land.' Her voice was flat, without a hint of emotion. She turned back to her tatties and wiped at an eye with the back of her hand.

'I could go into service, send money home,' said Annie. 'I can still study. I'll maybe have better chances on the mainland. I'd like to see Scartongarth thrive too.'

'I thought ye liked the teacher. Do ye want to leave him now?'

Annie didn't, she couldn't, but she spoke calmly. 'He's got a sweetheart. And I'm glad, I am, for I've plans other than marriage. No one has to have a man if they don't want to.'

'Oh, Annie, I hope ye win him, for I'll miss ye sorely if ye leave the island. And with Tess going…' The knife fell from her hand and she once more covered her face and began to sob.

Despite Bel's assurances that she was fine, Annie insisted on following her around like a mother hen for the rest of the day. Secretly Bel welcomed the attention and the knowledge that someone cared, but told herself that nothing could be achieved by self-pity.

'Could you light the lamp, Annie?' she asked, as she washed the evening plates. She couldn't admit that her hand was shaking so badly that holding a match steady was an impossible task. 'And there's no need to sleep beside me tonight. The sooner we get back to normal the better.'

'I don't mind. I think I'd rather.'

'No. I want to be by myself.' Bel didn't know how much longer she could keep up the pretence and Annie's mothering had become irritating.

Later that night, after Annie had gone upstairs, Bel lay in the box bed staring at the moonlit blue of the window. 'Mam,' she said, 'What should I do?' For a moment she thought she saw a shadow within a shadow, something with no edges moving between her and the darkest corner of the room. She shivered and pulled the quilt her mother had made up under her chin. The room seemed unusually cold. And then she felt it again, as she often had in times of stress, the soft, reassuring touch of a hand on her forehead. A sense of peace flowed through her and she closed her eyes. The next time she opened them it was daylight.

Poppy, the collie, lifted her head from where she lay on the rag rug and thumped her tail on the floor a few times. As she had done every day since her mother died, Bel rose and shivered in the early chill. Crossing to the stove, she opened the hob and piled kindling and dry peat onto the still glowing ashes. She used the chamber pot from beneath the bed, then took it outside and emptied it on the midden behind the byre where the animal dung was heaped before being spread on the land. Then she rinsed out the chamber pot with a can of water kept for that purpose and washed her hands in the rain barrel.

Back inside, she stirred the oats which she had left steeping in the large pan, and moved it over the flames, raked out the ashes and carried them outside to the ash-heap on the far side of the garden wall. These tasks were performed automatically, without conscious thought. The tedium of the early ritual gave her some normality back into her life.

'Bel, you're an angel,' said Annie when she came into the kitchen. 'It's fine to come ben to a warm fire and a singing kettle.' She pushed her mess of unruly hair back from her face and pulled her shawl more tightly over her nightdress. 'How did you sleep?'

'Aye, I slept well enough. I've just filled the teapot this minute and the porridge is on the boil. I told you, I'm fine.' She forced a smile to unwilling lips. 'I don't want to ever speak of Nick again.'

Annie didn't reply but simply hugged her, releasing her quickly when the door opened and Isa entered. 'Donald's away to visit his parishioners. I thought I'd give you lassies a bit of a hand. Bel! What happened to your face?'

'Ach, it's nothing. I slipped in the byre. Daft of me. I'm just a bit shaken, that's all.'

'You're sure? Are you hurt anywhere else?'

Everywhere else, thought Bel, but said, 'I'll be fine,'

Chapter Nine.

Early next morning, Bel went out to check the traps and found them depressingly empty. A wind had whipped up and rain threatened from the east. She saw Nick in the distance working on his boat and at the same time he saw her. She turned and retreated towards Scartongarth, but Nick was fast. He dropped what he had been doing and came racing up the slope angling outward so he arrived between her and the croft. In his outstretched hand, he held a fine-sized cod, his fingers hooked through the gills. Bel tried to skirt around him, but in her hurry her foot caught on a tuft of couch grass and she fell to her knees. She looked up to see Nick towering over her.

'Bel, here, I've got fish.' His voice was lower than usual, none of the brash confidence she hated. His eyes met hers and flew away like a bird. He held the fish out towards her. 'Maybe, maybe I came on a bit strong the other night, like.'

With the blood rushing to her face, Bel scrambled to her feet. She kept her head lowered. 'Ye hurt me.'

'Oh Bel, yer face. I'm sorry, I am. I didn't mean it. But ye must admit, ye've been keeping me going for weeks. And Annie, she came shouting like a cow at the bulling. What business is it of hers?'

Bel did not raise her head. She was near enough to smell the hot sour smell of him. 'I didn't ask her to.'

'I thought ye wouldn't. Ye would understand what drives a man wild when he wants a woman as much as I want ye.' He held the fish out to her as she regained her feet. 'Please take the cod, a peace offering, like. I'd buy ye much more if I had the money.'

She didn't want to take it. She didn't want to take anything from this man, but food was scarce and Scartongarth was hungry and it seemed like he wouldn't leave her alone unless she did. Trying her utmost not to show him her fear, Bel accepted the fish and pushed it into the sack she carried. 'Thanks Nick, it's fair welcome.' She still didn't meet his eye and turned to leave.

'Ye're surely no going away yet.' Nick grabbed her arm. His short, thick fingers dug into her flesh through the thin material of her blouse. 'Ye should be showing a bit of appreciation for a man who's been up since dawn. Come with me for a wee while to the cave yonder. I'll make up for the other night. I promise ye.' His voice softened. 'Ye'll enjoy it better next time. We could be good together, you and me.'

Bel swallowed over the dryness in her throat. 'There'll be no next time. I thought I liked ye, but...but now I don't. Now leave me be. I've traps to empty and a hundred other things to do.'

'Bel, I'm sorry if I hurt ye. I've wanted ye so much. Just give me the chance to show ye how sorry I am. I'll never hurt ye again as long as I live, I swear.'

Bel studied the hand holding her arm. On an island this size she would see him often, so she had to sort this now. She slowly raised her eyes to his. 'I thought I loved ye, but I don't. I can't be what you want, Nick, so I'll thank ye to leave me alone.'

'It's Annie, isn't it? She's the reason ye're rejecting me.'

'She's not.' Bel tried to struggle from his grasp. 'I've no time for this, I mean it.'

Nick gave a snort. 'I still want to wed ye, Bel. I stayed away because I was ashamed at what the wildness and the wanting ye did to my blood. There's no saying when the need takes a man. But I'll change. I will.'

His hand tightened until she gave a little cry.

'Give me another chance. Please, Bel, or does madam Annie tell ye what to do?' His voice, so soft and pleading a minute ago, became harder.

Bel forced herself to make eye contact. 'Ye're hurting me again.'

He let her go and wiped his hand on the leg of his dungarees. The calloused fingers made a scraping sound against the material. The lips she had once thought soft and inviting were now pressed together in a hard line.

'Has she got to ye, Bel? Has she set ye against me?'

Bel's mouth wouldn't form the words she really wanted to say. 'It's no Annie. It's me – I need time to think.'

'Think about what? It's like ye can't stand me to touch ye.'

Her eyes found the ground and she studied the smooth pebbles and broken shells making up the path. 'I don't like it, Nick. It hurt – ye hurt me. Leave me alone.'

He stared at her for a minute. 'Huh? But…but, aye, sometimes it takes the girls a wee while. Next time it'll be better, ye'll see. Come with me now, I'll prove it.'

'No, Nick.'

A muscle rippled along his jawline. His intake of breath was harsh and loud. 'Then don't take too long with this thinking. It sets a woman's head wrong, all that stuff going round in there.' He rapped a knuckle against her forehead. 'A man can't wait forever.' The look he

73

threw her held more anger than concern. 'Do ye still want me or no?'

'No.'

'Then I'll be away. There's plenty other lassies more than willing.' He kicked the stones on the path. 'Ye'll come crawling back when there's no another man on this island who'll look at ye. And I'll make sure they don't, I'll promise ye that.'

She shuddered at the threat in his words and watched him walk down to the pier, watched the swagger of his hips, the breadth of his shoulders. Was there something wrong with her? A bonny man, considered a catch, many an island lass envied the fact that he'd chosen her. And she'd hankered after him for a long time.

But he stole her innocence roughly and without feeling. Even his kisses had bruised her lips. There would be no escaping it if she married him. How could she put up with the pain night after night? Were all men the same? She wondered how other wives coped, but she guessed it was a woman's duty to put up with such things.

Chapter Ten

'It's the schoolhouse the night then,' said Tess. She was sitting in the kitchen of Scartongarth smoking a cigarette. 'Have ye tempted him yet?'

'No. He's just my teacher. I told you.'

'Is that why ye're all dolled up?'

'Dolled up? Nothing wrong with putting on a clean pinny is there,' said Annie with a laugh. She now went regularly up to the schoolhouse in the evenings. Alexander never showed more than the interest of a tutor and that suited her, or so she tried to convince herself. In the times when their eyes met, did she sense an affinity there or could it be her own imagination? Unlike other men she had known, he made no move towards her. It was as if a void existed that neither was inclined to cross. She found herself craving his approval and, every spare minute, she studied the books he had given her. At first it was born of the need to impress, but now she had grown genuinely interested.

'Ye'll give in yet,' said Tess, flicking ash into a cracked saucer, which she held in her hand. 'Hey, Bel, what ails ye these days? Come and keep yer visitor company. Annie'll be away up the road in a minute.'

'I'm sorry, Tess. But my head's sore. And...' Bel stared at the floor, her fingers twisting the cloth of her apron then releasing it. 'Nick's coming to speak to me and I'd like to see him on my own.'

'What?' Tess sat upright. 'I thought ye'd finished with him.'

Annie paused from where she was brushing her hair. 'Bel, please tell me you're joking.'

Bel closed her eyes. 'Ye'll have to know sooner or later.'

'What?' Annie and Tess both spoke at the same time.

'You're seeing him again? How could you?' Annie's breath quickened.

Since the attack, Bel had been pale and quiet. Her friends had done their best to cheer her up, but her mood constantly slipped lower.

'Bel,' Annie rose and stood beside her. 'I'm not leaving this house until you tell me what's in your head.'

'Me neither.' Tess stood beside them.

Bel lifted her eyes and they glistened. 'We...we're getting married.'

'Since when?' Annie could not believe what she was hearing. 'You hate him. Have you lost your senses?'

Bel started to sob. 'I have to marry him. I'm having his bairn.'

'No.' The word burst out of Annie's mouth. She looked at Tess who appeared equally horrified. Bel shook her head and wiped the tears from her eyes. 'I'll no bring a bairn into this world with no father and bring shame on my own head.'

'Oh, dear God, no,' Annie put her hand to her eyes.

'I've no choice.' Bel turned away and lifted the pan from the fire. 'There's so much work to do and I'm so tired. He'll help with the croft. At least there's that.'

'We'll help you. You don't have to marry him,' Tess said. 'I'll be here a while yet.'

'My mind's made up. I'll no hold you two back from yer plans.' Bel spoke quickly, her face flushed. 'I'm sure he'll be a good man in the end. I know he wants me for the croft, but once we have bairns there'll be little time for anything else. It will work out, Annie, if we're given the chance. I'm no bonny and clever like you. I'll never have the same opportunities.'

'But you are. There's more to life than this, there has to be.' Annie was still reeling.

'What's the point of dreaming? There is nothing more. I'm lucky to have Scartongarth, but I need a man to help me run it and I used to like Nick fine. Maybe I could again, and he'll give me bonny bairns. He's clever and all, was good at his lessons at school. And... what else can I do?'

'Other women live alone on the island.'

'Aye, and it's no easy on them either, but most have sons or brothers who give them a fry of fish. I know the islanders wouldn't see me starve, but I'll no live on charity. Scartongarth provided well once, but it needs a man's hand to bring it back.'

'Then get someone from an institution on the mainland. They can be good workers and you get paid for it as well.'

'I'd still need a man around to keep him in check. What if they give me someone who's dangerous?'

'It's not a good enough reason to marry.'

Bel gazed at the floor. 'I'm scared, Annie. My mam was never strong enough for farm work after Jimmy and I were born. And I'm just so tired.'

'Oh, Bel.' Annie knew she could never tell her now about Nick's advances.

Bel shook her head, her eyes once again taking on that faraway look. 'I wouldn't marry him otherwise. I don't think I would marry any man.'

Annie turned away, angry that her cousin had been put in this position. But who was she to interfere? Many an island woman married for the same reason and was happy. Or so they seemed.

77

'Tess, talk to her. I just can't.' Annie forgot about Alexander Garcia. Her body almost burst with the need to scream. She ran outside and harnessed Teddy, the workhorse, led him to the gate and used it to climb onto his broad back. Back in Canada, when she wanted to howl in frustration, she would mount her horse and gallop for miles. Teddy was young and fresh and unused to being ridden, but his feistiness suited Annie at this moment. He plunged forward tossing his head, his big hoofs digging into the soft ground. Annie loosened the rein and allowed him his freedom.

He galloped up the field, along the road, across the moorland. Annie did not pull him to a stop until he was in danger of plunging over the cliff. And she sat there, feeling the rise and fall of the muscles beneath her as the horse snorted and drew in ragged breaths. Then she shrieked into the sharp, salt-tinted wind. At this moment she could have cheerfully killed Bel's abuser. She turned the horse around and rode more slowly back to Scartongarth in time to encounter a grinning Nick Sinclair leaving the croft house. In her imagination she willed the horse to rear, willed his great hooves to crash on Nick Sinclair's skull and pound him until he turned to pulp.

He stopped when he saw her and waited until she dismounted. Unable to utter a word, she led Teddy towards the barn.

With a few quick strides he was beside her. 'Ye'll not be happy with the news, then.' He continued to grin.

Tears of frustration almost blocked her throat. 'I don't want to talk to you.' She pushed open the barn door.

'That's a shame. We both want ye to be bridesmaid. Would ye no do that for a girl ye claim to be fond of?'

Annie dampened her lips and turned hate-filled eyes on him. 'If you ever hurt her again...'

His hand shot out and he grabbed the harness. 'Ye'll do what?' His grin widened, mocking her.

Annie wished she owned a horse whip. She wished she had the means to wipe the smug look from his handsome face. In her mind she saw the weal rise across his cheek, the corner of the whip catch his mocking eye and rip it out. 'Let go of my horse and get out of my way.'

He released the horse and laughed. 'Your horse? In a couple of weeks he'll be my horse. Be nice to me and I might let you carry on riding him. In the meantime take good care of him. Oh, and that bicycle you use to get around, I'll have that back as well.' He walked away, still laughing.

She found Bel sitting in front of the fire with her head in her hands. She looked up as Annie entered. 'Dinna be mad at me, Annie. He promised he'd change. He's fair happy about the bairn and all.'

Annie sank in the opposite chair. 'And I can't change your mind?'

Bel shook her head. 'Be my witness, please?'

About to refuse, Annie looked into the pleading eyes, the pinched face, and melted. 'For you, Bel, I will, but only for you. But I can't stay here once you're wed. I'm sorry, but don't ask me.'

Bel nodded slowly. 'Just don't stay away because of him. I want ye to be godmother to my bairn.' She nibbled at her lower lip.

'Of course I will.' Annie crossed the space between them and hugged her cousin.

Chapter Eleven

Within the month, Reverend Charleston married Bel and Nick in the ben end of Scartongarth. Annie and Tess and one of Nick's brothers were the witnesses. There was no wedding dress or cake for Bel and she made her vows with no smile on her face. Nick, however, seemed jubilant. He had brought in a bottle of whisky from the mainland. Most of the island folks crowded into the small room, bringing presents of food and liquor. A few young men slapped Nick on the back.

By the time the night was over, Bel felt desperately tired. Annie hugged her before she left and said nothing, but her eyes betrayed her concern.

'I'll be fine,' Bel whispered with a forced smile. 'Nick's promised to change. He says he does love me and he's happy about the bairn. I'm sure he'll make a good dad.'

In spite of her words, as Bel watched her friends leave, she desperately wanted to beg them to stay, especially Annie. Turning to the room and the remains of the party, she wondered how she could avoid Nick's attentions this night. She just wanted to climb into her bed and sleep forever.

But he was looking at her with a bright glitter in his eye. Worse of the whisky, he staggered forward, lunging at her.

'Please, I'm tired.' Bel shrank from his grip. His hands closed on her arms and he pulled her roughly to him. 'You're my wife now, Bel. Come away to bed. I'll make you happy, I promise.' He half dragged her across the room.

Bel closed her eyes and allowed her body to fall flaccid onto the bed. This wasn't normal, it couldn't be; other women enjoyed the attentions of their men. She'd heard their jokes, their complaints when their men were away for months at a time. Biting her lip, she squeezed her eyes shut. She would lie here and suffer the indignities forced upon her sex for the sake of normality, and keep her strangeness buried within her.

Once Nick was fully satisfied, he rolled from her and began to snore.

Nursing her pain, Bel lay still, staring at the small oblong of faded blue night that was the ben-end window, while her groom grunted and snored his way towards morning. When finally she felt able to move, she rose and went to the back porch where she stripped and washed her burning body in the pail of rainwater. Over and over she soaped her skin and roughly scrubbed herself dry with the towel, desperate to wash every trace of him from her. When tiredness overcame her, she emptied the bucket out of the back door. Then she crawled into the box bed in the kitchen, huddled under the covers and pressed the quilt her granny had made against her mouth to stifle the sobs. Only when she felt the soft touch of her mother's ghostly hand on her hair, did she finally go to sleep.

The cockerel outside was already crowing when she felt the bed dip and a heavy hand on her shoulder.

'What are ye doing through here?'

She opened her eyes to see Nick's face loom over her, eyes heavy with sleep, the mark of the pillow still on his unshaven face. The sour whisky smell of his breath made her want to gag.

'I couldn't sleep, ye were snoring that loud,' she said, pushing herself into a sitting position, away from him.

He pulled the covers back and eased his naked body in beside her, his obvious arousal startling her.

81

He grinned at her shocked expression, misreading it. 'Surprised are ye? There's plenty more where that came from.'

'There's no time. I have to get up.' She tried to push him away, but he laughed and trapped her wrists in his big hands, pushing her back onto the bed. His eyes shut, his lips came towards hers and she twisted away so the harsh stubble scoured her cheek.

'Stop it, please stop it,' she screamed.

He drew back as if stung, confusion ghosting across his face. 'What's wrong wi ye?'

Bel wiped her cheeks. 'I'm sore. After last night.'

He laughed. 'Ah, I suppose I did expect too much too soon. But it'll get better, ye'll see. Ye'll be after me for more in the end. But now I'll let ye off with this.' He grabbed her hand and guided it to his throbbing member.

She forced herself not to vomit at the feel of it.

He moaned and grasped one of her breasts squeezing until she cried out. His body tensed and trembled, his mouth opened and he let out a long gasp before suddenly relaxing, dreadful sticky fluid covering her arm and leg. It took all her power to swallow the bile that rose in her throat. She was desperate to get away, to wash him from her once more. His presence had defiled the place where her warm ghosts came to her, let alone what he'd made her do.

He threw one heavy leg across hers, one heavy arm across her breasts, then fell asleep again, trapping her in his filth. God, she wished she'd listened to Annie. Survival was not worth this torture. What had she done?

Later that morning Nick left the house and swaggered down the road, whistling a tune. Bel dragged the tin bath from the back porch, filled it with warm water and carbolic soap and lowered her body into the suds to soak away the shame of the night.

After drying herself and dressing, she dragged the blankets from the bed. Blankets were usually washed in the spring when the air was dry, but she could not wait. She plunged them into the soapy water and trampled them until she was satisfied. There was little wind and they hung on the line outside like helpless sails.

Bel still felt unclean. She had agreed to marry a man she did not love and had submitted herself to his disgusting lust. Ignoring the many chores still to be done, she walked to the beach and stared at the water, somnolent for once, lapping against the pebbles.

'Oh, Jimmy,' she said aloud, 'why did you leave me?' Jimmy was her twin, her other half, her confidant. Down-to-earth in a way she had never been, she doubted he would believe what went on inside her head. He might think her mad and maybe she was. Maybe she was as mad as old Addie Andrews who never rose from her bed except at the full moon, when she went outside, lifted her head and howled.

Out in the bay, the waves beckoned her. She took a step towards them and another until they flirted with her bare feet. If she kept walking, it would all be so easy. The water would cleanse her. She kept walking until the waves reached her knees and she could not feel her feet. A sudden flutter in her stomach made her gasp and stop. For the first time her bairn was real, a living thing growing inside her, her responsibility. She stood still for a long moment, her hands trailing in the water. The sea had taken her father when she had been too young to have any memory of him and her mother had never been the same again. She wouldn't mind if the sea took Nick, she would have the sympathy of the islanders and her bairn would be decent.

She gasped with horror at the thought. What an evil person she must be. Perhaps she deserved all that had befallen her. She staggered back up the beach, trailing

83

green weed around her ankles. *Never, never, never think like that again, not for one moment*, she told herself.

As she approached the house, a cockerel crowed, hungry chickens raced around her feet, the cow bellowed from the byre, the dog ran to her, tail wagging, and licked her hand. She looked up at the sky, blue with shredded clouds stretched across it and seabirds circling and shrieking at an unjust world. Her first day as a married woman had begun and who knew what the future held? Maybe once the novelty had worn off, Nick would leave her be. Yes, she would keep her 'strangeness' locked up inside, and she would be a wife and have bairns and suffer what she must, and maybe, just maybe, he was right and eventually she would grow to care for him.

Chapter Twelve

Annie had a fairly large room in the manse, with a real bed all to herself. To her delight she also had a desk and a bookcase and downstairs, in the minister's study, there were any number of books that she could choose.

From the kitchen she could smell ham frying and hear her mother singing softly as she cooked. There was no farm work to do here other than a vegetable garden, so she had plenty time to study. She hadn't seen Bel since the wedding over a week ago and longed to know how she was faring.

She glanced at the clock on the mantel. The boats would not be back from the fishing yet.

'I'm going to see Bel,' she shouted to her mother as she came downstairs.

'I'm glad,' Isa called back. 'I've meant to go myself. I've been a bit worried.'

Annie marched out into the misty morning. Having made up her mind, she grew impatient and she missed the speed the bicycle had provided.

As she passed the shop, Tess came out and waved. 'Where are ye going?' she shouted.

'To see Bel. I've neglected her for too long.' She stopped and waited for the other girl.

Tess slipped her arm through Annie's. 'I went to see her the other day. She's no happy. Looks as weak as a kitten. I managed to time it when *he* wasn't there.'

'Come with me, we'll go and see her now. And if he's come home early, well, there's safety in numbers.' Annie wasn't afraid of him, but her stomach crawled at the thought of being anywhere near him. She had tholed the wedding ceremony with blood that boiled as if there was too much of it in her body.

'I can't come the day. My da's in one of his contrary moods.' She pulled a face. 'Do ye really think Nick's that bad? Bel might be the making of him. He's a rough lad, but he's a good worker and he's older now. A wife and bairn might be the settler he needs.'

'I hate him, Tess, and I can't help it.'

She found Bel bent over the washtub, elbow-deep in soap suds. Her pale face became more worried than pleased and as she stood up, her eyes turned quickly to the firth then back again. She dried her hands on her apron. 'Come away in and I'll put the kettle on. I made a bannock the day.'

As Annie sipped her tea she watched Bel. She constantly glanced at the window and her hands twisted in her pinny. She looked like a ghost.

'How's marriage?' Annie asked.

Bel glanced at the window. 'It's fine. I'm getting into the routine. How is it at the manse?'

'Good. I've got a big room to myself. I miss you though.'

'I miss ye too, but I'm married now. Things change. Would ye like another slice of bannock? I'll be making more butter in the afternoon.' She stood stiffly.

Annie wanted to cry, stop this, Bel. Sit down, tell me what's going on. Where was the easy relationship they had enjoyed no more than a week ago? How could Bel have changed so much in such a short time?

'You'll need to eat for two now. I could do the traps for you.'

Bel raised a trembling hand to her head. 'There's no need. I'm fine. I am really.'

'You'd tell me if anything was wrong,' Annie said.

'There's nothing wrong.' Then, in a more contrite voice continued. 'Please stop worrying. Life's different now that's all. Once we have the bairn, things'll be fine.' She glanced through the window. 'Nick doesn't want you coming here, though.'

'Do you want me to leave?'

'No, no, but just don't come when he's here, mind.' She glanced through the window again.

'I wouldn't anyway.' Annie wanted to add that she detested him, but what was the point? Bel had made her choice and there was little anyone could do about it now. 'I'd best be away, then.'

Bel's face filled with relief. 'It's best, Annie. He'll be back any minute.'

'Maybe you should come and see us up at the manse when you can.'

'Aye, aye, that'll be grand.' She smiled and a ghost of her old self appeared for a fleeting second. 'I will. Soon.'

On Saturday morning, Alexander met Annie as she stepped through the door. 'Good news.' He held up a folder. 'It *is* possible for you to go to university.'

Suddenly Bel's problems vanished from Annie's mind.

'That's great. How?

'You're bright, Annie. You've done so well. As you know I've been looking into ways to fund your education.' Alexander walked across the room and set the papers on the table.

'There's a trust been set up to educate the girls from the islands of Shetland and Orkney. I think we should apply for that.'

87

Her breath quickened. Could it be possible that her dreams would come true after all?

'What are my chances of getting it?'

'Very good I would say, when I tell them how well you've progressed. There will be some exams of course…' He did not get any further. She let out a whoop and folded her hands over her mouth in glee.

Alexander laughed with her and then became serious. 'I'll miss our sessions,' he said.

'So will I.' For a long moment their eyes met and held. 'We'll write,' she said. 'And I will be back.' The thought of not seeing him for months at a time dampened her spirits.

A silence only punctuated by the ticking clock, the whispering flames and the wind outside, fell between them.

He tore his gaze away. 'You'll meet many new people, lots of young men. Perhaps you won't miss me so much.'

'But I will.' She walked around the desk and stood before him, eyes trapping his once more. 'I will miss you.' She wanted to kiss him so much. She wanted this in the open now, she wanted him to say he'd wait for her, she wanted to swear she'd wait for him.

For a moment they stood like that. Unable to stop herself she leaned forward and stood on tiptoe until her lips almost touched his.

He sprung back as if stung. 'Annie, don't…' His voice came low, more like a plea for mercy. 'I'm older than you. I'm engaged to be married. You're my pupil. That's all.'

'I don't believe you. I've seen the way you look at me. I'm not a child.'

He sucked air through his teeth. 'You are a very beautiful young woman with a great life before you, but you still have a lot of the world to see. You're innocent in a lot of ways and I will not take advantage of that.' In spite of his words, she saw the flash of longing in his eyes and she knew she had him.

She stepped closer. 'Look at me and say you don't want me.' If he did that, she knew she would die, but she'd gone too far to back down now. She waited, each second an eternity.

He took another step back, then forward and suddenly his arms were around her and his lips on hers.

Annie gave a little moan and slipped her arms around his neck. She could not remember ever having been kissed like that before and all the magic she had read about was insignificant to the feelings surging through her at that moment.

She let her head fall back, her mouth slightly open, her lips desperate for more, everything else in her life forgotten.

'Oh, Annie, don't do this to me.' His breath came quickly, his eyes half opened, cloudy and dark. 'Go now, before I do something I'll regret – we'll both regret.' He grabbed her arms, turned her around and gave her a little push towards the door. 'I shouldn't have done that. Forget it happened.'

'I wouldn't regret anything.' She knew she would be unable to resist him at that moment, no matter what the consequences.

'Annie.' His tone was sharp, almost angry. 'I think it better if I don't tutor you anymore.'

She gasped. She couldn't let him do that, she just couldn't. 'I'll say no more about it if that's what you want. Don't stop teaching me, please.'

He ran his fingers through his hair and shook his head. 'Maybe William…'

Panic gripped her. 'I'll never mention it again, I promise.' Her lip quivered.

89

He closed his eyes, then nodded. 'We forget this nonsense,' he said. 'And if we can, we'll see. I hope I don't regret it.'

'Thank you. I'll be good and work hard. One day I'll make you glad you let me stay.'

But the memory of that kiss remained with her and made her hungry for more.

She was burning up to tell Bel her news, like she would have done in the past, but in spite of her promise, Bel had not come to the manse.

She couldn't let Nick ruin her friendship with Bel. Maybe Tess would think of something.

Tess was walking down the fields scattering the grain from the canvas seed-scoop, the happer, a flock of sea maws following her, lapwings tumbling about her. When she saw Annie, she stopped.

Annie ran across to her. 'I've something to tell you, but you're going have to wait until I get you and Bel together.'

Tess squeezed her arm. 'Is it something exciting?'

'Oh, aye.'

'Then we'll go and find Bel now. He can't keep us away. I don't care if he is home. We'll face him together.'

'Absolutely.' With fingers linked, they ran down the field.

They found Bel sitting on the stone seat at the side of the house, the water bucket by her feet. She looked up when she saw them and jumped to her feet. 'I'll put the kettle on,' she said.

Isa was shocked at the sight of her. In the short time since she'd seen her last, Bel had grown paler with dark circles beneath her eyes. 'Are you alright, Bel?' she asked.

'I'm so tired and sick. I'm not eating.'

Tess glanced at the fields. 'Is Nick still at sea?'

She shook her head. 'Came back an hour ago. He's out mending dykes.'

'Forget the tea. Come with us. It's a fine day.'

Tess took one arm, Annie took the other. 'We're going to sit on the beach, the way we used to after the chores were done.'

Bel looked around. 'I don't know. Nick...'

'Never mind Nick. Ye need a bit of time off, more so now than ever.'

Tess and Annie steered her towards the shore.

The three girls sat on the north quay, legs hanging over the side and Annie told them about her university place.

Tess gave a little shriek. 'I'm that happy for ye.'

'Aye, me too,' said Bel without enthusiasm. 'But ye'll be going away.' She continued to glance landwards and constantly plucked at the material of her skirt.

'But I'll be back every chance I get. Anyway, it's not definite that I will get it.'

Bel gave a wan smile and turned to stare out to sea, her body rocking slightly.

Tess lit a cigarette, drew deeply on it and offered it to the other girls who both declined. She shrugged. 'Sanny the Post has finally given up his round. Did ye hear? Magnus got his job.'

'I'm glad for Magnus,' said Bel. 'He's a fine lad.'

'Aye. He's no strong enough for the farm work. As weak as a kitten some days.'

Annie leaned back, resting on her elbows, turning her face up to the sun. She listened to the water lapping against the stone wall of the pier, the seabirds crying above her and the voices of her friends. She thought of Alexander Garcia. Of his dark eyes, of his lips on hers. This piece of news she wanted to keep to herself, hold it near her heart and relive it whenever she chose.

'Is Nick treating ye well enough?' asked Tess.

Bel gave a little sigh. 'Aye, he's fine. It's the bairn. Fair draining my strength, so it is.'

Annie sat up. 'And married life – is he still as rough with ye?'

Bel's bottom lip wobbled. 'He's treating me well enough.' She sniffed and a tear trickled down her cheek. Tess put an arm around the shaking shoulders. Bel began to cry in earnest.

Once the sobs had subsided, Bel wiped her eyes. 'It's not him, it's me, really. I suppose it's what men want. I'll never be a proper wife, ye know? But he'll no leave me alone. Night after night, I'm afeart he'll hurt the bairn with his demanding. And I'm getting no sleep. I just can't stand it.' She took a fresh bout of weeping. 'Apart from that he's fine enough.'

Annie and Tess glanced at each other.

'Does he hurt *you*?' asked Annie.

'He doesn't mean to. But I don't like it. I hate it. He's rough and …and… Ach, ignore me. I'd be happy enough if he'd keep his hands off me. He's a good man in every other way.'

'He forces you?'

'No. I don't fight him. It's a man's right, is it no?'

Annie didn't know whether it was a man's right or not, but she thought it shouldn't be. She had thought she would rather like the physical side. This morning, in Alexander's arms, she had wanted to go further, longed to. Would have if Alexander hadn't pushed her away. What had she been thinking? Now with university looming why would she risk having a bairn? Alexander was right. He was just looking out for her.

'And otherwise?' asked Tess.

'Otherwise the croft is getting better from all the neglect. Nick works hard and wants to come home to a warm wife, he says.' She covered her face and sniffed some more. 'I'm just not the right wife for him. I wish none of this was happening. I wish he would find another woman to spend his night with.'

'Maybe I can help ye,' said Tess.

'How? Ye'll no be thinking of sleeping with my man?' Bel looked at her in horror, then gave a little laugh. 'Though I'd thank ye if ye did.'

'Heavens, no. But I'll come and see ye tomorrow when he's at the fishing.'

'What are you up to?' asked Annie.

Tess stood up and stretched. 'It's a bonnie day, but I've wasted enough of it. There's a washing to do back at the croft, seeding to finish and bread to bake. I'd best go before my dad comes looking for me.'

'Aye, me and all.' Bel stood up. 'But it was grand seeing ye again.' Much more relaxed than she had been, she turned to Annie as Tess walked away. 'She can't help me. She's sometimes away with the fairies that one. But I'm happy for ye, Annie, though I'll miss ye sorely.'

'It'll be a while yet before the applications and all that go through. But we'll come and see ye often, Tess and me, when Nick's not there.'

'Ye don't have to do that. Nick's no that bad. He wouldn't mind me having visitors. He wouldn't. I was just being daft before. Oh Annie, I'm that glad ye came the day.'

With further promises to see each other more often, Annie left. How could she admit the other reason she didn't want to be in Nick's company? Whenever she was anywhere near him, she could feel his eyes crawling all over her.

Annie tried hard to concentrate on her reading. She had to think of her own future now. Bel had made her choice, and who knew, maybe fatherhood would make a man of Nick. Yet she couldn't help worrying. Her head filled with thoughts so that she had to re-read the same passage over and over and it still did not sink in. Apart from Bel, the memory of Alexander's lips pressed to her own was constantly with her. Finally she set down the book and went to help her mother in the vegetable garden.

As for Alexander, he knew he should pass Annie's education on to William Dick. Daily the girl was seeping into his blood. He loved Elizabeth and she would make a good wife, she was attractive, intelligent and kind, their families were friends and they shared the same beliefs. His life was already planned, orderly. He would work for a year, save up enough money to go to Spain, he would return, marry Elizabeth, find a suitable teaching job and raise a family. He had had his youth, his idealistic rebellions behind him, part of his student days. Why then did he allow himself to enjoy the company of the step-daughter of a Presbyterian minister and look forward to her visits so much? Why did he allow himself to kiss her like that?

But surely there was no harm in it, he told himself. She would leave the island, meet a man her own age and their time together would sink into the archives of his memories.

Chapter Thirteen

Meanwhile in Scartongarth, Nick pushed his plate away. 'This is no like me,' he said. 'I can't seem to settle. And I've no appetite.' He turned sunken eyes up to his wife. His hand shook and the spoon fell and clattered against the table.

'Aye, maybe ye're coming down with something.' With no more than a mere glance in his direction, Bel took away the plate and ate from it. She was hungry and the meagre portion left for herself had done nothing to satisfy her appetite. Her sickness had left her and she felt more in control than she had ever done.

'But I've no had a day's illness in my life. And... and...' He tried to stand up, but swayed against the table. 'It's this last while. Huh...I need to lie down.'

Bel's body tightened. The plus side of this marriage was that he worked hard to bring Scartongarth back to full production. 'But there's the fields to sow and the fishing to be done.'

'I'm ailing for something. I've even started a rash. Look.' He held out his arm and pulled up his sleeve. 'Maybe we should get the doctor, Bel.'

Without sympathy, she studied the red spots. 'We don't have the money. Ye'll be fine in a day or so. I'll make ye some chicken broth. There's a couple of old hens that's gone off the lay.' How she wished she had never married him. The love she once had had for him had turned to active dislike and was working its way towards hate.

He rubbed his forehead. 'I'm not a well man and that's the truth.'

95

'Ye're always grizzling! I thought that after we wed, I'd have a good hand to run the croft, but ye're as lazy as they come.' His recent apathy coupled with the frustration of her situation had given her the courage to talk back. She no longer saw him as the strong brash man she married, but someone pathetic and whinging.

'I am not lazy!' He banged his fist on the table, then pressed the heels of his hands to his eyes. 'Sometimes I feel I'm going mad. All these weird thoughts going round in my head.'

'Then go back to yer bed. Ye're no use to me as ye are.'

'And that's another thing. I'm no use to ye in bed either!'

'Well, that's no hardship for me. Anyway, all yer demands, it's bound to be bad for the bairn'

'There are other ways. It's a sad thing for a man to lose his manhood. Oh, Bel, I think I'm dying.'

Bel softened until she almost felt sorry for him. She was happy he left her in peace to sleep, but she needed more help on the land and these last few weeks his energy seemed to be seeping from him. Maybe now they could get a man from an institution. He could sleep in the barn and she'd get paid and all. 'Nick,' she began, but as she raised her head to broach the subject, Nick grabbed his stomach and crumpled onto the floor, the chair skidding on the flagstones and toppling over.

'Nick! Oh my God.' Bel's hand came up to cover her mouth, the other clutched at her apron as she backed away until the door behind her blocked her retreat. She fumbled with the handle and yanked the door towards her, stumbling outside. She looked wildly around before running up the brae to the road and grabbed the arm of the first person she saw. 'Help me,' she shouted. 'Nick's collapsed. Get the men to go for the doctor.'

An hour later, Doctor Denny stood up and scratched his head. 'I know what it looks like. But how is it possible?' His eyes imprisoned Bel's. 'Has he been taking anything, any medicines?'

Bel felt her face grow hot, but shook her head and stared at the floor.

'He's very ill. What aren't you telling me?'

'Nothing, I swear.' Bel's hand shook and she avoided the doctor's eye.

'Do you want him to die?'

'No, no, but...'

'But what?'

'I only wanted him to leave me alone.'

'What have you given him, woman?'

Bel went through to the back porch. She returned with a bottle which she handed to the doctor. 'I slipped some in his tea every night.'

Doctor Denny read the label. 'Potassium Bromide. Exactly as I suspected. Where did you get this?'

Bel hung her head. 'I can't tell ye, doctor. Don't make me. I'm sorry, doctor, I... didn't want to make him ill.'

'But why? This is outrageous. You could be sent to prison, do you know that?'

Bel started to cry. 'He's a rough man. And I was so tired... Please don't tell the law. It must be safe. They gave it to the soldiers in the trenches.'

'I doubt it was in the amount you've been feeding this man. He's suffering with bromism, chronic bromide toxicity.' He stared at her, an expression of disgust on his florid face. 'So you got it from one of the young men who have returned from the war?'

Bel lifted her head and glared back at him. 'Don't expect me to tell you. I will not. Get the law if you must, force me to have the bairn in a cell, but I will never tell!'

Doctor Denny shook his head. 'I won't report you. I'll let Nicholas deal with you himself.'

'Don't tell him, doctor. Please don't tell him. I won't do it again, I swear.' She grabbed his arm.

He shook her off. 'It's his right to know. I'll come back next week. I hope to find him greatly improved.' And with that he pushed the bottle into his bag and went into the bedroom.

The doctor had no sooner left, than the dreaded shout from the ben room echoed through the house. 'Bel!'

Hands twisting together, she made her way through the passage.

'I don't believe this. Ye poisoned me, Bel, ye poisoned me.' His voice was weak but the venom in it flowed strong.

'No, it was only to stop ye going on at me every night. I didn't know it would make ye ill.' Bel stared at him. Her hands no longer twisted, but clutched each other tight enough to hurt.

He struggled to sit up, his eyes blazing. 'Who is it? Who gave it to ye?'

'I'll never tell. Never.'

He threw the quilt off and pulled himself out of bed. Steadying himself against the wall, he came towards her and lifted his hand as if to strike her.

'Think o' yer bairn,' she cried, raising her arms to protect herself.

He lowered his fist. 'By God, I never thought you hated me that much!'

'I don't hate ye. I didn't mean to make ye ill. I just can't stand the things ye make me do.'

'Well, if sleeping with me is so repulsive, don't worry. I'll no be bothering ye again. Ye can sleep in the kitchen. The ice will form in hell before I lay a finger on ye, ye cold bitch.'

Nick turned and tottered back to the bed. 'Get me some food. It'll no be such an easy life I'll give ye once my strength comes back, I'll tell ye that. I've been bloody good to ye and ye know it.'

Bel almost ran to the kitchen where she stood shaking, allowing the tears to run unchecked down her face.

'But where did you get it?' asked Annie, as the two of them strolled along the shore.

'Tess. She told Magnus about me. I was mad at her for that, but he gave her something they gave the soldiers during the war to stop the urges, they said. He didn't take any himself, but it was still in his kitbag. I think I gave Nick too much.'

'And you feel bad? Please don't. He deserves it all and more. I'm proud of you.' Annie clutched her cousin's hands and laughed. 'At least he'll leave you alone now.'

'I didn't mean to make him ill, I didn't. I feel so guilty.'

'No, no, don't feel guilty. He deserved it, didn't he?'

'I thought he had a fever. I didn't know it was the stuff. I kept giving him more.' Bel wiped her cheeks.

'He wouldn't listen when you said no.'

'He saw it as his right.'

'It's not his right! Now he knows he can't push you around.'

'But it's not his fault I can't stand him to touch me. He's a good enough man in his way. It's the way men live.'

Annie sighed. 'Aye, and it's time something was done about it.'

'But, by, at least he'll no touch me again. Let him find some willing lass and I'll no object!' Bel suddenly giggled.

Annie laughed with her. 'I wish I saw his face when the doctor told him!'

'Aye, he was a picture, right enough.'

'Bless Magnus.'

'Aye, bless him. He's not like the other lads. He's quiet and kind.'

'Do you care for him, Bel?'

Bel's face reddened. 'I like him that's all. I'm sorry for him, being in the war and all. I wish I had taken him and not Nick, but now I'm a married woman with a bairn due any day.'

'I wouldn't judge you whatever you did. I never thought Nick was worthy of you.'

Bel stared at the ground. 'We have to do what we must. I'll be a good wife to Nick in every other way and a good mother for my bairn.'

'I know you will. I just wish you were happy.'

Tess appeared at the top of the rise, waved and came running towards them. 'I've got news,' she said, breathless. 'I came to tell ye I'm going away into service. I've got a job in a doctor's house in Wick. I'll get twenty-eight pounds a year, paid monthly and I'll get one afternoon a week off from four o'clock till ten o'clock and every other Sunday. My folks need the money and with Bel married and ye going to university soon, I want to get away and all.' She nudged Bel. 'I heard about Nick. Serves him right, eh?'

This time all three laughed. It was good to see Bel back to her old self.

'I'll be alright now,' she said. 'But I wish ye weren't leaving me.'

Tess squeezed her shoulder. 'But we'll meet when we come home and we'll be home often, won't we, Annie?'

'As often as I can. I want to be godmother to this wee tyke.' She set her hand on Bel's stomach.

'Ye'll both be godmothers. I insist. But I'll miss ye so much.'

'I'll miss ye and all. But,' Tess nodded towards the fields around them. 'Look at Scartongarth. Whatever my opinion of Nick Sinclair, he's a grand worker. It's yer dream, Bel, to have the croft back the way it was. Aye, it's exciting. It's a new life for all of us.'

Chapter Fourteen

'No, Da, ye can't stop me going.' Tess glowered at her father who sat before the fire rubbing his misshapen knees. 'I'll send money home. It'll help.'

'But who's going to look after me?' Tears formed in his rheumy eyes, softening her heart.

'Magnus is here. Between ye, ye'll manage.'

'A house needs a woman's touch.'

'Dad, there's nothing here for me. At least on the mainland I'll have a job.'

'I'm not long for this world, then ye and Magnus can run the croft together. There's little chance of either of ye getting wed. Him with his poor health and ye with yer big teeth like a horse.'

Tess rubbed her forehead. After all these years she should be used to her father's jibes, but they still stung.

'Aye, I favour ye in looks, yet ye still got a wife.'

Her father started forward, grasping the arms of his chair. 'I was a fine figure of a man in my day. It's that my looks do not sit well on a lass. And Magnus there, he's the spit of your mother, far too like a girl. Why couldn't it have been the other way round, eh?' He glowered at her as if her lack of beauty was her own fault.

Tess sighed. She had to go, if for no other reason than to get away from her father's constant belittling. Nothing either of them did pleased him. 'I'm going, Da, and there's an end to it.'

'Then ye'll not come back here, I'll make sure of that. And don't expect a penny in my will, either.'

'I don't think I'll ever want to come back and as for yer will, what have ye got to leave?' Her voice had risen. She had to get away from the place where her father's disapproval ate into her confidence on a daily basis.

'I'm glad yer mother didn't live to see the day when ye left me to fend for myself.' He muttered some more about disrespect and no gratitude. She didn't speak to him again that night.

Next morning, she pulled out her old, battered kist, the one her mother used when she herself was a downstairs maid, and packed her few possessions in it. She had been told she would need to wear a uniform and this she purchased with the money she had squirreled away from her share of last year's lamb sales. She left, dressed in a blouse and skirt that belonged to her mother.

Magnus had arranged for Jock from two crofts up to take her to the pier with his horse and cart. 'How're you going to get this kist to the doctor's house?' he asked. 'Are they coming to meet ye?'

'Na, I'll need to go on the bus.' Her belongings weighed very little, it was the oak kist itself that added the weight. As Jock and Magnus hoisted the kist onto the cart, her father appeared at the cottage door and tottered towards them on legs so wide apart at the knees that, when he stood upright, they almost formed the letter O.

'Dad?' she said. 'Will ye come with me to the haven? I don't want to leave on bad terms.'

'Aye, I'm coming right enough, but just to make sure ye're off the island. Help me up, Jock.' With much heaving and pushing, he eventually sat on the seat beside the driver.

Tess smiled to herself. She knew the effort the climb had cost him. Along the road he stared ahead without speaking. At the haven, with the help of both Jock and Magnus and his face twisted in pain, he eased himself down.

Tess stood before him. 'Bye for now, Dad. I will be back.' She stared at him, willing him to say something kind; she had to tell herself that underneath his gruff exterior he really did care for her.

As she looked into the wizened, weathered face, she realised for the first time how much he had aged since her mother's death. 'I love ye, Dad,' she whispered.

Without warning, he put his arms around her, hugging her awkwardly but fiercely, which surprised her. Even if it were not for his current discontent, her family had never gone in for open affection and the last time her dad had given her a cuddle had been when she was a wee girl.

'I'd come wi' ye, lass, to help ye with the kist, but my legs.' He indicated the offending limbs.

It was his way of apologising for his cruel words the night before and the closest thing to an apology she would get. 'I know, Dad, I know.' With his arthritis, getting on the boat would be beyond him. 'Between me and Magnus, we'll manage.'

Turning quickly as her own eyes blurred, she allowed her brother to help her onto the boat. Jock lowered the kist down into their upstretched hands.

'I'm sorry to leave ye with his foul moods,' she said to Magnus as they watched the shoreline grow smaller.

Magnus gave a laugh. 'I've coped with the Germans. I can cope with a bitter tongue. He is fond of us in his way.'

Tess nodded. It was the way he used the truth to hurt her that she could barely stand.

Once the bus dropped them off, Magnus helped her carry the kist up to the door of the doctor's house and rang the bell. An irritable-looking older woman dressed in a white blouse, navy cardigan and skirt, dark stockings and black lacing shoes, answered the door. Her face was thin and long, with greying hair rolled in a sausage shape around her head, glasses perched on a narrow nose.

'I'm the new maid,' Tess said.

'What are you doing coming to the front door? Get round the back.'

'Please couldn't we … just this once. My brother's disabled and this kist is awful heavy.'

The woman's face turned beetroot. 'You'll not last here a week with that attitude, girl. Get round the back now.'

Tess looked at Magnus. Beads of sweat dotted his face and he was breathing heavily.

'Is there anyone who could help, then?' Surely there had to be a manservant of some kind, she thought.

The woman's mouth fell open. 'This is not a hotel and you are not a guest!' she slammed the door.

'I'll drag the kist along the ground,' Tess said. 'You rest.'

'That bitch,' Magnus muttered. 'Are ye sure ye want to work here?'

'It'll have to do till I find somewhere else.'

'Then give me a minute to get my breath. How do we even get round the back?'

The only way seemed to be down the drive to the road and up a side lane. They made their way around and finally found a heavy door. Tess thumped at it a few times. This time it was opened by a woman dressed in pale blue and white with a cap covering her hair.

'Come on in, hen,' she said. 'I'm Mrs Mowat, call me Elsie. Ye'll be the new girl. And who's this young fellow?'

Surely this must be the cook, for food was obviously no shortage in her kitchen. When she led them in, Tess was sure she felt the floor tremble beneath them. But in complete contrast to the fiend upstairs, her smile was wide and welcoming.

'My brother. ?He was hurt in the war and he's not very strong.'

Magnus elbowed her. She'd forgotten how he hated to have his disability pointed out. Back home she had done it to tease and had fallen into the habit. 'Sorry,' she whispered.

The first thing she noticed about the large kitchen was the size of the range. With two ovens, it filled one side of the room. A long wooden table with eight chairs around it sat in the middle of the floor. Tess surmised that at one time, this house would have had many more servants.

'Sit yerself down and I'll brew ye a tea. I'll give Jemmy the gardener a shout and he'll take yer luggage. Yer room'll be through the back. Doctor MacGregor's a fine man, but his wife, ye've got to watch for her. And as for her companion, Mrs Wilson, she's a real harridan. Calls herself Mrs but she's never had a man in her life if you ask me. Thinks she owns the place, she does. A decent roll in the hay would do her the world of good!' She smirked to herself.

Tess rubbed her aching arms. 'I think I got a flavour at the front door.'

Elsie stared at her. 'Ye went to the front door?'

Tess nodded. Elsie let out a hoot of laugher and slapped her thigh. 'I've no heard the like of it. That's ye in the bad books right away.'

Tess made a grimace.

Magnus glanced at the clock on the wall. 'Thanks for the tea. I'd best be going, if I'm to catch the bus home.' He set his hand on Tess's arm. 'Ye take care, lass.'

106

'Aye, ye too. And take care o' Dad. I know he can be a contrary bugger, but it can't be easy wi no wife and the arthritis.'

'Don't ye worry. We'll rub along fine.'

'And Bel. I have a feeling she'll need a friend.'

Magnus grew pink. 'I'll keep an eye on her.'

'I'll walk ye out.' Elsie led the way and they disappeared through the door.

Elsie returned with a bent old man with earthy hands and wearing dungarees. He winked at Tess. 'Where's this kist of yours then?' His eyes fell on the wooden box. With a strength that belied his age and build, he lifted the kist off the floor, balanced it on his shoulder and carried it through another door.

'Once work's done for the night, the door between ye and the house is locked. Ye don't get back into the kitchen until her upstairs come and unlocks it, so there's no chance of a midnight snack. Ye have an outside toilet, but it does flush.' He opened another door to a small room with walls the colour of weak, milky tea, a single bed and a chest of drawers.

'Mrs Wilson goes home at night, so ye'll be on yer own. But don't go sneaking any young men in, her upstairs has ears like ye wouldn't believe.'

He set the kist on the floor with a thump, wiped his brow and caught his breath.

'What do I do now?' Tess asked.

'Put on yer uniform and go back to the kitchen. Elsie'll keep ye right.' He gave her a wink as he left. 'I hope ye stay longer than the others.'

Those words hardly boosted her confidence.

She studied the duty list Elsie had given her. Rise at five thirty. Clean the flues. polish the steel fender and the fire tools, set and light the fires, black lead the range, prepare cook's table, lay the upstairs tables for the family. Have this done by eight thirty. Take time for your own breakfast. Kitchen staff eat whatever has been left over from upstairs dinner the night before. Clear away and wash the breakfast things, wash front door and step and polish knocker, make up beds and collect laundry, prepare cook's table for lunch. The list went on and on. Tess was no stranger to hard work, but she wondered how she would ever get all the chores done in the time allotted. Her last job in service had been looking after one amiable old woman.

Tess soon found out that nothing was good enough for Mrs Wilson, 'her upstairs'. Her tongue was as sharp as her nature was sour. And when Tess eventually met Mrs MacGregor the mistress of the house, she discovered that she was even worse. One of Tess's less pleasant duties consisted of taking the mistress for a walk in her bath chair when Wilson had a day off. The woman constantly complained. Tess walked too fast or too slow, the wind was in her face, she was too cold or too hot. She derided Tess for being clumsy, for being ugly, for being untidy, for not completing her tasks in time, which was completely untrue. It seemed the woman had a grudge against the world and the maid became the target of her dissatisfaction. No wonder she couldn't keep staff, Tess thought.

Bobby, the message boy who brought up the deliveries from the grocers, made Tess laugh and she looked forward to his visits more and more. She loved his cheeky wit and he, it seemed, loved hers.

One day he sidled up to her. 'Eeh, Tess,' he whispered when Elsie was in the pantry checking the supplies, 'Fancy going to the pictures with us on yer next day off?'

Tess wondered who 'us' was. 'Who's all going,' she asked.

'Just me, like, and ye if ye'll come.'

'I'd like to,' she answered. She'd never been to the picture house.

His face split into a grin. 'Charlie Chaplin next week.'

On her afternoon off they went to the matinee of Charlie Chaplin in '*The Kid*'. Bobby led her to the back of the theatre and once the lights went out, he put an arm around her shoulders. Her first instinct was to resist, but then she decided she rather liked the feel of his arm there. The moving picture on the screen fascinated her and when Bobby leaned over to kiss her and blocked her view she pushed him away.

'Ah, Tess, lass,' he said. 'A wee kiss, what's wrong wie that?'

Tess thought there was nothing at all wrong with it, but right at this minute the moving screen held more fascination for her.

'I want to watch this.'

'Later then?'

'Aye, later.' She snuggled against him and he tightened his arm. She thought she would rather enjoy the 'later'.

Once they were in the lane between the house and the high hedge, he pushed her against the wall and kissed her again. This time she allowed the kiss, allowed him to fondle her bosom. She even allowed him to lift her skirt, but grew wary when he started to fumble with his own flies.

'Ah, come on,' he panted, his breath hot against her cheek.

'I'll no have a bairn,' she said.

'This way then.' He guided her hand to his crotch. Having never touched a lad's private bits before, she gasped, but enjoyed the velvety feel of it and allowed him to show her what to do.

'Pictures again next week?' he gasped as he buttoned himself up.

109

'Aye, that would be fine.' She went back indoors thinking that next time she would make him do something for her first. She could now cope with anything the old bitch or her upstairs threw at her.

Chapter Fifteen

It was early November and the sky hung overcast and ominous, storms threatening from the west. Annie, on deciding to learn Spanish, was trying to memorise her verbs. She heard the door downstairs opening and Donald's voice called up to her. 'Annie, Annie, I met Nick. It's Bel. She's in a lot of pain and she's crying for you.'

Annie grabbed her jacket and ran downstairs. It had to be serious if Nick had come for her. 'Is it the bairn?'

'What does a man know about these things? But Nick is away for the howdie.'

Isa came out of the kitchen pulling her coat over her apron. 'I'm coming too. Bel's like another daughter to me.'

Together they hurried down the road. The first fat drops of rain struck their faces and the wind cut through them, promising worse to come. By the time they reached Scartongarth, Alexina, the howdie, was already there. A large pan of water sat on the stove simmering to the boil and Bel lay in the ben room grasping the pillow as she twisted around, her face slick with sweat. She held out her hand. 'Annie, Isa.'

Isa knelt beside her. 'How long have you had the pains?'

'All night. Just niggling. But it's real bad now. I didn't know it would be so bad.'

'Hush,' said Isa, stroking Bel's forehead. 'It'll be worth it when you hold your wee one in your arms.'

111

Several hours later, Annie sat by Bel's side as Isa made even more tea.

'It's taking awful long,' whispered Bel, sweat pouring down her face, her fingers grasping the bedcovers as yet another spasm grabbed her.

'You'll be fine,' said Annie, although she wasn't sure at all.

In the doorway, Alexina beckoned to her. She led her through to the kitchen. 'One of you find Nick. Tell him to send for the doctor. I'm worried. The bairn's stuck at the shoulders.'

Nick returned within the hour, his face white. 'We can't get the boat out. The sea is too rough. They're going to keep trying. Can ye manage? Will she be alright?'

'I'm sure she will be. It was just to make sure, like.' But Alexina looked far from confident. She was young and did not have a wealth of experience under her belt.

Another hour passed. By now Nick was pacing the kitchen. He turned when Annie entered. 'Is he born? Is Bel alright?'

'This bairn's no coming easy.'

'Can I see her? Can I see Bel?' Gone was the brash, confident Nick she knew and in his place stood someone who showed some human emotion.

'For a moment. Then go, hurry. See if the men have launched the boat.'

He almost ran into the room and fell on his knees in front of the bed, grasping Bel's hand as yet another contraction gripped her. 'Why is this so hard? I thought it would be like my ma, easy, couple of hours and then a fine fat bairn.'

'Come on, go.' Annie pushed his shoulder. He rose to his feet and with another glance at Bel headed for the door.

Isa followed him. 'If you can get to the mainland, get Chrissie. She was the best howdie we ever had. She's got a wee house not far from the shore at Mey.'

'Aye, I know where she bides.' Nick gave a brief nod before running from the house.

'Annie,' gasped Bel, her face red, sweating, her breath coming in painful gasps. 'If I die, promise me, promise me ye'll take my bairn.' She grasped Annie's hand, squeezing hard enough to break the bones as another pain arched her back.

'You're not going to die. Just hold on there, Bel. The doctor and Chrissie, they're on the way.

'Promise me!' Bel screamed, her eyes shut tightly. As her body sank back, her voice calmed. 'They're by the door. Can't ye see them? My ma and da. They've come for me. Promise me ye'll take the bairn. Nick's no got a way about him.'

'I promise,' whispered Annie, wiping Bel's forehead, her glance flying to the door and back. 'But you'll be fine, you'll be fine. Tell her Mam, tell her she'll be fine.'

Isa had just entered.

'She's imagining things. She's seeing her mam and dad at the door,' cried a panic-struck Annie.

Isa took a seat by the bed. 'Hush, lass. They've not come for you. They're just watching over you. They want to see their new grandbairn, that's all it is.' But when her eyes met Annie's, they were filled with worry.

The clock ticked, seemingly extra loudly, the fire spat and an errant flame shot up the chimney. The spasms that shook the girl on the bed, now only brought about a moan. Isa boiled more water and wiped Bel's face and upper body, while Annie held her hand as the pressure grew ever weaker.

113

After what seemed like a lifetime, the door opened. Isa shot to her feet. 'Thank God, Chrissie.' She looked beyond the other woman who had rushed to Bel's side.

'Where's the doctor?'

'On another call. He'll be here as soon as he can.'

Annie marched to the window and clenched her fists to hide her frustration. The men had risked their lives to fetch the doctor and he couldn't come. Nick stood by the open door, his fingers grasping the post, his face strained. 'Is she all right? Is my bairn alright?'

'Out,' Isa laid a hand on his shoulder, easing him backwards. 'It's not a man's place to be by his wife at a birthing.'

'But is it always this bad? I know I'm no the man I should be, but I wouldn't know what to do without her.' His voice trembled.

'She's a fragile lass, but Chrissie never lost a patient yet.' She pressed on his shoulder until he was far enough out so that she could close the door.

With a degree of surprise, Annie realised that perhaps Nick really did love Bel.

'Hold her shoulders, get her something to bite on,' called Chrissie. She looked up at Alexina. 'When it goes on too long, ye have to bring the baby out by other means. Put yer hands high up on her stomach.' Alexina immediately complied. 'Now, Bel, when I say push, Alexina'll help ye.'

Chrissie stroked Bel's face. 'Bel, lass, I may not have said it often since ye grew up, but I brought ye up and I love ye like my own. Ye can do this. Now.' She looked at Alexina, this'll no be easy.' Her eyes slid to Annie and Isa. 'Best if ye go. Get the kettle on and a tea brewing. I'll call if there's more to be done.'

From the kitchen the silent women and Nick sat without looking at each other. The kettle boiled and no one stirred. From the other room came a long thin wail.

'Isa, Annie,' called Chrissie. Both rose simultaneously and ran through. Chrissie held a limp blue baby over one arm, rubbing its back. When there was no response she lifted the child by its heels and slapped its bottom. It jerked, gasped and emitted a feeble wail.

'A wee lassie, Bel, ye've got a wee lassie.' As she spoke she cut the cord that attached the child to its mother.

But the figure on the bed did not move. Chrissie thrust the baby at Isa who immediately wrapped her in the blanket, while Annie stoked up the fire. 'Is Bel....?' Annie spoke over her shoulder, afraid to finish the sentence.

Chrissie rubbed Bel's wrists and called her name. 'She has a pulse.'

'Should I get whisky?' asked Annie.

'No, no whisky.' She checked the afterbirth. Bel moved and groaned. 'Ah, ye're back with us, lassie. Ye've got a wee girl.'

Isa laid the baby on Bel's chest and tucked the blanket around them both. 'There's no better medicine,' she whispered. The faintest smile ghosted Bel's lips.

'Will she be alright?' asked Annie, moving to the bedside.

Chrissie checked Bel's pulse again. 'Growing stronger. We'll give her some fennel and warm milk. You'd better tell the father now.' She picked up the baby and handed her to Annie. 'Bel needs her sleep.'

Annie carried the bairn through and held her out for Nick to inspect. He had been pacing the floor, his hair standing on end with the constant running of his fingers through it. Without looking at the child, his eyes asked the question.

'Bel's going to be fine.'

115

Relief seemed to collapse him. He closed his eyes and tilted his head. 'The Lord be praised,' he said. 'And the bairn?' For the first time he seemed to notice the bundle in Annie's arms. 'A lad?'

'A lass. Isn't she bonny? Just like her mam.'

'A lass.' He looked at the small wrinkled face and turned away. 'I wanted a son.'

'We don't always get what we want,' snapped Annie.

'Aye, well, maybe next time,' said Nick. 'Can I see Bel?'

'For a wee while then, she's exhausted.' Annie followed him into the bedroom and laid the child beside Bel.

Awkwardly, Nick lowered himself until he was sitting on the bed.

Bel opened her eyes. 'Nick. Are ye happy with her? What'll we call her?'

'Call her whatever ye want,' said Nick. 'As long as I can name the next one.'

'Jamesina Mary, James after my da. And Mary for my ma. We'll call her Sina for short.'

'Sina,' he said, looking at the child. He touched the soft downy head. 'She'll have a brother next year. The second'll be easier. Ye'll see.'

Bel shook her head. 'I don't think so.' Her voice was weak.

'Aye well, we'll see. I'll go tell the lads, wet the baby's head, like. Ye're sure ye're fine? Ye're a good lass and I do love ye, Bel, ye know that. I mightn't show it in the way ye want, but it's the only way I know how.'

'Aye, in your way,' said Bel, her eyelids already drooping.

'Ye'll need to feed the bairn. Come on, I'll help ye.' Chrissie lowered herself down in the space vacated by Nick.

116

The clock tick sounded loud. The fire sparked and settled. Annie sat in the rocking chair cradling the child, watching the small mouth opening, the starfish fingers reach out and close. From the other side of the room, Bel was silent, too silent. Annie rose and crossed to the bed. Bel's face, white as chalk with eyelids threaded by tiny blue veins, looked like she had hardly a breath in her. Annie laid her hand on the side of Bel's neck, felt the slight flutter of pulse. Was this normal?

'Chrissie,' she called.

Chrissie rose from where she sat in the kitchen, drinking tea. She hurried into the bedroom, felt for a pulse and pulled the bedclothes back. A bright crimson patch beneath Bel was spreading.

'She's bleeding badly. Get pillows, anything, we have to raise the mattress.' She slapped Bel's cheeks gently. 'Come on Bel, wake up, wake up, lassie.'

By now Isa had joined her and together the women lifted Bel's legs and packed the pillows under her back and hips and legs until the lower half of her body was significantly raised. 'Keep her warm.'

Isa covered her in blankets and coats, and stocked up the fire.

'Get the men. Send them for the doctor again, and tell them not to come back without him,' shouted Chrissie.

When Bel opened her eyes she thought she could hear music in the distance. She looked around and everywhere was bathed in a pale white light. In the centre of the light stood her parents, smiling, holding out their hands to her. She tried to sit up and found it remarkably easy. Her mother beckoned to her and she moved forward and into the waiting arms. Her mother's body was warm and solid. Somewhere in the distance she heard her name being called and her eyes followed the direction of the sound. Annie and Chrissie were

117

leaning over someone on the bed. She looked around the rest of the room and saw Isa with a baby in her arms. Bel turned her eyes back to her mother..

'I'm not leaving.'

'It's time, Bel. Ye have to come with us.'

'But my baby…'

'Ye can stay beside her all her life, the way I've stayed beside ye.'

Bel watched the scenario taking place around her, watched as Chrissie straightened up and put an arm around a frantic Annie who was still pleading with the body on the bed to open her eyes, heard the words Chrissie spoke. 'Come away, Annie, she's gone.'

Nick sat with his head in his hands. 'What am I to do now?' he said. 'How can I bring up a bairn and run the croft?'

'I promised, she made me promise to take the bairn.' Annie spoke, realising at the same time that keeping that promise would mean the end of her dreams.

Nick lifted his head and his red eyes brightened slightly. 'Wid ye move in? So I can see the bairn every day like?'

She shook her head. 'No. I'll stay with my ma at the manse. You can still see Sina every day.'

He nodded slowly, rose and pushing his hands in his pocket, walked to the window. 'I'll take her off your hands when I find another wife.' Without a glance at the child, he slouched out the door, head hanging, his shoulders hunched.

Annie watched him through the window. He went over to wood pile, picked up the axe, swung it high and brought it down on the same log again and again, faster and faster, until the log was little more than a pile of sticks and, only then did he fling the axe from him and sit on a nearby rock, hands covering his face, his shoulders shaking.

Chrissie and Isa did what needed to be done for Bel. Now she lay, serene and beautiful, her fair hair spread on the pillow. Annie refused to leave the room and sat before the fire, cradling the child and staring into the flames. She suffered the aftermath of death, the impossible hope that a dreadful mistake had been made, that any minute, the figure on the bed would stir, groan and demand to see her baby.

The door creaked open and she heard the whisper of feet as someone entered the room. Annie recognised the soft tread of her mother. Isa took a seat in the opposite chair. 'Don't give up on your university,' she said in a low, slightly cracked voice. 'Donald and I will bring up the bairn.'

How like her mother to think of practical things, even at a time like this. Annie held the precious babe gently against her chest. 'I promised,' she whispered. 'Bel entrusted her to me.'

Isa stood up and touched the child's cheek. 'She's a bonny wee thing.' She gave a deep sigh. 'I'd best go home and tell Donald. He'll no have had any sleep. There'll be arrangements to be made.'

Annie heard her go, heard the door shut, heard the murmur of voices in the next room, heard the clock strike three times. Finally she rose, crossed to the bed where she eased herself in beside the still form, placed the baby between them and fell asleep.

The chill on the breeze from the sea stole through Annie and made her shiver as she watched the line of black-clad men carry the coffin towards the graveyard. She imagined them lowering Bel's body into the ground, in the same plot as her mother and heard the thud of the

119

dark, damp earth falling on the place where she lay, hiding her from the sun. Bel always loved the sun.

'I want to go with them,' she said.

'A graveside's no a woman's place.' Isa stood by her daughter, close but not touching. 'It's our duty to get the tea ready for when they get back.'

The outside chill followed Annie into the house, where she saw her cousin everywhere, pulling the kettle over the flames, laughing her little laugh. No, the essence of Bel would stay in this house. She wouldn't be with the men being lowered into the cold damp ground.

Chapter Sixteen

On the day the letter came, Tess was in a foul mood. She had not slept much the night before due to toothache and every noise cut through her head with the sharpness of a blade. Mrs Wilson had already read the riot act because the door knocker had been left with a bloom on the shine. On top of that she had a headache, so Tess would have to take the Missis out. There was no point asking for time off to visit a dentist, no one cared about a mere servant having pain. Just before two o'clock the postman delivered a letter from Annie, telling her about Bel.

Tess let out a long wail.

'Whatever's wrong?' asked Elsie.

'My best friend, she's passed away having her bairn.' Tess almost fell into the chair and, putting her elbows on the table, she covered her face with her hands. 'I can't take the old witch out today, I just can't.'

Elsie Mowat set her hand on Tess's shoulder. 'I know it's hard, love. But the gentry, they don't see us as humans. I'm sorry about yer friend. Did the bairn survive?'

Tess nodded.

'The best thing is to carry on as normal. There's nothing else for it, lass. But wait till the doctor comes home. He's a fair man, might give ye something for the toothache and a wee while off to go home as well.'

The bell in the corner jangled calling her to her duty.

'I'm coming,' shouted Tess, and dragged herself up from the chair.

The Missis was particularly bothersome today. She wanted to go down by the river, but as usual, everything Tess did was wrong. Mrs MacGregor demanded Tess pull the chair behind her rather than push it so that the wind didn't blow on her face. That same wind was sharp and did nothing to help Tess's aching tooth. The bath chair hit a stone as she turned it.

Mrs MacGregor smacked Tess across the legs with her umbrella. 'For the Lord's sake, girl, why are you so clumsy? You wouldn't have lasted a minute in my young day. Now get this chair straightened or you'll be back in the gutter where you belong. You island girls are all the same; ignorant as well as ugly. It comes from the inbreeding.'

Tess stopped. She turned the chair around so that the wind blew straight into the woman's face and seriously considered tipping her into the river. Instead, she applied the brake. 'Ye're nothing but a mean, cantankerous old bitch,' she said. With that she spun around and marched back up the road to the house, through the kitchen and into her bedroom where she threw her belongings into her kist. Elsie stood open-mouthed when Tess dragged her kist into the kitchen. 'What's going on?' she asked. 'Where's the Missis?'

Tess dashed her tears away. 'I've had all I can take. I left her at the riverside, face to the wind. By, she's lucky she's no swimming with the fishes now!'

'Ye never?'

'Aye, I did. And I'm no waiting to face the music either.'

'But where'll ye go? Ye'll no get a reference now.'

'I don't know. I'll see the gardener. Surely he'll let me put the kist in the shed till I find a room.'

Cook suddenly burst out laughing. 'By, I've longed to do something like that to the owld bitch myself. Good on ye, lass.'

When she told Bobby he laughed even harder. 'Come with me to the harbour. My uncle's a maister, in charge of the squad. He'll take ye on as a herring gutter. He definitely will when I tell him that ye put one over on Mrs MacGregor! Ye *have* gutted fish before?'

'I was born on an island. What do ye think? Mind ye, I was never fast.'

'Ye'll soon get the hang of it. Most of the houses in Lower Poultney take in lodgers. Ye'll find a room no bother.'

'I think I need a dentist first,' she said, clutching her face. And together they walked towards the town.

Chapter Seventeen

The days passed into weeks. Annie had not let the baby out of her sight since she had been born. Sina was a fussy little thing and often sick.

'What's wrong with her, Mam? She's no gaining any weight.'

'She needs her mother's milk. The cow's milk's maybe too strong. We'll water it a bit more.'

Sina continued to cry a lot and gained weight slowly.

Annie herself had little appetite. Her mind was full of if-onlys. If only Chrissie had been here from the beginning, if only the doctor had been available sooner, if only Nick hadn't forced himself on Bel in her early pregnancy, if only a wet nurse could have been found for the baby.

Isa set her hand on her daughter's shoulder. 'The bairn's poorly, but I'm capable of nursing an ailing bairn. Your brother was born early and needed a lot of care and look at him now.'

Annie took heart at her words. Dan was indeed a strong, healthy young man.

'Bel wouldn't have expected you to give up your dream.' Isa studied her daughter sadly.

'It's too late to get into university this year or get the grant anyway. Alexander is going to apply again next year.' Annie continued to gaze at Sina who stared back at her with trusting blue eyes. 'Maybe by then she'll be a big strong lass and I won't feel so bad about leaving her.' She coaxed the baby to drink a little more milk. 'Ach, what am I saying? University is a dream and not for the likes of me. I'll most likely not get the grant anyway.'

'Annie, you were so determined. You could go far.'

'Maybe I'll settle for marrying well – if I meet the right man.' In her mind she saw herself and Alexander standing before the minister saying their vows.

A sudden loud knock startled them both and the door burst open. Nick stood in the doorway, his cap in his hands.

'Have you come to see your daughter?' asked Isa. If he had it was the first time.

He didn't look at the child. 'Money's getting tight. The lambs didn't bring in as much as we thought.'

'What are ye saying?'

'Milk for bairn. I can't give ye anything this month.'

'But she's yours. You have to provide for her.'

He turned his cap around in his hands. 'There's something else. Ye may have heard I've been keeping company with Jean MacKay. When we get wed, we'll take the bairn to bide with us.'

The breath escaped Annie's body in a rush and her arms tightened around the child. 'No ye can't.'

He raised one hand and scratched his head. 'It's the money, see? The cow's milk is beginning to dry up and the tinned stuff is damned dear and no easy to get. There are repairs to do to our croft house as well. Jean reckons the bairn'll never make old bones anyway. She thinks it would be better, cost us less if Sina lived with us.'

'But ye've had nothing to do with her…' As she said the words, Annie knew neither he nor that hard-faced bitch he was keeping company with would spend money on medicine.

'Then keep her, if ye want, but ye'll get no more from me or mine.'

'You forget,' Isa's voice had turned cold, 'the croft is not yours. You can't inherit from Bel, it was never hers.

It should have been Jimmy's. I wouldn't have said anything if I thought you'd do right by Sina, but looks like that's not going to happen.'

Nick's lips twisted. 'If ye're trying to blackmail me it won't work. The croft is mine.'

'We'll see what Jimmy says about that. I'll away to see him and a lawyer in the morning.' Annie's heart raced. She couldn't give up Bel's child, she just couldn't, especially to someone who didn't believe she'd make old bones anyway. And the croft should be Sina's inheritance.

'Look, my lady, nothing was done legally after your grandad died. You're right, it should have been Jimmy's but he wanted none of it.' He stopped for a breath. 'We went and got everything in my name the week after we were wed. I'd no trouble, Bel being my wife and all.'

'You fly bugger! You didn't let the grass grow, did you?' So you get everything? The animals as well?'

Nick shrugged. 'It seems that way, yes.'

'Get out,' screamed Annie. 'Get out, and if you want Sina, you'll have to fight me for her.' At that moment she hated Nick as much as she had ever done.

Nick shrugged. 'As long as we know where we stand.' He turned and walked away, his steps slow.

Annie followed him, slammed the door behind him, and fled into the kitchen where her mother stood, white-faced.

'I can hardly believe it. Our croft, the house my great grandfather built, all gone to that man,' said Annie.

'We're all too trusting. If only Jimmy and Bel had sorted things out sooner it would be Sina's inheritance,' said Isa. 'It might be anyway if he has no more bairns.'

Annie shook her head. 'Nick didn't want a girl. He'll no even look at her. He'll marry that Jean and she'll give him a son sure as eggs is eggs. If she has to, she'll keep producing bairns till a boy is born and all the girls will have hellish lives.' Her eyes filled with tears.

Isa laid a hand on her shoulder. 'He'll not take Sina back if he doesn't have to pay anything. Neither of them want her. You'd best leave things be. If you make trouble for him, he could take her out of spite.'

'I could kill him, yes I could.' At that moment Annie believed herself capable of murder. The baby made a small noise and when Annie looked down at her, Sina's mouth twisted into the semblance of a smile, the small hand reached out and touched Annie's lips. She kissed the fingertips and she knew she could not do anything to risk losing this child.

When Donald returned from his parish duties, he listened quietly to their tale. 'Our earthly possessions matter little in the grand scheme of things. I gave up a lot to become a minister and I've never been happier. We've got what we need and we'll provide a stable, loving home for this little one.' He touched the tiny hand and the fingers closed around his. Once more the mouth twisted in a small smile.

'She knows me already,' he said, mirroring the smile, his features softening, his eyes full of love. 'You're right, Annie, we are the best family for this child.'

Annie cuddled the baby and enjoyed the security and peace surrounding her. She had so much to be thankful for, but deep down, she knew there would come a time when it would no longer be enough.

127

Chapter Eighteen

The harbour was the busiest place in Wick. The steady clang from the coopers' hammers as they made the barrels, the clomp of heavy hooves and the rattle of iron wheels against cobbled streets, the whoops of the children as they birled their hoops along, or kicked a can, or chased each other with severed fish heads. Scorries, fat, noisy herring gulls, filled the air, growing more confident as the day went on. Dogs barked and women sang.

The herring drifters sat side by side with the newer steamers and between them they filled the harbour. Barrels three tiers deep were piled along the front and along the sides and into the distance along the coast. Behind them were the troughs where the gutters worked, three to a team. What seemed like hundreds of women, scarves round their heads, rubber aprons flecked with silver scales, bandages round fingers, worked with an amazing speed that Tess could not match no matter how she tried.

'Ye'll hev tae' keep up,' whispered Georgina, the packer. 'If ye don't yer keepin the whole team back.'

'I'm sure I'll get the hang o' it,' said Tess as yet another herring slipped through her fingers and landed at her feet.

'Ach, lass.' Maggie, the third member of the team shook her head. 'ee'll never make a gutter. Yer too cack-handed.'

Tess glanced at her big hands and thick fingers. 'I'm sorry for keeping ye back.' It had been over a week and she was no quicker than when she started. The girls in her team were kind, although, as they were paid according to what they produced, her lack of speed reflected in their pockets at the end of the week.

Once more she returned to her lodgings with a heavy heart. 'It's no use, Lizzie,' she said to her landlady. 'The maister's threatened to sack me if I can't speed up. I'll need to find something else and I'll no get into service again if that owld bitch has anything to do with it.'

'Don't get too down about it, lass,' said Lizzie. 'Ma cousin's man's sister is the Matron in the fever hospital. I'll pit in a wordy for ee. They're aye looking for fowk.'

As Tess scrubbed the smell of fish from her body that night, she inwardly prayed that she could indeed get another job. She had cut her fingers more often than the fish and having to pee on them to stop them going septic was none too pleasant. Her father had always berated her for her clumsiness. She just couldn't return to have him say, 'I knew it!'

Chapter Nineteen

By January, winter had a firm grip on the land. Bitter gales with snow and ice on their backs swept the island from northern shores. Waves as high as the cottages pounded the shore and sent yellow ropes of spume across the land. The manse enjoyed water pumped in, but it froze in the pipes.

Boats could not get to sea, so salt fish and smoked pork became the staple diet. With no milk and watery porridge for sustenance, Sina put on weight slowly and her eyes sunk and became dark rimmed. She vomited often and coughed relentlessly. Annie sat with her night after night, refusing to let anyone else nurse the baby. It was as if while this child lived, Bel stayed by her side.

In early spring, when Sina reached five months old, she was diagnosed with asthma. By then Annie had already accepted that her life would have to change. She would have to get a job, earn enough to support them both and pay for the medicines Sina so desperately needed. But whenever she thought about leaving Sina with her mother, she would see an image of Bel on the bed clinging desperately to life, wringing the promise out of her. She could hear herself swearing an oath, little knowing how things would turn out. There had to be a way of keeping both the baby and her dream.

There seemed to only one course of action. On the mainland there were, she had heard, housekeeping positions with attached cottages where the child would be welcome. She settled down to write a letter to Tess, ask her if she knew of such a position.

She still went to the schoolhouse two evenings a week and continued with her studies. Sometimes she and Alexander would discuss something he'd given her to read well into the small hours. There were times too, when the talk would become personal and although he didn't encourage her, she still harboured the strong feeling that they were meant to be together forever. Concentrating on her studies, however, became increasingly difficult. Every minute she was away from Sina, the child filled her head.

'Are you still going up to the schoolhouse tonight?' asked Isa as the wind battered the manse and the rain lashed at the windows. 'It's enough to lift you off your feet.'

Annie glanced at Sina. The child slept sound enough in her cradle, but she had been coughing earlier. Now each breath came out in a whistle.

'I'll be no more than an hour,' she said. The thought of not seeing Alexander at all was unthinkable. 'She's no too bad, is she?'

'I've told you many a time, I am capable of looking after a sick bairn.' Isa laid a hand on Sina's forehead. 'She's not too hot and Donald's here.'

'You go,' said Donald. 'I'll come for you if she gets worse.'

'Thanks, both.' Annie stood, pulled on her coat and scarf and tucked her books inside her coat for protection. Outside the wind drove her back against the kirk wall, and sent the breath down her throat. After the muggy dampness of the manse kitchen, the freshness was welcome. Lowering her head and clutching her scarf, Annie struggled up the half mile to the schoolhouse. She had to talk to Alexander about her decision.

131

'Things are different now,' she explained. 'Sina doesn't sleep and I'm so tired. I wanted so much...Oh why did Bel have to die?'

'I know. But it's her father's duty. He could pay a woman...'

'No!' Annie was emphatic. 'I made the promise.' Her eyes filled. 'Sina'll no be a baby forever. It'll get better and I still want to learn.' Right now she couldn't see past the next feed, the next asthma attack.

'I can't give her up,' said Annie, gazing into Alexander's deep brown eyes, willing him to understand. 'I've asked Tess to find me a job on the mainland. I always said I would not go into service, but there are positions where I can take the baby. Seems I have no other choice, have I?'

Alexander grabbed her arms. 'You can't go.'

'I have to. We need money for medical bills. University isn't the only way out of poverty.' However long it took, she knew she would never subject herself to a life of drudgery, having Sina made it a little bit more difficult that was all.

She gave a sad laugh. 'Maybe a rich man will see me and want to marry me.'

'You're not serious? I thought you would only marry for love?'

'But I can't have the man I love, can I?' She trapped his eyes.

He looked startled and drew in a breath. 'Annie...maybe there is a better way.'

'If only there was. I've thought and thought...'

He bent so that his eyes were level with hers. 'I've been thinking too, thinking this last while, but I wasn't sure until now how you felt. I want to marry you. We can raise the bairn together, adopt her, make it legal, give her sisters and brothers. We won't live on the island forever, not if you don't want to.'

A thrill ran through her body. Marry Alexander. He wanted her, loved her. But the suddenness of his proposal threw her. She had longed for him, dreamed of him, fantasized about this moment, yet now she was struggling for words to explain her feelings.

'I want to marry you more than anything, I do, but ...'

'But?'

'I still want to have a worthwhile job one day. I know I have to care for Sina, but having more bairns, it's not what I want.'

With his eyes still trapping hers, he straightened his back. 'Who knows what the future holds, Annie. I said nothing before this as you're young. I believed once you were away from here you would soon forget me and I didn't want to stand in your way. But, as you say, things are different now and I couldn't stand seeing you waste your life in service.'

'And Spain? Your dream of going back there?'

'I won't give up on my dreams and neither should you. I don't want a wife who'll settle and bake cakes and produce bairns if it means losing you. I want you, Annie, whatever your conditions. If we believe we can, we can do it. We can do it all.' He reached for her and pulled her into an embrace.

Annie pressed her forehead into the space where his shoulder met his neck and breathed in his warm, clean smell. 'If you are willing to take Sina on, I'll marry you in a heartbeat. I think I've loved you since the first moment I laid eyes on you.'

'My pay isn't much but it'll be adequate for all three of us.'

'It'll be enough for now. But what about your fiancée?'

133

'She's never made me feel the way you do. I hate hurting her, but I can't marry her under the circumstances.'

At that moment, Annie needed him like she needed her next breath. 'I will, I'll do it.' She gave in to his embrace. With a low groan he eased her away from him. 'Our wedding night will be special,' he said. 'Until then, don't tempt me too much.'

She hurried home, brimming with the news. The wind had risen to gale force and she struggled from the shelter of one small cottage to the other, pitting all her weight against the wind between buildings.

She burst into the manse, shut the door with difficulty and almost fell into a steamy kitchen.

'Thank God you're back,' said Isa. 'She's bad, really bad.'

Annie rushed forward and took the limp baby from her mother's arms. 'Why didn't Donald come for me?'

'I sent him for Alexina first. She's the one with the medical knowledge.'

Annie held the baby against her feeling the struggle each breath cost the small lungs, wishing she could breathe for her. 'Come on, darling,' she whispered. 'I've got such grand news. I'm going to be your mammy and what do you know, you're going to have a new daddy. He's a good man and he'll love you as much as I do. Oh, God, please, please get her over this.'

The door opened and Donald and Alexina blew in. Alexina immediately took the baby and rubbed her limbs. The bony little chest was straining to rise and fall, the stomach caving in with each effort to draw air into the starved lungs. 'We need a doctor,' said Alexina. 'But the boat will never get across the sound on a night like this.'

Annie couldn't take her eyes from the child. 'I shouldn't have left her.'

Alexina shook her head. 'It wouldn't have made any difference. I'll try a poultice on her chest.'

'Isn't there anything else you can do?' Poultices had had little effect in the past.

'There is something called Epinephrine which you give through a large glass contraption called a nebulizer. I've been trying for ages to get one. They're costly and I'm not a registered nurse. I would think the doctor's got one.' She set her hand on the babe's head. 'If only she had her mother's milk.'

By four o'clock in the morning, the storm had died, and the men had gone for the doctor. Annie continued to gaze at the infant in her arms. She could sense little movement and the lips were faintly blue. Alexina parted the blankets. The chest hardly rose and fell, but it was still there, the flutter of life.

'I think I should take her,' said Isa, but Annie's arms tightened as the length of time between each tiny breath lengthened and then stopped.

By the time the men returned, there was no more movement.

Donald put his arm around Annie. 'She's with Bel now. You've done your best, no one could have done more.'

Annie shook him off and turned, her eyes blazing. 'Are you going to say she's in a better place? That it's God's will?' Her arm tightened around the still form as if by holding her, she could somehow stop her from growing cold, stop the life force from escaping.

'I wasn't going to say that. Who am I to guess God's reasons? I wish I did know. I wish I could tell you. All I can say is that she's at peace.' He cupped his hand over the baby's head. 'The angels must have missed her. Give her to your mam, now.' His voice was low and broken and the sound of his pain released something inside Annie.

135

Isa eased the little body from her daughter's reluctant arms and pressed her cheek against the fuzzy head. 'Sleep well, little one.' She whispered brokenly.

With a long wail Annie collapsed against the minister. He held her while the tears soaked the collar of his jacket.

'I loved her too,' he said.

Annie's hair muffled his words.

Jamesina Mary Sinclair, aged nine months and two days was laid in the same grave as her mother on a fine April day when young shoots pushed through the earth, leaves began to bud, birds built their nests, and ewes' bellies grew fat, pulsating with new life.

Annie rode the unbearable waves of grief and when the wave subsided, she relaxed into blissful numbness for a short time. The only real peace she knew was in the moments between opening her eyes and attaining full consciousness. And a distant sense of liberation brought with it the added agony of guilt.

Chapter Twenty

'Do you still want to marry me?' Alexander leaned slightly forward, his knuckles pressed against the desk, his brow furrowed.

'Of course, one day, for there's no one else I want to marry. Maybe just not now.'

'I guessed as much.' He straightened up. 'You can still go to university. I wouldn't hold you back. I'll send the application for the bursary if you like.' He began to lift papers from the desk, his eyes anywhere but on hers.

University. It had once been her dream. She had seen it on the horizon and then it had faded from view.

'I don't want to go to university any more,' she said.

Alexander lifted his head and came round the desk towards her. 'Are you sure? Take your time, Annie. You're still raw after losing the child. Don't make any rash decisions.'

'It's not rash. I've been thinking of nothing else for days.'

'Then what...'

'I want to be a nurse.'

'What? A nurse? Are you sure?'

Annie pressed her eyes closed to stem the tears. 'I watched my best friend die. I watched her baby die and I could do nothing. I felt so...helpless. I have to make their lives mean something. And I helped out in a hospital when we lived in Canada. I loved it.'

'I think nursing is a grand profession, but I had hoped...' With a sigh he allowed his arms to fall by his sides.

'We can still get married. We can get jobs in the same area, after I've done my training.' She held her breath, willing him to say yes, that he would leave the island and come with her, that he wanted her that much.

There was no such concession. His next words struck an ice shard through her heart. 'Don't you know about the marriage bar?'

'Marriage bar?' She had never heard the term.

'Professional women have to choose between marriage and a career.' He stopped and let his words penetrate.

'I thought that was just for teachers or lawyers.'

'It covers all professions for women.'

'You're saying I have to choose, you or nursing?'

'You'll always have me. I'm saying we can't get married, have a family, even live together if you want to work in a hospital.'

'I won't feel this way about anyone else.'

'I know deep inside you'll never settle for being just a wife. Maybe it's that spirit that makes me love you. I'll wait for you until you know for certain what it is you want from life.'

Annie's anger burned. 'It's so unfair.'

'Life is seldom fair.' Alexander became brisk and business-like, his voice cool. 'If your mind's made up, I'll make enquiries for you.'

Taken aback by the change in his manner, Annie sharpened her own voice. 'I want to do this. It's the only thing that makes any sense. If Alexina had been a registered nurse, she might have been allowed the equipment that would have saved Sina and other bairns like her.'

'Dear Annie, I do understand. I won't stand in your way.'

138

She slipped her arms around his neck and pulled him down until his lips were close to hers. 'I will marry you someday. I swear, I'll never marry anyone else.'

She felt his body stiffen, almost pulling away. 'You can't make promises like that. There's a whole world out there, why would you want to shackle yourself to a simple schoolteacher so much older than you?'

'Because you're bonny and you're clever and you're different from any other man I know and you make me feel things I've never felt before.' She tightened her arms, pressed her body against him and, encouraged by his obvious arousal, tried to kiss him.

With a sudden, low moan he crushed her to him. Their lips met and she put her soul and being into that kiss. When they drew apart, they were both shaken, breathless. And the closeness that came in glimpses was back there and they were one. At that moment she would have done anything he asked of her.

'Annie, Annie,' he whispered, his voice unsteady. He put his hands on her shoulders and pushed her to arm's length. 'Annie, I'm a normal man. I want you more than anything else right now, but don't let's risk spoiling your dream.'

She reached for him again. At that time, there was nothing more important than being in his arms.

The door opened and they sprang apart.

Mr Dick stood there, scowling. 'Seems I returned just in time,' he said through tight lips.

Alexander rubbed his forehead. 'Nothing was going on. Annie, I think it best if we're not alone from now until you leave.' He spoke with the voice of a stranger, as if the intimacy of a moment ago had never happened. 'It's for the best.'

She turned and glared at Mr Dick, her face as hot as a stove in winter. 'I'll bid you goodnight, gentlemen.' She picked up her coat and with her chin in the air, swept from the room.

After she left, Alexander held up his hand, palm turned towards Dick. 'I don't wish to discuss this. I know what I'm doing.' He walked into his own room and with knuckles pressed against the sill, stood at the window, watching Annie walk down the road. For one mad moment he had almost thrown away all his resolves. That girl had found her way into his very blood and he wanted her as he wanted his next breath, yet his head told him to back off. She was such a mixture of warring emotions. A woman-child with more surfaces than a prism. Even after everything she had endured, he doubted that she was mature enough to know what she really wanted. If he followed his natural desires, he had no doubt that he could have persuaded her to stay, but once the glow of attraction had faded, would she ever truly be his? He recognised a restlessness in her that once stirred his own blood, but he had lived his youth, dipped his toe in the grimy world of experience and finally decided that shaping young minds was one of the most worthwhile things he could do. Apart from the planned visit to relations in Spain, he was ready to settle down. Teaching was his life. Annie, on the other hand, had not yet found her way.

He lit the candle which sat in front of a picture of the Madonna and child, dropped to his knees and clasped his hands. 'Holy Mother,' he prayed, 'Give me the strength to do what is right.'

Part Two

Chapter Twenty-One

The train journey had been long, hot and dirty. The iron monster coasted into Buchanan Street Station and settled amid billowing steam, its whistle fading to nothing. Clutching her case, Annie stepped onto the platform amid the surging mass of humanity all intent on where they were going, none looking as lost and confused as she felt. The throng carried her forwards, towards the entrance.

He stood by the door and she recognised him at once. She would have known him even if he hadn't been holding a card with her name printed in bold black letters. Reverend Donald Charleston's brother, Frank. He and his wife had offered to take care of her until she knew whether or not she'd passed her interview.

Although having the same black hair and dark eyes as the minister, his face was more drawn, harder somehow.

'I'm Annie Reid.' She stopped before him, her fingers gripping the handle of her case so tightly she could hardly feel them.

'I'm very pleased to meet you.' Frank's eyes appraised her for no more than a second before he lowered the card and reached out to grasp her hand. He had one of those grips, thankfully brief, that made her wonder whether he'd left any uncrushed bones in her hand.

'It's kind of you to give me lodgings.'

'Only too pleased to help. My brother seldom asks me for anything.' He gave a curt nod, took her case and turned towards the entrance. 'You're Donald's stepdaughter and nursing is a noble profession. This way.' He indicated that she should follow.

Annie had been up since dawn and, after the quiet of the island, the bustling crowds, steady stream of motor vehicles, trams and the odd horse-drawn carriage was disorienting. She almost ran to keep up with his long strides, her new shoes crushing her toes.

Frank stopped beside a motor car. 'This is our transport.'

Her distorted reflection from the shiny hood mocked her. 'Oh my, it's very posh.' The words were out before she could stop them. Annie had never ridden in a motor before and she had not envisaged her first trip to be in anything this grand.

He gave an amused smile. 'A Ford model T.'

The name meant nothing to her. Letting her eyes wander over the length of the vehicle, she tried to imagine it on the rough roads of Raumsey. My, wouldn't that be something.

Her admiration seemed to please him. 'My one extravagance.' Still grinning, he opened the door to allow her to enter.

'And how is the Reverend Donald?' he asked, once they were settled in their seats.

'Both he and my mother are well.' Annie used a polite voice, one she'd been practising ever since she knew she was coming to Glasgow.

'I've always meant to visit them, but my life's been busy.' Frank peered into the road ahead and moved the gear stick.

Annie didn't answer as she looked around the chaotic streets and breathed in thick city smells. Everything was not totally new as she had passed through cities on her way from Canada, but now she revelled in the experience, finding the bustle, the noise and the prospect of living here exhilarating.

'George Square. And the statue is of Sir Walter Scott,' said Frank, as she gazed in awe at the majestic buildings, the statue, the pigeons which seemed to be everywhere.

'Our home is in Pollokshields, just west of St Andrew's Drive,' Frank said. 'I don't suppose you've heard of it.'

'Donald told me your address.' It had meant nothing at the time. It could be a palace or a slum, but she had surmised it would be nice, him being a banker in the city and all.

'The villas of Pollokshields are all built to different plans. No two are exactly alike. It'll be a change to what you're used to and, I hope, a pleasant one.'

'The manse on Raumsey is very nice.' Smarting at his assumptions, she sprang to the defence of her island home.

'I'm sure it is, I'm sure it is. But unlike the rest of the family, Donald never had much ambition.'

'He seems very happy doing what he does. He's a good man.'

'I'm glad. He never wanted to follow in father's footsteps. Quite a disappointment for the old man. Had a calling, he said.' The car turned into another street. 'We live close to Maxwell Park, a nice green space, where my wife often walks.'

'It sounds wonderful,' said Annie politely, but unenthusiastically. Nice green spaces were no novelty to her.

They passed from the city streets into quiet avenues with trees planted along the kerbsides, sunshine and shadows alternating across the road. Eventually he pulled into the drive of a large house in a street of other large houses. More trees grew in the gardens, the sun dappling the ground beneath and birds twittering in the branches.

'Beech, sycamore and lime,' said Frank as Annie gazed up into the leaves above her. 'Do you have anything like this on the island?'

Annie shook her head. 'But we'd all sorts of trees in Canada.'

'Of course, of course.'

The door opened and a slim, smartly-dressed woman with faded blonde hair and a string of pearls around her neck stepped out, her hand extended. 'How nice to meet you, Annie. I am Margaret, as I'm sure you know.' She spoke in a low, whispery voice. They shook hands and Margaret's felt cool and limp. Her lips did not part when she smiled. 'Daddy will show you to your room and Daisy will get tea. We do have a cook, but this is her day off, so the girl fills in. Reliable help is hard to get nowadays; the war changed everything.' She led the way indoors leaving a waft of rose water in her wake.

The hallway was wide with polished wooden floors. Paintings, mostly of Scottish landscapes with deer or highland cattle, hung on the walls. Frank caught her eye. 'Come along. I'm sure you'll be very comfortable here.' He led her up the sweeping staircase.

The bedroom was the most luxurious that Annie had ever seen with its cornices, flowered wallpaper and ornate fireplace. On a dresser sat a jug and basin, a face flannel and a thick white towel. A vase of lavender standing on the dressing table scented the air.

'Freshen up and then come downstairs for some tea.' He hesitated at the door. 'I know it's all very different to what your used to, but don't let it overwhelm you. You seem like an intelligent girl, you'll soon adapt.' He smiled at her then, as one would at a child.

'Thank you,' she said through gritted teeth.

Tired and mesmerised, Annie longed to throw herself on the pink brocade cover on the bed and close her eyes.

Instead, she removed her coat and blouse and washed away the grime of her journey in lukewarm water.

The drawing room was as overwhelming as she had expected. Red velvet curtains hung at the bay window. Slightly to one side sat an upright piano with built in candelabras on either side and a square of satin material let into the woodwork on the front.

'Do have a seat,' said Margaret. 'Now, my dear, tell me about Canada and Raumsey. I've never been to either, you know, though I have a sister who emigrated to Vancouver. Did you live anywhere near Vancouver?' She poured the tea, her long bony fingers trembling slightly.

'I'm sorry, no, Mrs Charleston.'

'Call me Margaret, please. We're almost family after all.' She sucked in air through her nose and gave a little smile that, once again, did not show her teeth.

Tea was served with neat little salmon sandwiches with the crusts cut off and several small cakes on a three-tiered, silver cake-stand. Although Annie was ravenous, she ate slowly as her mother had instructed her to do.

The door opened and a young man wearing a three piece suit and tie entered. With a small moustache and his hair slicked back, he reminded her of the men in the magazine kept under her pillow at home. His eyes immediately fell on Annie and opened wide. Grinning, he reached towards her, hand outstretched. 'Ah, you must be the island girl. I say, you are rather a pleasant surprise.' He raised her fingers to his lips and kissed them.

A long-suffering look appeared on Margaret's face. 'Annie, this is my son, Henry.'

'Pleased to meet you.' Annie retrieved her hand and took a hurried sip from her cup.

147

'I believe you are the stepdaughter of my uncle, the reverend.' Henry helped himself to a cup of tea. 'I must say, I admire him for having the strength to stand up to my grandfather instead of allowing the old boy to dictate his life.'

'For heaven's sake, Henry,' snapped Frank. 'I'm sure Annie doesn't want to hear our family history.'

Henry swallowed his tea, set down the cup, threw himself onto a chair and lit a cigarette. 'If she's staying in this house, she can hardly not be aware of the undercurrents, eh, my dear?' He blew a smoke-ring into the air and watched it as it dissipated.

'I really don't...' Annie began. She glanced at Frank's angry face, then back at the polished top of the small table. She noted an almost indiscernible semi-circle of white where someone, at one time, had perhaps set a hot cup.

'I must apologise for my son.' Margaret blotted her lips with a napkin in a series of small quick pats.

Suddenly Henry rose, took a seat at the piano and flexed his fingers. 'Any good on the ivories, Miss Reid?'

'I would like to say yes, but I never had the chance to learn.'

'I was forced to learn.' He ran his fingers over the keys. 'I never quite got the hang of it.'

Annie studied her teacup. The pale rose design, the gold edging.

'He had every advantage.' Margaret bunched the napkin in her hand.

'But you like music, Miss Reid?' said Henry, ignoring his mother.

Annie gave a little cough and raised her eyes to meet his. 'Yes...very much.'

'Then, with my illustrious parents' permission, I shall escort you to the theatre one night. Harry Lauder is performing in the Britannia Music Hall. Have you heard of him?'

'Yes. I have. My mother and Donald have a gramophone in the manse. She plays his records all the time.' In spite of the tension in the air, excitement grabbed her. Actually attending a concert was more than she had dreamed possible. Silently praying for approval, she glanced at her hostess.

'Henry, do you really think…' His mother began.

'The girl hasn't been to the city before. What's the harm in showing her a few sights? You and father can come with us if you feel she needs a chaperon.'

'I…I would love to go,' said Annie.

'I'm not sure…' Margaret's voice trembled, but whether with nervousness or anger Annie could not tell.

'Of course she must go.' Frank's voice cut in. 'But only if my son stops being a buffoon. If not, we shall take her ourselves.'

'Maybe we really *should* take her ourselves. What do you think, Daddy?' said Margaret.

Annie thought it strange that she referred to her husband as 'Daddy.'

'She'll be fine with Henry.' Frank looked at Annie. 'You must forgive my son, he makes it his aim in life to embarrass myself and my wife. Now, I'm sure you would like to get unpacked and settled. I'll be upstairs in a minute to light your fire. Dinner is at seven o'clock.'

His tone of voice left Annie in no doubt that she had just been dismissed. She stood up. 'Thank you for the tea.' Henry shot her a wink and she smiled, not sure what to make of this branch of the Charleston family. There had been a definite tension in the air, something she did not care to analyse.

As she left the room, she overheard Frank say, 'Annie Reid is in our care for the foreseeable future; we are responsible for her and I ask you to remember that.'

Henry laughed. 'Just making her welcome, father dear. I know how you want me to marry the lovely Cynthia.'

Annie ascended the stairs still smiling. She found Henry handsome and amusing, but if this family thought she was a naïve innocent, ready to fall for his manufactured charm, they were wrong. They had nothing to worry about; her loyalty to Alexander ruled absolute.

Henry did not appear for dinner which was a simple meal of cold ham and potatoes, served by a thin, young girl, no more than thirteen or fourteen and who Margaret introduced as Daisy. When Annie thanked her, she was rewarded by a wide smile.

They ate from matching plates with silver cutlery and she tasted her first glass of wine from a long stemmed glass. She took her time, terrified that she would do something wrong, watching her hosts before she lifted a knife or fork so that she would use the right one. Who could have imagined that the minister came from such a background? This was the life she had aspired to, yet now it felt alien, lacking the warmth of the close-knit family in which she had grown up.

'Have you had much in the way of education, Annie?' asked Margaret over dinner.

Annie recounted the difficulties in Canada and how she studied with Alexander on the island.

'You must be very grateful to my brother for taking you in,' said Frank.

'I am. But there are bursaries.' Annie's scalp tingled. She hoped they did not assume that Donald had funded her studies, nor did she want to explain that Alexander's tuition came without charge.

'I have heard there is help for the less fortunate.' Margaret set her cutlery down on her plate. 'We are glad to ease the burden and accept you into our home, aren't we, Daddy?'

'Of course we are. You must ask us if there's anything you need.'

'I'll do the washing up, shall I?' asked Annie, rising and lifting her plate both from habit and a desire to be away from the table.

'Not at all, my dear.' Margaret batted the air. 'That's what we pay a servant for.'

'I don't mind helping out...' Annie set the plate down and resumed her seat, heat suffusing her cheeks.

'You are our guest. We wouldn't hear of it.'

Daisy came in and removed the dinner plates, then brought dessert, a sponge pudding with custard. Once they had finished, Frank stood up and looked at Annie. 'Feel free to join us in the lounge for coffee and perhaps a glass of sherry.'

'Thank you, but no. I have a nursing manual that I need to read.' The desire to escape was stronger than the desire to study.

That night, in her big empty room, the excitement faded. Never having been away from her family before, the emptiness of the large room seemed to close in on her and brought back the pain of losing both Bel and Sina threefold. Struck by a sudden sharp pang of longing and, in a moment of doubt, she wondered how she would exist for three years without Alexander. Even the sounds of the city, faint and distant in this peaceful neighbourhood, unnerved her, leaving her with the feeling that something was off, missing. And then she realised what it was. She had grown accustomed to the constant, deep, steady breathing of the sea.

Her mind drifted to that last night on the island. She and Alexander had walked in the soft gloaming, her arm linked with his, their bodies close together. 'Do well, Annie,' he whispered into her hair. 'Make me proud.'

She turned to face him, lifting her lips for a kiss.

The kiss had been light, without passion and with a shuddering sigh he drew away as he always did. And the cool space where he had been filled her with disappointment and slight confusion. If he felt the same as she did, how could he bear to let her go?

Now she relived that night and with the memory, the ache of her longing returned. With a little moan she wrapped her arms around herself. Soon weariness took over and she slipped over the edge of consciousness.

Chapter Twenty-Two

The next morning, as the family ate breakfast of eggs and toast in the sun-filled dining room, Margaret set her hand on her husband's arm and looked at him with something like adoration. 'Will you be able to take Annie for her interview, Daddy? I don't feel comfortable with her finding her own way.'

Frank set down his napkin. 'Sorry, dear; I have a meeting first thing. You'll have to accompany her. Order a taxi.'

'No need for that.' Henry turned from where he helped himself to eggs from a platter on the sideboard. 'I'll take her.'

Margaret's mouth pursed. 'Didn't you promise to go with your father to the bank today? You really have to be more responsible.'

'There's nothing that won't wait until tomorrow, is there, Father? You can't expect our guest to use public transport.'

'Really, I'm fine,' said Annie. 'I'd like to take the bus. I need to learn how to make my own way round the city.'

Frank cleared his throat and studied Annie for a second. 'Henry's right. We can't let you go alone. After all, we have a certain responsibility.'

Henry beamed. 'We'll leave right after breakfast. Give us time for a wee tour before your interview.'

Secretly relieved that she wouldn't be left to the mercy of a strange, busy city, Annie nodded her thanks. 'You're all very kind.'

Henry had his own car. 'An Austin ten hp. Not the latest model, I'm afraid,' he said as he opened the door.

It seemed that owning cars was very important to this family. As she settled beside him she thought once more of how Donald had turned his back on all this, choosing instead to be a minister on a small island. 'When you said Donald stood up to his father, what did you mean?' she asked.

'My grandfather was a stern disciplinarian. I was afraid of him. I'm sure his own family was too. My father certainly knuckled down and followed in the family line. Now Father expects me to do the same.'

'And you want something else?'

'Forget about my family problems. I took you out for a pleasant journey.' Henry drove her through the streets, pointing out the magnificent buildings. 'You have to look up,' he said.

She did so and understood what he meant. Over the top storeys, were many statues set into the elaborate stonework, watching centuries of life evolve in the streets below. And more pigeons. This, it seemed, was a city of pigeons. 'It's amazing,' she breathed. It felt strange to be treated like this, almost like a lady.

'What do you make of my family?' Henry turned up another street.

'It's kind of them to take me in. Your father is very different from Donald, but he seems nice.'

'And my mother, what do you think of her?'

'She's nice as well.'

'She's the charitable lady, so wrapped up in good works she forgot she had a son.'

'Oh.' Annie could think of no other reply.

'Don't mind me. I enjoy tormenting them.' He gave a small laugh.

'Tell me about them.'

He sighed. 'My grandfather was a merchant banker. He was rich, but he lost heart when his wife died young and he turned his energies into controlling his family. Donald was never interested in banking, I believe there was a bit of a to-do when he insisted on going into the ministry. My Aunt Elizabeth, another rebel, died for her beliefs. My father stepped into the old man's shoes. He's been successful himself, but the war has drained his resources somewhat. When I returned home, he had a job all waiting for me.' A wistful smile flitted across his mouth.

'You don't sound too keen.'

'To be honest, I'm not.' He gave a snort. 'But I'm not trained for anything else. Just to annoy them, I've become interested in politics.'

'Donald's interested in politics.'

'I think we would get on rather well, but to be honest, politics used to bore me to distraction. Predictably, my parents have been set against it, so that makes it rather fun.' He turned and looked at her. 'But I'm not the empty-headed disappointment they seem to think. I feel differently than they do, that's all. They want me to follow in my father's footsteps, work in the bank and marry a girl of good breeding with money.'

'Surely there's nothing wrong with politics.'

Henry gave a hoot. 'There is if your beliefs are at odds with my father's. He's a staunch Conservative, therefore I choose to be a Socialist.'

Annie felt surprised at his words. Now she partly understood the undercurrent of tension she had sensed earlier.

'Don't you have any beliefs of your own?'

He shrugged. 'Not when I started, it was just a lark, but I've been going to hear Maxton talk and I must admit, I'm rather drawn in by the man. I do believe that every man deserves a fair chance to better themselves and how can they do that without a fair wage? People like my father won't listen. They are afraid of revolt, especially after what happened in Russia, yet they can't see that the best way to prevent an uprising is to give the workers decent living conditions.'

'Who's Maxton?'

'He's the Independent Labour Party MP.'

Annie had never heard of him. 'My fiancé's very interested in what's going on in Spain.' She needed to turn the conversation towards something she knew about before she made a fool of herself.

'Fiancé, oh, then I have a rival.' Henry fell silent for a beat, then said, 'Why Spain? Isn't there enough problems in Scotland?'

She told him about Alexander and gave his reasons.

Henry didn't speak again until they pulled up in front of the hospital. 'Here we are.' He turned to face her. 'I admire you, you know. You're doing something worthwhile. With your looks, you could marry money and become a lady of leisure, but I already think you're worth more than the empty-headed flibbertigibbets in my social circle.'

Two years ago, she would have been just that, Annie thought and there still might be a modicum of that social climber left inside her. She wanted a better life for herself, but she also wanted a career that gave her self-satisfaction. 'Things happened that made me realise what's important. I never want to have to rely on a man for the bread I eat.' She thought again of Alexander and her heart lurched.

'Good for you. I have a meeting I want to attend,' said Henry with a laugh. 'I'll collect you here at two o'clock.'

'There's no need. I'd like to find my own way back. I will have to learn sooner or later.'

'I insist. There's plenty time for you to find your independence. Good luck with the interview.' His smile was wide and his eyes twinkled. He had a mischievous, little boy charm that she couldn't help but warm to. She decided that she liked Henry Charleston and admired his rebellious nature.

She stood before the large, imposing building and she smoothed away a stray hair, ran her hand down the side of her coat, took a deep breath and strode forward. At the top of stone steps leading to the front door of the Royal Infirmary, she asked a porter for directions. She was ushered down a faintly antiseptic-scented corridor and into a narrow room where another four girls waited. A bench with a woman in uniform sat before yet another door with a plaque on which the word 'Matron' was engraved in gold and black lettering.

'Give your details to Sister McCormack, then wait till you're called,' hissed a starched figure who stood at the door of the room and introduced herself as Sister Gibb. Around ten minutes passed while the Sister at the desk wrote endlessly in a folder and the would-be nurses fidgeted and coughed quietly.

The door opened.

'You're late,' snapped Gibb, as yet another girl edged her way in.

Annie gasped when she saw the latest arrival. 'Tess!'

'Annie.'

'No talking or you won't get as far as the interview.' The fiend in starched white raised her voice.

Tess took a space beside her friend.

'What are you doing here?' whispered Annie.

'Same as you, by the looks of things.'

'Silence!' Gibb's boomed out. 'You two, if you wish to become students here you will need to show more decorum.'

157

'We'll talk later.' Tess clasped her hands in front of her and said, 'Sorry, Miss.'

'Please address me as Sister, not miss.'

'Sorry, Miss...er... Sister.'

When her turn came, Annie gave a list of details. Name, age, education. 'Wait for Matron to call you,' she was told and sent back to stand with the others.

One by one the candidates were summoned.

Finally, 'Anne Reid. Matron will see you now.'

Matron was a plump bespectacled woman, with a stern face, sitting behind a heavy mahogany desk. Dressed in black, her head topped by her white headdress, she made an imposing figure. Behind her, a grandmother clock counted the seconds. A fire smouldered in the grate.

The mat beneath her feet was threadbare, undoubtedly trampled on by generations of trainee nurses before her.

'Anne Christina Reid.' Matron looked up from the papers on her desk and laced her fingers together. 'Take a seat.'

Annie nodded and sat down.

'Relax, girl. I don't bite.'

Annie swallowed, moved further back in her chair and wiped her damp palms on her skirt.

'Tell me, Miss Reid, why do you want to be a nurse?'

Annie cleared her throat. She did not care to repeat her reasons. The death of Sina and Bel was her own personal pain, something she carried close to her heart, not something to share with strangers. 'I want to help people,' she said. 'I'm a hard worker and I'm interested in medicine.'

Matron lowered her eyes and adjusted her glasses. She picked up a sheet of paper. 'So I see from your letter of application. I have no doubt you're a hard

158

worker, but so are most of the girls who apply. What makes you special?'

Her eyes met Annie's and she waited.

Slightly perturbed by a question she had not anticipated, Annie took a deep breath. 'I'm nothing special, Matron, but I want to become a nurse more than anything else on earth. If you give me a chance I promise I'll not let you down.'

The Matron studied the papers before her. The relative silence in the room stretched. 'Your tutor at...' She looked up. 'Evening class?'

Annie knew what Alexander had put in the report. 'Yes, Matron.'

'Your tutor has given you a glowing reference. Recommends you highly.'

Her eyes never left Annie's face. It was as if she was reading Annie's mind and finding her wanting.

'I did my best.'

Matron straightened her shoulders and drew in some air. 'The hours are long, the situations often heart-breaking and you will be expected to keep the rules of the hospital, which are strict. Tell me, Miss Reid, do you have a young man?'

Annie crossed her fingers in the folds of her skirt and shook her head. 'No, Matron.'

'I would keep it that way. If you want to be a nurse here, you will need no distractions. Too many young girls decide they want marriage after all and don't serve their three years. Then it is a waste of good training. I think they only come here with romantic notions of cool hands on fevered brows and the hope of snaring a doctor. The reality, Miss Reid, is very different.'

'I don't want to waste my training.' Or snare a doctor, she mentally added.

159

'I believe you are the daughter of a clergyman and you will be staying at an address in Glasgow?' Matron looked down to the papers on her desk.

'Yes, Matron.'

'Pollokshields.' Matron raised her eyebrows. 'Relations?'

'Uncle and aunt.' It wasn't exactly a lie.

Matron's face lost some of the severity and she almost smiled. 'Very good, Miss Reid. Do you have any questions?'

'The marriage bar, does it cover all nurses?'

'If I said yes, would that change your mind?'

Annie shook her head and lowered her eyes.

'If you wish to work in a hospital, yes. However, if you decide you want to marry and, provided you've qualified, you may be a district nurse or become a midwife. The skill will never be lost. Does that answer your question?'

'Yes, thank you, Matron.' She thought of the women of Raumsey and the surrounding islands. She thought of Sina and Bel and tried hard not to let the relief show on her face. If Alexander would wait three years for her, they might be able to marry after all.

Matron set her folder to one side and picked up another. She peered at Annie over her glasses. 'Very well. I'll let you know.'

Outside, in the weak sunshine, Annie had some time to wait before Henry returned. Her interview had been over sooner than she expected. She watched the nurses come and go dressed in their starched white hats and aprons, covered by black cloaks, their lacing shoes clicking against the cobbles. Ambulances drew up, stretchers were carried in and energy flowed through the scene. She wanted more than ever to be part of all this.

160

Eventually Tess came through the doors and ran towards her. 'How did you do?'

'I'm not sure,' said Annie.

Tess pulled out a packet of cigarettes and shook one into her hand. 'I'm gasping. I didn't want to go in there smelling of smoke.' She lit the cigarette and drew deeply on it. 'Imagine both of us being here, eh? I heard about Bel and the baby. I couldn't manage to come home with the weather and all.'

The now familiar lump rose in Annie's throat and she quickly changed the subject.

'How was it, being in service?'

'Hated it. The wifie was a right bitch. I lasted three months. Then I tried my hand at the herring gutting for a while, but I gave that up too. Cack-handed, they said I was. Bloody cold work too and my fingers...' She twisted her hand in the air. 'Cut them to ribbons. The girls had a right laugh though, always singing and cracking a joke. Off to Yarmouth and up to Shetland. I always wanted to see a bit of the world. Think I might have enjoyed it if I ever got the hang.'

'How're you here, then?'

Tess shrugged. 'I got a job in the fever hospital in Wick. Not many wanted to risk catching something themselves, so I got in easily enough. I had all the wards to clean and the washing to do, but island lassies are no strangers to hard work.' Her face became solemn and she stared at the ground. 'I was good with the patients, all the poor bairns. I was a natural, Matron said. She recommended me for proper training and wrote a few letters to various hospitals on my behalf. Then I met an island lad one day and he told me you were coming here. I was delighted to be accepted too. Where are ye stopping the night?'

'Donald has a brother in Pollokshields. He's offered to put me up until I hear whether I've got in or not.'

161

'Ye're lucky. I've got to go back north tomorrow. I'm sleeping in the workhouse tonight and I believe it's pretty dire, still it's better than the penny line.'

'Penny line?'

'Aye, a woman on the train told me. If the early incomers hadn't enough money for a bed in the workhouse, they could pay a penny to be tied up to something like a washing line and someone would release them in the morning. Otherwise they'd have to sleep on the streets among the rats and chances were the ground would be wet and muddy an' full of sewage an' all.'

'I don't think that can be true.' Annie was aghast. Immediate visions of clothes lines with people hanging like rag dolls along the length of them sprang into her mind and she laughed at the ridiculousness of it.

'The woman swore it was true. I was seriously worried when I counted my pennies. Mind you, it probably doesn't happen nowadays. Come on, let's find a tearoom and have a something to drink.' She linked her arm through Annie's and they set off along the street.

Annie couldn't imagine being strung up on a line to spend the night. She would not have relished a night in the workhouse either and silently thanked God that her mother had met the Reverend.

Tess gave a hoot of laughter and her plain face lit up making it almost pretty. 'So glad you're here, Annie. We're going to have a rare time.'

'What if they turn us down?'

'Then we'll try another hospital and keep on trying. I've got to get in. I'm no' bonny like ye; doubt if anyone will ever want to marry me. It won't matter so much if I'm doing something I love.' A shadow passed over Tess's face, a sadness that transferred itself to Annie and dampened her mood. It was there for an instant and then

162

gone. It was true Tess was no beauty in the conventional sense, but her ready laugh and friendly personality more than made up for it. Once you got to know her, Tess shone anyway.

'Any man would be blessed to have you, madam.'

Annie forced a laugh. 'Come on, let's find the tearooms. Do you think they'll have coffee? I've never had any since I left Canada and I fair miss it. But I'll no stay too long, Donald's nephew is picking me up.'

'Donald's nephew? Is he good looking?'

'He is actually, and nice, if a little daft.'

'Maybe ye've landed on yer feet already, lass.'

'Don't be silly!' Alexander was too ensconced in her heart for there to be any room for someone else. She thought of him at least once every hour and wished he was by her side. She imagined them doing things together, him showing her around instead of Henry. Most of all, she remembered the strength of his arms, the pressure of his lips and how much she had wanted that last kiss to go on forever. And yet there had been a detachment about him, a drawing away, as if, in spite of his words, he did not share her passion. She had to believe it was because he respected her and wanted things to be right. But, oh, how her body had burned for his touch, still burned at the memory. 'Anyway, I doubt if Henry thinks of me in that way.' She pulled herself back to the present.

Chapter Twenty-Three

'How did you get on?' asked Henry when he picked her up.

Annie recounted her day.

'I'm sure you will have made quite the impression. I've managed to get us tickets for the theatre tomorrow night.'

'My, that's grand.' The theatre. Then a thought struck her. 'I don't have much money. I don't know how long it'll be before I hear from the hospital.'

'You will be my guest and I'll be proud to have you on my arm.'

'And then there's the clothes. Do the ladies dress up?'

He laughed again. 'Like clowns, you mean?'

Her face grew hot. 'I don't think I'll go thank you,' she said stiffly.

'You will go. I command it. And don't worry, all sorts of people go to the music halls these days. Since the war ended, people want to celebrate.'

She feigned meekness. She wanted to go with a passion. Surely it wouldn't give him the wrong idea if she accepted his offer just this one time? The dress her mother had made for her before she left was very nice.

They returned to Pollokshields in good time for tea.

This time it was served by a slim, cheery-faced woman in a maid's uniform.

'This is Myrtle, Daisy's mother,' said Margaret in her whispery voice. 'She does the cleaning and most of the cooking around here. I've already told her you will be staying with us a few days.'

Myrtle smiled at Annie. 'Glesga'll be a change frae the north, for ye, hen.' Her eyes flew to her mistress and she fell silent.

'I'm looking forward to my time here,' said Annie, warming to the woman at once.

'Thank you, Myrtle,' said Henry. Myrtle shot him a fond smile and bustled out.

'She's not been in service before, so she doesn't quite know how to behave. She worked in a munitions factory during the war, but she is a good help.' Margaret reached for the teapot.

Her face took on a disapproving look when Henry told her that he intended taking Annie to the theatre the following night. 'Are you sure you should?' she said.

'Oh, Mother,' said Henry. 'You and Father can come as chaperons if you don't think she's safe with me.'

'Your father will be going to his club.' Margaret spoke through narrow lips. 'I trust you'll bring Annie straight home.'

'Honestly, Mother, you'd think I was intending to sell her into slavery.'

'I'm ashamed to say that you do, shall I say, have a certain reputation with the ladies.'

'Greatly exaggerated, Mother, I can assure you.'

Margaret turned and studied Annie. 'Well, as long as you don't get any romantic ideas about my son. I hate to say this about my own flesh and blood, but I'm sure he would let you down badly. It would never work out. For one thing you are totally the wrong class.' She immediately covered her mouth with a shaking hand. 'Please, dear, I didn't mean that in a derogatory way, not at all, it's just that, well, you're used to a different lifestyle.'

Henry muttered something under his breath.

165

At least she had the decency to look embarrassed, thought Annie, her scalp and face prickling. With difficulty she managed to hold her tongue. Totally the wrong class indeed.

'I have a sweetheart back home. I have no designs whatsoever on your son.' She stopped before she said more. Until she knew whether she was to get into the nursing or not, she was reliant on the Charlestons' charity and despite the woman's snobbishness, she was kind enough.

'Perhaps I put that badly, my dear. I just worry. You are under my care.' She bunched her napkin and dabbed her lips.

Annie drank her tea and ate her sandwiches in silence, then made her excuses. As she climbed the staircase, she heard the voices from below. Margaret's trembled slightly.

'Where have you been all morning, Henry? I hope you've not been to one of those meetings.'

'I'll make my own mind up about which meetings I will or won't attend.'

'We've given you every advantage, a good upbringing, yet you're mixing with... with low-lifes. Are you doing this to hurt us? It was that girl, that Irish trollop who turned you against your family, wasn't it? That girl from the gutter?'

'That girl, as you call her, is a very nice lady who just happened to be born poor. I tried to help her, that was all there was between us. And no, I haven't seen her for months.'

'And Annie Reid. She's a delightful child, but please don't make us regret taking her in. I have to say I had my doubts, but your father was adamant.'

Not wishing to eavesdrop any longer, Annie hurried to her room. What had she been thinking? That they looked on her as an equal? She washed and dressed in her frock, brushed her hair until it shone and stared at her reflexion in the mirror. 'Annie Reid, you are every bit as good as them,' she told herself. 'One day you will have everything you want and it won't be because you married money.' The eyes that looked back at her shone with a renewed determination. She spent the next hour poring over her text books and did not return downstairs until she was called for dinner, which was much more lavish than the night before and was served by a harassed-looking Myrtle.

'You're very quiet tonight,' Frank said. 'Did your interview go well?'

'I think I did well, thank you.' Annie answered.

'Annie, you and I will go up town tomorrow and get you some appropriate clothes for the theatre. My father owns a warehouse and I have a ticket. I can get clothes for factory prices. You can pay me back once you get a wage,' said Margaret.

Annie realised Margaret was trying to make amends for her harsh words earlier, but any sympathy she had towards the woman was shattered by her next words. 'If you are to stay here any length of time, I want you to make a good impression. After all, you are living in our house and a daughter of the kirk.'

She had a strong desire to tell Margaret where to stuff her 'appropriate' clothes. But Isa's voice still rang in her head. *'These people are very kind to take you in. Do not disrespect them no matter what. Remember they are a product of their environment as we are of ours.'*

'Yes. Thank you very much.' She spoke through clenched teeth. After all, it was not charity. She would pay the woman back, every penny, and it *would* be nice to have something new.

Next day they walked along the avenue and out onto the main road where they took a bus into Sauchiehall Street. Annie gasped when she saw the price of the blouse and skirt Margaret chose for her. They were beautiful, but much more expensive than she would have dreamed of, even with the discount.

'I can't really accept that,' she said.

Margaret batted the air. 'My dear, you must learn to pay for the best and look after it well.'

'I'll pay you back as soon as I can.'

'Don't worry about it, dear. Donald would not have asked us to keep you if you were less than honest. Now let's go and have tea. I know a wonderful place. You'll love it.' Her face was flushed and she looked happier than Annie had seen her since her arrival.

They went to the Willow Tearooms for tea in delicate china cups. She was awestruck by the grandeur of the place, so much so that she could hardly taste her tea or the little triangular sandwiches. But Margaret was animated, enthusiastically pointing out this and that while Annie absorbed the atmosphere, visualising the ghosts of fine ladies and gentlemen drifting among the tables.

When they left, Margaret gripped Annie's elbow. 'I've rather enjoyed today, my dear,' she whispered. 'You know, I've always regretted that I never had a daughter to take shopping.'

It was then Annie realised how much Margaret enjoyed playing the lady bountiful and the clothes *were* lovely. She thought of her own mother, who would want her to be polite and grateful, she who never had the chance for such indulgences herself.

That night over dinner, Annie quickly became aware of the change in Margaret's mood. It seemed the presence of her husband and son filled her with apprehension.

'You do look lovely,' she said when Annie reappeared after dinner dressed in her new clothes.

'Thank you very much.'

168

'Beautiful in fact.' Henry's eyes swept the length of her as he took her arm.

'Your father and I are trusting you to take good care of our charge.' Margaret began the characteristic bunching of the napkin in her hands. She glanced at Frank who said nothing, but shook his head as if resigned. Gone was the woman Annie had glimpsed this afternoon.

Annie's emotions swung widely as Henry drove along the streets, alternating between excitement of the theatre and unease about Margaret's disapproval. 'Why is your mother so concerned?' she asked. 'Are you a danger to young women?'

'Young, middle-aged, old.' He gave an unhappy snort. 'Such is my parents' opinion of me. They think I'm a bit of a reprobate.' He became silent for a heartbeat, then continued. 'They want me to settle down and marry someone they approve of.'

'Are you a bit of a reprobate?'

'I've had a few girlfriends, that's all. Really no scandal to speak of. My parents sent me away to boarding school when I was eight. Then on to Oxford. I entered the army as an officer, but the war was almost over by then. I take my pleasures where I can. That's my life in a nutshell.' He faced her and smiled. 'You're like a breath of fresh air, Annie, after all the stuffy circles my parents want me to move in. Say you'll come out with me tomorrow. I'll give you the guided tour of this fine city.'

'Won't you have to work?'

'I'll go in the day after. One good thing about working for family, they're not likely to dismiss you.'

'Let's go on Saturday. I don't want it to upset them, my being here.'

169

'For your sake, fair one, I will do as you ask.' They parked some streets away and walked to the theatre. Rain had fallen earlier and the lights from the lamp posts shimmered and fragmented in the shallow puddles.

'I couldn't help overhearing. You were arguing last night, after I left the room.'

Henry's face tightened. 'How much did you hear?'

'Something about an Irish girl and meetings.'

'I wish I wasn't an only child. They pin all their hopes on me, want to turn me into a duplicate of themselves.'

'So you go to the opposite extreme?'

He looked at her in surprise. 'Perhaps. I never thought of it that way.'

Henry took her arm and guided her through the throng to stand in a queue. Annie loved the building and the buzz around her at once. She was a bit perturbed when Henry led her to the more expensive seats and tried not to mind the way the extravagantly-dressed ladies glowered at her simple attire. Although her skirt and blouse were of the best quality, she still wore the reasonably-priced coat and shoes that Donald had bought her. Who did these women think they were anyway? She was every bit as good as them, better in fact, as she did not look down on anyone. Then she overheard a woman with a dead fox around her neck and a cloche hat on her head. 'Isn't that Henry Charleston? Looks like he's found another girl from somewhere.'

'It's disgraceful that he flaunts his conquests the way he does,' replied her companion.

'Maybe that's the Highland girl Margaret has given shelter to. Going to the nursing, I hear.' The third woman. spoke in a loud voice. 'I'm surprised at Margaret allowing her out with Henry though.' With another disdainful glance in Annie's direction, they moved away.

170

'Don't mind them,' whispered Henry, tucking her arm through his.

'I don't.' Angrily, she lifted her head. 'Was that why you brought me here? To flaunt me – to make some sort of point?'

'Of course. I love ruffling feathers.' Then he stopped and looked down at her, his face serious. 'They have no right to talk about you like that. As my guest, you will walk into the best seats with your head held high.'

Annie wasn't sure if she wanted to be used in this way. It seemed both Henry and his mother had their own agenda. Only Frank treated her like a real person. Once inside the theatre, however, she began to relax and enjoy the acts, especially Harry Lauder. By the time they left, she no longer cared about disapproving looks, no longer cared whether Henry was using her to make a point, no longer imagined Alexander by her side; she didn't think he would enjoy the music hall anyway. He was much too serious, too intense. Instead she thought of Bel. 'You would have loved this,' she whispered to the ghostly presence she so often felt by her side.

'Beg your pardon.' Henry leaned down, cocking his ear towards her.

'I was thinking about my cousin, Bel. She's the main reason I chose to be a nurse, you know.'

'Ah, the girl who died. I'm sorry.' They walked in silence for a while. 'You've such a conscience, Annie. You'd make a good socialist.'

'I won't be able to vote anyway, so what's the point of me being anything political?'

'Things will change one day. Nothing wrong with believing.'

Annie thought of the poverty of the islands, the lack of medical supplies and compared it to what she saw as the lavish lifestyle of the Glasgow Charlestons. Almost as if he read her thoughts, Henry said, 'You see how we

171

live. Yet we're poor compared to many others. Some of the merchant bankers of the larger branches and many of the traders live far more lavishly, I can assure you. On Saturday, I'll take you to Burnside and Bearsden, and after that, I'll show you streets where the poverty is greater than you could ever imagine.'

'I'll look forward to it, but no more staying away from work on my behalf.' Although he was older than her, she already thought of him as a silly wee laddie searching for something to believe in. He appeared to enjoy the accoutrements of wealth far too much to be a committed socialist.

That night she fell asleep with the songs of Harry Lauder floating in her head.

The following day, with Margaret attending one of her many charitable functions and with the others at work, Annie went in search of the servants.

Both of them were in the kitchen. Myrtle was peeling potatoes and Daisy shelling peas.

'Please don't rise,' said Annie as Myrtle made to leave her seat. 'I'm from the islands, I'm not posh.'

'Aye, but ye live in a fine manse.'

Annie laughed. 'Compared to this house, it's not that fine. And before that, things were a whole lot different.'

'But yer still a guest of the missis.'

'Please, can I join you?'

'Aye, hen.' She indicated the girl who smiled shyly at Annie. 'Daisy's the oldest of ma weans. She comes in tae do the washing and on my days off she does the cooking. She gives me a wee hand when she can. Yer aunt's a fine woman, always lets me take a bit extra home wi' me for the lads. The missis would give Daisy a full-time job, but things are looking bad for everyone now. She aye gives her a penny or two extra in her

172

wages though. Ma man's no been able to find work since he came back from the war. He's lost a leg an' all.'

Annie took a seat at the table and helped the child to shell the peas.

'Ah, no, hen, ye shouldn't be doing that work,' said Myrtle.

'Back in Raumsey, I did much more.'

When Myrtle looked surprised, Annie told her about the croft and the struggle to survive.

Myrtle shook her head. 'She's a charitable soul, Mrs Charleston, so she is.'

It was as Annie thought. She was just another one of Margaret's charities. It made the woman feel good to let Annie sleep in her house and eat at her table, but woe betide if she were to marry her son. Well, she would have no worries on that score.

For the next few days, Annie spent her spare time in the kitchen with Myrtle and Daisy. She found Daisy to be a bright child, eager to learn and more than interested in Annie's dreams.

'I wish I could be a nurse too,' she said.

'Then you can,' said Annie. 'You're clever enough.'

Daisy stared at the vegetable she was dicing. 'I can't stay on at school. I have to get a full-time job and make money. I'm getting a start in the Singer factory, next week.'

'Is that where they make the sewing machines? My mother has one of them. Do you think you'll like working there?'

The conversation went on until it was time for Annie to join her hostess for a light lunch.
'

On Saturday, as promised, Henry took Annie out in his car. They visited Glasgow Cathedral and Provand's Lordship. In each case he enthused about the architecture. Afterwards he drove her out into the

173

country, into the clear air and towards the village of Lenzie.

He turned off a rutted track and towards a stretch of water where he parked. 'Come on,' he said. After exiting the car and opening the passenger door, he offered her his hand.

Through the trees the water sparkled in the afternoon sun. 'Lenzie Loch,' said Henry as he flipped up the boot and took out a large basket covered by a checked cloth. 'I brought us a picnic. Go on, down by the water.'

In the shade of the trees, they found a suitable spot where he spread a rug. From the basket he produced bread, cheese and a bottle of champagne. 'Harder to get things since the war, but I have my sources.' He handed her a glass and opened the champagne. The cork shot off with a loud pop and some of the liquid fizzed out.

Annie gave a little scream and then laughed as Henry poured her a drink. She had never tasted champagne before and she sipped it slowly. 'The bubbles are going up my nose,' she said and giggled.

'That's what makes it special, the bubbles. Drink up, have some more.'

She sipped the second glass more slowly, enjoying the taste. Although the day was warm, the air had the first breath of autumn and she shivered.

'You're cold?' Henry took off his jacket and placed it round her shoulders.

She thanked him, enjoying this attention. She looked at his handsome profile and wished it was Alexander sitting here with her drinking champagne on the banks of Lenzie Loch, listening to the water lapping gently against the shingle and the birds twittering in the trees.

The alcohol made her drowsy. She lay back. Somewhere in the distance a piper was playing and the music travelled over the water. She drifted off.

'You look beautiful lying there.'

174

Waking with a start, she found Henry studying her, his face too close for comfort.

She tried to sit up but his body kept her pinned to the ground and he didn't move.

'Maybe we should go,' she said, unnerved by the warmth of his breath against her face.

He whispered, 'I really want to kiss you.'

'I already told you I've got a sweetheart back in Raumsey.' She set her hands on his chest and pushed. This time he drew back with a sigh.

'And you ought to be staying true to the lovely Cynthia,' she added, shaken.

He gave a pah. 'I'm not attracted to Cynthia. She's my mother's choice, not mine.' His eyes were still on her, drinking her in.

Annie stood up. 'Let's go now.'

He looked chastened. 'I'm sorry if I've overstepped the mark or if I've become a bore.'

'You're not a bore, Henry. I find you funny. I loved being shown around and I loved the picnic. But you are just a friend; you'll never be anything more. Come on, your parents will be wondering where we are.'

'I've enjoyed myself today.' There was a wistfulness to his voice, something verging on sadness.

For a second she wanted to reach out to him, to touch the pain she sensed beneath the carefree exterior. 'I did too, Henry. I really did.'

'And you're not angry with me?'

'Of course not.' But inside she was trembling. For the briefest minute she had enjoyed the feel of his body against hers and she had wanted to kiss him. Only, in her head, it would not be him she was kissing. Her body was alive with all the sensations of a young, healthy woman, and the realisation scared her.

He picked up the basket and rug and together they strolled to the car.

175

'It's Sunday tomorrow,' he said. 'You'll want to go to church, no doubt.'

'I don't mind whether I do or not.'

'It's mandatory, I'm afraid. Appearances must be kept up.'

'In that case I shall go and be glad to.'

He opened the car door and helped her inside. 'Then we *shall* go and listen to the fine minister preach against the Great Papal Plot.'

'What are you talking about?'

'Our local minister is a staunch supporter of the Reverend John White. There is a train of thought that all the Irish Catholic immigrants have come here in order to swamp Protestant Britain with Catholicism. Does my reverend uncle not believe the same?'

'Not at all.' She shook her head, not understanding the strange new world she had entered. On Raumsey there was very little division between poor and not so poor and the only religious differences were between those who went to the kirk and those who did not. Neither had she seen much evidence of this division in the prairies of Canada.

'Do you believe that?' she asked.

'Of course not. Reverend John White is a staunch Tory. I wouldn't believe anything the man said.'

'Do your parents believe him?'

'Every word.'

It was with great relief therefore when, the following Sunday, the minister delivered his sermon in a straight forward manner and said nothing at all about the Great Papal Plot.

The letter arrived on Monday morning. Annie's fingers shook as she opened the envelope and she screamed.

Margaret came running from the drawing room. 'Why, dear, whatever's the matter?'

176

'I've been accepted. I've been accepted for the nursing.'

She rushed to the kitchen to share the news with Myrtle.

'I'm glad for ye, lassie. You'll make a grand wee nurse, so ye will. Ah hope this'll no be the last I see o' ye?'

'I'll come and visit on my day off.'

'Ye see and dae that, hen.'

'I promise.' Annie hurried out. The next thing she had to do was write to her mother and Alexander. She could hardly wait until Henry came home from work to share the news with him.

Chapter Twenty Four

There was a general shuffling in the room as the trainee nurses took their seats. The matron sat behind a desk. Once all the girls were seated, she stood up, her eyes scanning the faces before her. To Annie she seemed even more formidable than she had previously. 'Good day, nurses. At least I hope you are all going to become nurses.' Pausing, she let her eyes sweep the room again. She held her head high and her chin jutted out giving the appearance of looking down her long nose at the unfortunates. 'If you think this is an easy job you will soon be disillusioned. It's hard work. Many of you won't last the course. It won't take long to sort the wheat from the chaff.'

Annie sat straight, shoulders back. Her heart was full and had been ever since she received the letter of acceptance. She would be wheat, she promised herself, the best wheat that ever grew in Glasgow Royal Infirmary.

'From now on, you will be known by your surnames and you will obey any order given to you by a Sister.' She stopped and cleared her throat. 'You may be wondering why the term 'Sister' is used for the officially registered nurses.'

Annie had never wondered why. She accepted it as she had accepted that Matron was called Matron and nurses were called nurses.

The voice carried on. 'Centuries ago, nursing was done by nuns. As you may know, King Henry the eighth dissolved the monastic and conventual orders and nursing was taken over by prostitutes and criminals, but the term, Sister, remained.'

Annie knew little of Henry the eighth. However, she listened, eager to soak up every piece of information.

'We have to thank Miss Florence Nightingale and her companions for beginning the process of turning nursing into the respectable profession it is today.' Here she stopped and fell silent for a heartbeat. 'However,' her voice returned, stronger than ever. 'There are still men of authority who think of nurses as women of low morals.'

There were a few nods of agreement.

'So you will be careful to uphold the standards of that magnificent woman and her stalwart team. I will not tolerate any behaviour which will bring the good name of nurses and particularly the Royal into disrepute. Is that understood?'

Murmurs of 'Yes, Matron,' rippled round the room.

'Sister Beasley is your housemother; follow her and she will see you to your rooms. Good day.' With that she turned and swept from the room.

Sister Beasley had narrow shoulders, a large backside and a pudgy face with small intelligent eyes. Her voice was like a bow being scraped across the untuned strings of a violin.

Tess clutched Annie's arm and hissed, 'She's an ogre.'

'Hush.' Annie put her finger to her mouth. Sister Beasley spun around and glared at them. 'What did you say?'

'I said, ye're like my mother.'

Sister Beasley continued to glower at her for a further minute. 'No talking please.' She led them outside by a back door and into a big, old building with small windows that badly needed a wash. Inside, the hall was wide and high and dull and cold. Sister Beasley showed them the kitchen, the dining room, the toilet and bathroom which had a real bath and running water. Finally she took them to the sitting-room. The furniture was well worn, as was the lino on the floor. Sad-looking, pale brown curtains and discoloured screens hung at the window. Like the rest of the house, the walls were painted in shades of brown and green and badly in need of redoing. On a heavy, scratched sideboard sat a gramophone, a stack of records to one side. The walls were bare except for a large print of King George at his coronation.

'You can spend some of your leisure time in here. You will not sit in your bedrooms. On your days off you may go into town, but you must be back before lights out at ten, otherwise you will be faced by locked doors. You will find me strict, but fair. The Home Sister holds a responsible position.' She stopped and stared at them each in turn. 'I am responsible for seeing that you behave yourselves. And never let me find your beds in a mess or your drawers untidy. There is a list of rules taped onto the back of your room doors. Please acquaint yourselves with them. Follow me.'

Sister Beasley led the way upstairs directing the nurses to their various rooms. Her voluminous grey skirts swished with each movement of her heavy hips. As she walked, she delivered a further litany of rules and regulations. The higher they climbed, the narrower the corridors grew. They were all the same shades of dark green and pale brown with paint that flaked in places from the plastered walls. Up here, the air smelt musty and damp.

'Nurses Reid and MacLean? I have put you island girls in together along with an Irish girl. I thought that would be best.'

Annie and Tess looked at each other and grinned. Maybe Sister Beasley wasn't such an ogre after all.

180

They were to share a room in the attic. At first Annie looked at it in despair and decided they had been put here as a punishment. Lit by a single skylight, the room was as dingy as the corridors had been. Three iron beds had their tops under sharply sloping eaves. She would have to take care when sitting up, Annie thought, imagining her head colliding with the plaster. At either side of the door, was a chest of drawers suffering advanced attacks of woodworm. A third chest sat directly under the skylight.

'The room's small,' said Sister Beasley, 'but it's quieter up here. If you want tea you can make it in the kitchen; the range is usually on. Your uniforms are on your beds. I'll leave you to get unpacked.'

Once she had gone, Tess threw herself on the bed and it creaked in protest. 'This is going to be grand.' She sat up and lifted a long piece of something that looked like white cardboard.

'I think that's the hat,' said Annie.

'Will we try our uniforms on? I can't wait to see if it improves me, makes me look smart. I can't look any worse, can I?'

'Tess, why do you always say unkind things about yourself?'

'It's true, isn't it? I've had a few lads but none wanted me in the daylight.'

Aye, thought Tess, the bitter memory of Bobby still stung. She had got off work early and thought she would surprise him by waiting outside the grocers where he worked. When he finished for the day, he had exited with another message boy and they were laughing together. 'The ugly ones are easier,' said Bobby. 'They're so grateful for a bit of attention.'

'Does she, I mean, she lets ye?' asked the younger lad.

181

'She's well up for…' Bobby's words died on his lips when he saw Tess.

Filled with a rage she could not control she screamed and launched herself at him, knocking him to the ground and punching him in the face hard enough to break his nose. Durrand, the shopkeeper, had to pull her off him in the end.

'Tess,' Bobby cried, clutching his nose. 'I wasn't, I didn't mean…'

Fighting tears of humiliation, she marched away, holding her head high. What had she been thinking? That a bonny lad like Bobby would really like her? It was true she had let him have his way, not because she was grateful, but because she thought she loved him and foolishly believed he felt the same way about her.

He had tried to speak to her the next day. 'Please, Tess, let me explain. I really like ye. It's not what ye think…'

She had bunched her fists. 'Get away from me before I give you a black eye to go with yer broken nose.'

'Tess…please.'

She took a threatening step towards him and drew her arm back ready to strike.

'I'm going, I'm going. I didn't mean it. I'm sorry. I just wanted to be like the other lads, big like. Please give me another chance.'

Shooting him a look that would have withered a tree, she turned on her heel. She immediately went to the Matron of the fever hospital and accepted the offer to put her forward for proper training. The sooner she got away the better.

She banished the memory and lifted her voice so that there was a false smile in it. 'But no matter what I look like we're in Glasgow. We'll have to find time to explore the city.' She studied Annie who was opening her case. She had managed to fool her friend and one day, hopefully, she would manage to fool herself.

Although Annie's main concern was being the best nurse she could be, she also wanted to explore this strange new world beyond the hospital walls. She couldn't wait to show Tess the things she had shared with Henry. She examined the contents of her case. There wasn't much: her dress, underwear, a couple of blouses, a skirt, black stockings, black leather shoes, blunt-ended scissors, a pen, pencils, a watch, a set of books on anatomy, physiology and hygiene, a nurses' dictionary. All things Donald had bought for her. One day she would be able to pay him back. One day her family would be proud of her.

'Just you do well,' Donald had said when she protested that the cost was too much. 'Your mother and I don't mind tightening our belts for a bit, in fact we insist on it.' She thought of how kind he had been in the aftermath of losing Sina. A serious man, he could never make her laugh like her dad did, but he was warm and generous and she was glad that her mother had found him.

The uniforms were starched and crackled as they put them on. 'The collar's going to chafe my neck.' Tess ran her finger around the rigid rim.

Annie thought that too. The long skirt and stiff aprons were hardly designed for comfort. They laughed as they tried, without success, to assemble the headgear.

The door opened and Sister Beasley stood there. 'For goodness sake, girls.' She bustled in and took Annie's headdress from her hands. 'Like this.' Within seconds, she had it assembled. She turned and studied the beds and her expression turned sour. 'They were made up properly for you. I will expect your beds to be made with the precision you will be taught to use on the wards and kept that way.'

She grabbed the top cover of Tess's bed, now wrinkled, dragged it off and as the horrified girls looked on, she threw blankets, pillows and bedding onto the floor exposing the bare springs. 'This,' she waggled a stubby finger, is what to expect if the beds are not kept in precise order. I will not tolerate a badly made bed. I will strip it and continue to strip it until you get it right, understand?'

'But I only...' began Tess.

The Sister's face grew redder still. 'And never, ever have the audacity to speak back to me.'

'Sorry, Sister,' said Tess, as she met Annie's eyes and clamped her lips.

'Remove your uniforms and set them out for morning, then present yourselves in the mess hall. Food will be served shortly.' With that she dashed away.

By the time Tess had remade her bed, the door opened again and a dimpled, red-faced girl with long black hair and round blue eyes struggled in. 'Whit d'ye think o' all these stairs?' she gasped, set her case down and held out her hand. 'I'm Bernie Finnegan.'

'From Ireland?

'Ma Mammy and Da are frae Ireland right enough, but I wis born in Clydebank.'

Chapter Twenty-Five

The mess hall was large and drab and filled with voices. Five bare tables filled the space. At one side was a serving hatch. Nurses poured in and found themselves seats. The three girls made their way to the only vacant bench which was thankfully close to the serving hatch.

'Don't sit there,' hissed a nurse as she passed by. 'That's for the higher rank, the sisters. Come on, squeeze onto the bench at our table. We're the lower ranks, probationers.'

Thankful for her advice, Bernie, Annie and Tess followed her.

The girls soon discovered that they were expected to serve those who had been there longer. The mess-room maids concentrated on the sisters. That night, however, since they were not in uniform, they were spared the ordeal.

As they ate sausage and mash and listened to the conversations around them, Annie's heart sank.

'That staff nurse had me in tears again. I tell you, I'm taking no more of it,' complained the girl to her right, whom she learned was Nurse Andrews.

'Aye, well, ye should have the one on my ward. Made my life hell since I came here. I tell ye, if my mammy wasn't sae prood o' me I'd be down the flea market.' Doris Finnegan was from Pollokshaws. She had fiery red hair and freckles. She leaned over to speak to Annie. 'See you, hen, you new? You must be mad wanting to be a nurse. See now, if you want to stay oot later than ten, leave your windie open and you'll get in that way.'

'But I live on the top floor,' said Annie.

'I live on the bottom. Tell me and I'll leave mine for you. But you'll have to risk running into Beasley in the corridor. And,' her voice dropped to a whisper, 'mind and get the mail before she does. She'll censor them as fast as look.'

The broad Glaswegian dialect was different from the north and at times Annie had difficulty understanding it, especially when several girls got together and spoke quickly. Thankfully she was not alone; there were girls from the west coast with soft, proper speech, English being a second language to their native Gaelic, girls from Ireland, a few from the north of England and one from Aberdeen who spoke the Doric and whom no one understood.

As she ate, Annie listened to stories about bowels and bladders, cruel sisters and the Matron from hell.

The first duty of the probationers was the sluice room. Annie had been allocated West Ward, which consisted of women in various stages of recovery after surgery. It was her job to collect the bedpans, wash them thoroughly, warm them with hot water ready for going out again. The wards held twenty beds to either side and another ten down the middle aisle and not one bed was empty. The demand for bedpans was steady. Only patients ready for discharge used the lavatory. Sister Macintosh and her charge nurse were both tyrants who, it appeared, were there to make the probationers' lives hell.

'Hurry up with those pans, Reid.'

'They're ready.' Annie turned to her with a smile, pleased that she'd completed her task so quickly, but if

186

she expected praise or even some sort of appreciation, she was in for a let-down.

'This is not clean! Go up inside the handles.'

'But, I did...' Annie knew she had washed them carefully.

'You will not, I repeat, not speak back to me. Get the lot washed again before Sister sees how inept you are!' The charge nurse tipped the pile of clean pans so that they fell on the floor with a clatter, bringing the Sister with a face full of fury into the sluice room. 'What's going on here? The patients need quiet.'

'I'm afraid Reid is clumsy,' said the charge nurse sweetly. 'But I've set her straight.'

'You'll not last long here if you act like that.' Sister Macintosh pointed her finger at Annie. 'Get this pile washed and stacked.'

No sooner had she started the second round of washing, than the charge nurse was at the door again. 'Reid, patient in bed number four wants a pan. I have other things to do than to keep looking for you. Get her attended to before she soils the bed.'

Words of protest sprung to Annie's lips, but she trapped them behind her teeth and glowered instead.

'Now!' shouted the charge nurse. 'And less of the attitude.'

Annie grabbed a pan and made for the door.

'Just a minute. Have you warmed that pan?'

'There wasn't time...'

'Then make time. You do not give a patient a cold bedpan. Are you stupid? God alone knows why they send you island girls down here, you're all bloody useless.'

And so it went on. By the end of the day her hands were raw with scrubbing already clean bedpans, her feet ached and her back ached and her bones ached. Some of the patients had been kind and thanked her for her

187

attentions, others had sworn at her and threatened to report her for taking so long to bring them the means of relieving themselves. That she could cope with. However, she found it hard not to give both the charge nurse and the Sister a piece of her tongue.

As Annie left the ward at the end of her shift, Sister Macintosh called her over. Despite her aggravation at the charge nurse, Annie knew she had worked hard and was sure the Sister was going to say something kind. She must have noticed the abuse she had endured throughout the day.

'Not had a good beginning, have you, Reid?'

'Wha…no, Sister.'

'Come into my office.'

Annie followed her.

The Sister turned on her, eyes gleaming in her hawk-like face. 'I don't know where you were dragged up, but you were obviously taught nothing about cleanliness or obedience. Any more of this and you will be sent to Matron. A bad report to the committee will mean you have to leave, understand?'

Annie could not have replied even if she were allowed to. Her mouth fell open in astonishment. The blood rushed to her face. It had been her first day and, with no idea what she had done wrong, she did not feel she deserved these words.

For the next ten minutes she was subjected to a barrage of complaints that ranged from slovenliness, lack of attention to detail, attitude to her superiors and the likelihood that she would never become a nurse.

Annie wanted to say, 'Fine.' And go pack her bag that very night, but giving in was not her way. She no longer only wanted to give the harridan before her a piece of her tongue, she wanted to kill her slowly, poke red hot irons in her eyes, both her and the charge nurse.

188

Back in the nurse's home, she dragged herself up the many stairs, believing more than ever that she had been put at the top of the house as a punishment for being a Highland lass. With a sigh of pure exhaustion she reached the final landing, opened the door and burst into tears. Her bed had been stripped to the springs, her drawers emptied on the floor. Both Bernie's and Tess's belongings had been treated likewise. Mentally, Annie added Sister Beasley to her imagined hit list. She dragged the horse-hair mattress back over the springs and fell on it, face down. By the time the other girls returned, in no greater humour, Annie was fast asleep.

In the mess hall that night, they discovered that being sent to Matron was something that happened on a regular basis. 'If you think the sisters are bad, wait till you cross Attila.'

Annie soon learned that Attila was Matron's nickname.

Chapter Twenty-Six

After a week that passed in much the same way, Sister met her as she entered the ward. 'Today you will have a variation of job, Reid. First you must clean all the lavatories, then come and help with the nitting.'

Annie was delighted. Knitting sounded like a nice change. Her mother had taught her the skill at her knee and she was surprised that this talent would be needed here. Perhaps it was some sort of therapy for the patients. Tolerating the pain in her red, raw hands, she scrubbed the lavatories with such concentration that even Matron herself would be hard pushed to find fault, she thought. 'Finished, Sister.'

To her surprise Sister Macintosh didn't check her work. 'Not before time. You will of course have removed nits from heads before?'

Annie opened her mouth, 'Ah, of course...'

'Excellent. Start at this end of the ward. Nurse Parker has already begun at the other end. Get a tray and a comb from the office. I'll get you some sassafras oil. Get a move on then.'

'Yes, Sister.'

Annie was all too familiar with the delousing technique. Her mother had been meticulous in regularly subjecting Annie and her brother to the horrors of the small-toothed metal comb. Such were Isa's administrations, it was doubtful if Annie ever had a live louse in her head.

She soon learned to crack the nit with her nails and set it on the clean towel. A triumphant shout from the other end of the ward made her jump.

'I got a live one!' shouted Nurse Parker. Some of the patients clapped and joined in the nurse's joy at finding a live louse.

'Ye'll soon get the hang of it, hen,' said Annie's patient, a sweet woman with a soft, wrinkled face.

'Another one!' Annie shrieked, holding it up trapped between finger and thumb. Without any shame at having lice, the patients united in the merriment. It was almost a competition to see who found the most. After a week of constant harassment, it was good to be able to laugh.

Sister Macintosh eyed them disapprovingly, but said nothing. However strict she was with the nurses, she appeared to have compassion for her patients. She would not put a stop to anything that gave them respite from their suffering.

During the first few days, Annie had harboured thoughts born from frustration and anger at her superiors, thoughts that perhaps she had made a mistake by entering this job. In the Charleston's household, she had seen another way of life, the way of life she had once aspired to, but believed it to be an impossible dream. If she married someone like Henry, she could have a life of leisure and do charitable works like Margaret and no one would have the right to speak to her the way the sisters in the hospital did. But these were spur-of-the moment notions with no substance. Because then she remembered the pain of losing Bel and Sina and the frustration of not being able to help them would hit her again. With renewed resolve, Annie found it easier to hold her rebellious nature in check.

Her first three months were probationary and who needed to stand up for oneself if it meant dismissal?

On her first day off, Henry came to pick her up in his car. He drove a different car today. A sporty two seater, in bright red, which he informed her was a Morris

Cowley. 'I've made some investments in the stock market,' he said, his face beaming. 'I think I'm rather good at it. I've actually earned my father's approval for once and a nice wee bonus for myself as well.'

'I'm glad for you.' Annie climbed into the passenger seat and settled back.

'My parents sent me to take you home for afternoon tea. But first, the grand tour.'

'You mean there's more?'

'Kibble Palace, the botanic gardens.'

In spite of how tired she was, the excitement of seeing more of this grand city chased away the cobwebs. Just being out of the confines of the hospital grounds was like an escape from within prison walls. Annie laughed with the sheer pleasure of the sense of freedom.

'What's so funny?' asked Henry, grinning at her.

'It's just a good day,' she said. 'That's all.'

'I like to see you happy. What do you say we make this a regular thing?'

'I can't take you from your work.'

'It's an escape.'

She laughed again. 'That's just how I feel.'

It was a fine day and they walked slowly through Kelvingrove Park. Trees had just turned into their autumn colours and the first of the yellow leaves floated to the ground to lie in a carpet of autumnal grandeur or settle among the graceful swans on the Kelvin River.

'Are you happy here?' asked Henry.

'It's what I want to do and I'm getting to like Glasgow more and more.'

'No I meant right now. Here, with me?'

Annie thought for a minute, then glanced at him, almost shy. 'Yes, yes I am,' she admitted in surprise.

He grinned in that little-boy way again. 'Then let's go and look at some flowers.'

'I didn't think flowers would interest a man.'

From the edge of her eye she saw that his face had turned towards her. 'How could they not, when I have the most beautiful rose by my side?'

She faced him and he winked. 'Oh, Henry, stop being so foolish.' She laughed and punched him lightly on the arm, but she felt the pinkness flood her cheeks.

After two hours of walking round the gardens, it was time to go. 'I've never seen such wonderful flowers. Can we come back some time?' She would have happily spent all day among these glorious plants. It was a world away from anything she had seen in the past.

'I enjoy showing you things,' said Henry.

She looked up to find his eyes on her.

'You've got a sense of wonder... it's...refreshing.'

She gave a little laugh. 'I'm just a simple country girl.'

He smiled fondly. 'No, not simple. You're like a flower opening up.'

'Are you sure you aren't a poet?'

'At heart maybe.' Henry gave a laugh. 'Come on. Mother wants you back for tea. She'll be wondering where we are.'

Back at the Charlestons, Margaret politely made conversation, asking her about the nursing, although Annie got the impression that she was barely interested. She was glad when she could finally escape to the kitchen to find Myrtle, who greeted her warmly. 'Hello, hen.' She dusted her floury hands on her apron and came round the table to give Annie a hug. 'Oh, oh my, look what I've done.' She stepped back with a gasp.

Annie looked down at the dusting of flour on her clothes. 'Don't worry, it'll rub off. Now, how's the family?'

'Grand. Daisy's happy wi' her job in the Singer factory. We've a wee bit more spare cash now. She's a

193

clever lass. It was a shame to take her out of school, but she wanted to help.'

'She's a lovely girl. You're blessed to have her.'

'Ain't that the truth! Things're finally looking up. Maybe ma wee Johnny'll be able to stay on at school.'

Annie thought how unfair it was that Daisy had to sacrifice her schooling so that her brother didn't have to. The lads certainly seemed to have the best of it.

Chapter Twenty-Seven

Winter was upon them all too quickly. Annie had never lived in a city before and the winter confines of Glasgow contrasted depressingly with the wide open spaces of both the Canadian prairies and the island of Raumsey. Chill winds blew through the slate-grey streets, the sky lowered with dense clouds and the creeping damp found its way to her bones. All too often they suffered typical Glasgow fog, thick, yellow and suffocating.

Without any form of heating, their room grew chilly and draughts found a way in through the rattling skylight. Annie longed for the cosy kitchen of the manse and the large range with its outpouring of heat. Thank God she had little time to reminisce, for when she thought of home, she felt the stab of longing for her mother, for Bel, for the small warm body and morning smiles of the baby she had loved as her own. Most of all, she longed for Alexander. His face was the last image in her mind as she drifted to sleep each night and the first one in the minutes between waking and rising. She read his letters several times and kept them in a box under her bed.

But chasing the homesickness away was the flamboyant Henry with his little-boy-lost smile. Thankfully he had taken her at her word and, although she often caught him looking at her wistfully, he never again exceeded the boundaries of friendship.

In spite of missing home, it was a magical time for the girls. Even after five years, Glasgow was still caught up

195

in the post-war glow; dance halls, picture houses and music halls were thriving. Visits to any of these, difficult on a limited budget and because of the ten o'clock curfew, had to be relegated to afternoon matinees, unless Henry took her which he was more than willing to do.

Every second month she went out with him and he always had somewhere exciting and new to take her. In an effort to drink in all there was to experience, the probationers often did not go to sleep after a nightshift, but instead went up town just to walk around the centre and gaze in the windows of the stores, then back to catch a couple of hours rest before the next shift began.

It meant dragging herself through the night more dead than alive, but to Annie, it was worth it. Sometimes, if she was alone on her time off, she would take a tram to Kelvingrove Park. On calm days, she found herself a seat by the water and imagined Alexander sitting beside her, holding her hand. How Bel would have loved to hear Annie's news. Only here, alone did she allow herself a moment to reflect on the past and shed a tear.

It was good that Annie was blessed with the energy of a fireball, because, as well as their work and the pleasures of the city, the young nurses had to attend lectures and find time to study.

Although she loved the thrill of it all, Annie soon realised that if she was to do well, she needed to apply herself completely. At first, she wrote a letter every night to Alexander, but as the weariness overtook her, the days between letters grew longer until it was often no more than a couple of times a month.

Once her three months' probation was over and she passed her exams, she was no longer a skivvy but assigned to the wards as a nurse.

Flushed by her success, she immediately wrote two letters, one to her mother and one to Alexander.

Her mother's reply, full of joy and congratulations, came by return of post, but it was some weeks later before she got news from Alexander. Clutching his letter, she ran upstairs to her room and tore it open.

Darling Annie,

I miss you so much. I'm so glad you passed your first tests and are now on your way to becoming a registered nurse. There's something I need to tell you, but I want to tell you face to face. If you will write to me and name the most convenient day, I will travel to meet you. I hope we can spend the day together.

Her heart sang. What could he have to tell her? Perhaps he had gotten a job in a school in Glasgow and they could see each other more often. That had to be it. She re-read the words several times, trying to sense some clue. Since their time apart, he had grown in her imagination. His jaw line had become firmer, his shoulders broader, his eyes darker and full of deeper meaning, his passion for her all-consuming. He would follow her here, since here is where she had to be. She believed that, because it was what she wanted and she couldn't contemplate it being any other way. But how she longed for his letters to be a bit more passionate. His letters never made her giggle and blush the way Bernie did when she read the words written by her young man.

The rest of Alexander's letter contained news of home, similar stuff to that which was in her mother's letters.

'You look right pleased with yerself,' said Tess as she rearranged the bedding Sister Ogre regularly threw onto the floor.

'Alexander's coming to Glasgow soon. Oh Tess, I can't wait to see him, it seems a lifetime.'

'Will ye be able to keep yer hands off him?'

Annie felt her face turn pink. 'I wanted to marry him. I wish I could be with him all the time, but being a nurse is my goal and I don't plan to give up on it.'

'Well don't take any chances.'

'No, I can't risk it.'

'There are ways nowadays. Ye can be together and ye don't have to have a bairn.'

Annie had heard whispers between nurses and off-the-record advice given to poverty stricken women after yet another unwanted birth. 'I know of ways, but isn't that just for married women.'

'Do ye think I live like a nun?'

'Tess, you don't?' Annie put her hand over her mouth.

Tess straightened her shoulders, defiance in every movement. 'Ye don't think badly of me, Annie?'

'Not if you love him.'

Tess let out a hoot of laughter. 'Love? That's something I'll no risk again, but men have their uses.'

'What? Oh, Tess! But what if you have a bairn? Will he marry you? Would you be happy to give up the nursing?'

'Probably no to all those questions. Marriage is not for me. And I won't have a bairn. I know what to do.'

'Oh, I can't believe you're saying this!' Yet as she spoke, hope leapt within her. Alexander was a man. He must know of such things.

'Look, go to the library on your next day off and ask for books by Marie Stopes. Then come and see me. Reggie has the catalogues. I'll order something for ye if ye want.'

Annie's stomach churned. Could she dare? Yet living here made her see things differently. She suspected many of the nurses led less than moral lives, yet they were good people.

A butterfly fluttered in her stomach. 'Yes, please do that, Tess. But tell no one.'

'D'ye think I'm daft?' asked Tess.

She walked into the library wondering on which shelf she would find the book written by Marie Stopes. After a while, the prim-mouthed librarian approached her. 'Is there anything I can help you with?'

Annie's face grew hot. She was glad she had worn her gloves, hiding the fact that she wore no wedding ring. First clearing her throat, she made her request, immediately averting her eyes, waiting for the rebuff.

To her surprise the prim mouth smiled, completely transforming the face. 'It's not on the shelves,' she said. 'My boss is Catholic and he strongly disapproves, but I brought in a copy of my own and it's been very popular.' She led Annie to her desk and opened a large handbag. 'It's a best seller, you know. About time women were in control of their own destiny. I managed to get a few copies of *Married Love*.' She pulled out a book wrapped in brown paper. 'Return it only to me. If it's my day off, say nothing.'

That night Annie read until her eyes were sore and when she was too tired to read any more, she fell asleep feeling liberated.

Chapter Twenty-Eight

The day he arrived she rose early and washed carefully in the freezing cold. She brushed her hair and allowed it to fall about her shoulders. Having no make-up other than a scraping of face powder, she pinched her cheeks to make them pink. Outside, a dusting of snow had fallen in the night and the air smelt fresh and new. The sharp wind slapped her face and hurt her lungs.

She took the tram up to the centre of town and arrived as the clock struck nine. His train had been due in ten minutes ago. In her hurry, she slipped and almost fell twice. In the relative shelter of the station with crowds surging towards her, she suddenly felt faint and clutched a pillar until she regained her breath. Her eyes scanned the multitude before her. What if he had already left, thinking she had failed to turn up?

'Annie.' She heard her name, turned all the way round and he was there, coming towards her. She let go of the pillar and ran towards him, her heart floating in time with her feet, warm and glowing in spite of the cold. She stopped before him and the other occupants of the station faded into nothing. He reached out and took hold of her hands, his face softening as his gaze drank her in. A snowflake settled on one eyelash. 'You look wonderful,' he whispered.

He was taller than Henry, his face held so much more strength and the time they had been apart drifted away. His eyes seemed darker than she remembered and then his face was too close to see. She shut her eyes and waited for the touch of his lips, cold, light as a feather.

After the first shock she moved her own lips. Her heart swelled as she gave herself to the incredible sensation of a kiss given by someone she had been dreaming about for so long. One of his arms moved around her shoulders, the other slipped to her waist and his touch was electric.

They parted and laughed, eyes fusing them together, their breath billowy in the freezing air. In that moment, a whole world belonged to them.

'How long are you here for?' she whispered.

He drew back and took her hands in his again.

'Just today and tonight. Come on, let's find a tearoom where we can get out of the cold.'

She constantly glanced at him as they walked. Flakes of snow, soft as moths landed on his hair and the shoulders of his dark coat. One landed on his nose and he blew it away. He looked as good as the image of him she had held in her heart, better because he was here, in the flesh and his hand was holding hers.

'In here,' he said, nodding at a doorway.

They chose a table by the window and sat opposite each other hands joined across the table top.

'How are you, Annie Reid?' His voice was soft, her name like a caress on his lips.

She tightened her fingers around his. 'The best since I've been here.'

'Your mother sends her love.'

'Is she well, happy?'

'She's both.'

'What have you got to tell me?'

Silence fell between them. His eyes dropped to the table and something cold started inside her.

'Alexander, what is it? I was hoping you were going to tell me you were moving here, that we could see each other on my days off. Isn't that what you're going to tell me?'

201

He shook his head and she felt the seed of hope shrivel and die.

'You've not met someone else?' The thought would kill her. She forgot to breathe as she waited for his answer.

'Of course not. I needed to see you again. Find out if this is what you really want.'

'I'd hoped …' She stopped and stared at their hands joined together and lying on the table. 'I thought, maybe, there was a way we could be together without me giving up my nursing.'

'What do you mean, Annie?'

She felt tension travel along the fingers that held hers. 'This is my only chance of a career and I love it. Helping save a life, or giving comfort to those in pain, knowing I can do it, that I'm important to that person at the time…I've got to finish my training.'

'I knew what your answer would be.' He kept his eyes on her as if waiting for her to say more.

Her mouth had dried. Her heart raced. Could she find the courage to say what was in her heart? She took a deep breath and moistened her lips. If she didn't say the words now, she might regret it for ever. In the end, she simply blurted it out. 'I want to be with you. There is a way I can have both, if we're discreet.' She swallowed and there was nothing to swallow. 'If you got a job near here we could be together whenever I had time off.'

He opened his mouth as if to speak, but she held up her hand.

'I don't have to get pregnant and it won't be the same as being married, but we still will be one day.' She spoke quickly. She had to say it all before her courage failed her.

His face paled. He snatched his hands away from hers. 'God, you're forward, Annie. I'm surprised you even suggested we should break the Lord's commandments.' His look of horror and the shock in his voice startled her.

All last night she had been imagining how their life could be, she had to make him understand. 'I've been reading books by a woman called Marie Stopes.' She sensed him stiffen, saw anger in his eyes.

He took a few quick breaths. 'I've heard of that woman. She's an abomination.'

'What?' It was Annie's turn to be shocked. 'She isn't afraid to speak her mind, she's strong and she's trying to help women. If Bel had the means to stop bairns, she would have never married Nick and she would still be alive.' Pinpricks crept up her neck and filled her scalp. 'I think it's a good thing, why don't you?'

'There was no excuse for what Nick did to Bel. But believe me, this woman's doctrine can only cause trouble.'

'But... we could be together, don't you want that too?' Her mind swirled. What had she said that was so wrong? 'If you loved me...'

'Annie, stop.' He pushed his fingers through his hair.

She shook her head. This was not going the way she had imagined. 'I thought you were forward-thinking. Have you even read anything she's written?'

'Of course not, but I've read about her.' He took a deep sigh. 'We cannot be together in the way you suggest outside marriage. And even if we were man and wife, abstinence is the only way to control the number of children we have. It's not for man to change the Lord's law, or woman either.'

A cold hand closed around Annie's heart. 'Lord's law? But... you never even went to the kirk on Raumsey.'

'I'm a Catholic, Annie. Do you know what that means? I wouldn't go to a Protestant kirk, but I kept the

203

Sabbath.' Alexander stared at the ground. 'Promise me, you'll read no more of Marie Stopes' books.'

Annie stared at him in dismay. A few minutes ago it was as if they had never been apart, now she didn't recognise this man before her. 'I'd no idea you felt like that. I thought you wanted me, too.'

'Oh Annie, I do want you, more than you'll ever know. Why do you think I've not come to see you before now? You're too much of a temptation. I'd go against my parents to marry you, but I won't go against my own beliefs.' He gazed at her, his face a mass of warring emotions.

She drew her hands away and hid them in her lap.

'I'll wait for you until you tell me with certainty that you'll never marry me. But know this, I have strong convictions and I will abide by them.'

'If you forbid me to read the books I want, if you forbid me to form my own opinions, if the constrains of your religion are more important than me, then I'll *never* marry you.' Each word, born from anger, was a shard of glass in her heart, ripping it apart.

Alexander's face flushed. 'I know how important your career is to you and I'm willing to wait, three years, four years, as long as it takes, but I can no more go against my beliefs than you can.'

'Then there is no more to say.' Annie clutched her handbag in shaking hands and stood up, each angry breath trembling its way into her lungs. She had meant to tell him that they could get married someday and she could carry on as a midwife, but he had angered her too much. It had been her own impatience that had prompted this confrontation. She wanted to be with him now and had imagined that he felt the same.

'I'll come back for you. Whatever you say now, I will come back.'

204

Once more their eyes met and his held both sorrow and incredulity, perhaps even anger and she realised she had never really known him at all.

'What…what was it you came to tell me?'

'I'm going to Spain for a couple of years. I've been accepted as an English teacher in Barcelona. It seemed the best time, while you're doing your training. I thought there might be a chance that you'd changed your mind, that you'd want to get married and come with me. But I know you need to do this and I need to give you time to grow up.'

A scream of frustration rose in her throat and remained trapped there. How had she been such a fool to think he felt the same way for her as she did for him, that he really understood? And grow up? How dare he? For a time she forced her lips to remain still as she held his gaze. With ice in her voice, she said, 'I suppose this is goodbye.'

'Not goodbye. I'll come and see you when I return, I promise.'

She shrugged. 'What's the point?'

He followed her to the door where he kissed her lightly on her unresponsive cheek. 'Until we meet again, then?'

She nodded and said nothing. But I will be waiting, she thought, I'm just too angry to tell you that.

He closed his eyes as if in pain and for a moment she thought he was going to say more, but he turned away. She watched him walk towards George Square and then the traffic and the shoppers swallowed him up. For a long time she stood and stared into the thickening snow swirling in the space he left behind. For all their long discussions, religion had never been one of their topics. Why had she just assumed it was as unimportant in his life as it was in hers? But hadn't she always sensed a holding back, as if he was living behind a barrier that prevented her from touching his soul?

Tess was pulling on her nightdress when Annie returned. 'Well, did ye meet him?'

Annie pushed past her and flung herself onto the bed, finally giving vent to the sobs she had held in since she left the park.

Sitting down beside her friend, Tess rubbed her hand over the other girl's shoulder. 'What happened?'

'Please, Tess, it's over. He's away to Spain. He never did intend to stay here. He was... not like I remembered him. I never knew what he was really thinking.'

'But surely he'll be back.'

Annie shook her head. Her humiliation churned at her belly. 'He's a strict Catholic. And I offered myself to him. He must hate me for being so forward.'

'A Catholic? And ye didn't know?'

'How was I to know? We never talked about religion and why should it be a barrier? My mam lost her faith when her sister died and we seldom went to the kirk, yet she and the minister are happy.'

'Sounds like your teacher's not worth it. There'll be others.'

'Please, Tess, I can't talk now.' All she wanted was to nurse her pain and humiliation alone.

'Alright, pet,' said Tess. 'I wanted to tell you a bit more about the Marie Stopes movement. I've got leaflets here.'

'What's the point?' muttered Annie, as her heart contracted with another wave of pain. 'I'll not be needing her help, ever again.'

Chapter Twenty-Nine

At the same time as Annie hugged a pillow already wet from her tears, Alexander knelt in the front pew of St Andrew's Cathedral, hands clasped, head bowed. Unable to find words to express his feelings, he allowed his heart to bleed out its sorrow. He had been shocked at Annie's proposal. Now he felt that perhaps he had acted too hastily. He knew when he first met her she was a girl of high spirits, with no strong ties to her own religion, but to offer herself to him so blatantly was too much. Had he totally misjudged her, or did his feeling blind him completely to what kind of girl she really was? His own views had been liberal, he saw himself as a forward-thinker on many issues, but he was locked in the belief that his wife had to be of the highest moral standards.

Annie might find someone else to live with her the way she wanted and that possibility filled his heart with outrage. Three years should be long enough to find out whether she would wait for him, or whether she was fast, corrupted by the world and Marie Stopes. He had made the most sensible decision, so why was his heart torn in two?

His mother had been angry when he broke up with Elizabeth and furious when he told her he was in love with a Protestant. At least *she* would be happy now. He rose, lit a candle made the sign of the cross on his chest and went to catch his train. He wanted out of this city before the temptation to return to her became too difficult to resist.

On the journey south he had time to reflect on his actions. He hated the fact that they had parted on bad terms. He should have understood that they came from different worlds. On the island it didn't seem to matter, but here in the real world there would be problems that might be too difficult to overcome and Annie's proposal was the tip of the iceberg. He argued with his rebellious heart, listing all the reasons that a relationship between them was a bad idea and he had to go on listing them as he tried to convince himself this was the right thing to do.

Chapter Thirty

With her dreams shattered, Annie threw herself into work and study until, by bedtime, she was too tired to think. Spain had been a distant possibility, a place where they would go together someday. She had expected him to agree with her plans for no other reason than she willed it so, had never considered rejection. Now she moved from day to day trying to concentrate only on the task of the moment.

Every three months the nurses changed over and were allocated different wards and Annie loved the new challenges each set of medical problems brought. After surgical, she was sent to the children's ward, which she loved most of all. Alexander and her humiliation waited, just beyond the horizon of her consciousness, behind a door shut, but never bolted. The only tears she shed were for the undernourished children, often with bruises on their frail bodies, who came to them with various complaints that better feeding and housing might have prevented. She watched their health improve and hated it that they were returned to the same situation which had brought them to the hospital in the first place.

The diphtheria cases were the most heartrending. The first time Annie watched a tracheotomy she was nervous, but the process was a revelation when the small blue body began to turn pink once more. Now it was a case of careful nursing, but despite their best efforts, the children seldom survived.

'There's another child admitted today,' said the Sister. 'And the mother is asking for you by name. You'd better come; she's causing a scene and if you can't calm her we'll have to get security to throw her out.'

Annie quickly finished the bed bath she had been administering. 'You'll be more comfortable after that, Matty.' She smoothed the sheet and blanket around her patient who gave her a weak smile, then she hurried after the Sister.

The woman was grey-faced and struggling with a porter who was forcibly restraining her.

Annie gasped. 'Myrtle!' Her thoughts immediately flew to Daisy. 'What happened?'

'They won't let me in. I want to be with ma wee laddie.' She calmed down and grabbed Annie's arm. 'Please, save ma wee laddie. Let me be with him, he's scared o' strangers.'

'I'll look after her, Sister.' Annie led her away from the harassed porter. 'There's things they have to do and you can't be there. I'm sure they'll let you in as soon as he's settled.'

'He can't breathe,' cried Myrtle. 'Oh, Annie, love, can ye make him breathe?'

'We can do that,' said Annie gently. 'What's his name?'

'Johnny, he's Johnny. Och, I'm sorry for making such a fuss. But he was my last, he's my baby. He's aye been delicate.' She wiped at her eyes. 'Why will they no let me stop with him?'

'It's kinder on the bairns if they don't see their parents. It upsets them.'

'But, Annie, ye don't understand. He's never been away from family, he's a wee bit special, ye know?'

'How's the rest of the family?' asked Annie, knowing how diphtheria could spread.

'Daisy's poorly. She took to her bed today, but she'll listen out for the others. I'm so worried. Ma man died two months since. I couldn't bear it if I lost Johnny too.'

'I'm sorry, I didn't know.' Annie was shocked that Henry hadn't told her, but how high would the death of a servant's man feature in his list of importance? With all his fine talk, Henry was a hypocrite. 'You wait here. I'll go and see if you can sit with him a while.'

'Aye, Annie, love. And I'm sorry for making a fuss.'

The trachea was in place, Johnny was washed and in the ward, but his small frail body remained barely responsive. 'You can let the mother see him as soon as you get all the details,' said Sister in a low voice.

It was unusual to let a visitor in outside visiting hours and Annie saw the rare streak of compassion in this otherwise austere woman. She also knew this meant the child did not have long to live.

Myrtle was pacing the corridor. She turned at the sound of Annie's voice. 'You can sit with him a wee while.' She led Myrtle to Johnny's bedside.

'Johnny, ma wee man. Oh my sweet Jesus, I hope the others are alright.'

'I'm off duty in an hour. Give me your address. I'll go and check on them.' Annie laid her hand on the child's brow. 'His colour's better.' She smiled and hoped her smile transmitted more assurance than she felt. Johnny had been starved of air for too long.

Two hours later, Annie walked through streets of high tenement buildings where women with babies at their breasts stood in doorways. Children played in the road, kicking tins and jumping ropes. When she came to the right address, she climbed the stone stairs in the dark close that stunk of cat's pee and overfull lavatories. A girl of six or seven with untidy ringlets and a dirty face answered the door.

'Your mammy sent me,' said Annie.

'Is Johnny going to die?'

Annie couldn't answer. 'Can I speak to Daisy?'

'Aye. Ye'd better come in.'

Annie was ushered into a small room reminiscent of the kitchen in Scartongarth. In one wall was a similar box bed and on the opposite an iron range, black and shining, an armchair on either side. A table sat before the window. A china cabinet held a few ornaments and a tea set. The room was spotless except for an open jar of jam on the table beside a knife, a plate and the jar lid. Two younger boys squatted on the floor eating thick slices of bread liberally spread with jam. A blowfly buzzed and banged against the window glass.

'Oor Daisy's in bed,' said the girl, 'Through there.' Annie was directed into another room with a double bed, a single bed, and nothing else. Annie heard the laboured breathing before she saw her. 'Daisy, Daisy,' she stepped over and laid her hand on the fevered brow. There was no doubting it. Daisy, too, was very sick.

She returned to the front room. 'Do any of you feel ill?' she asked. The little girl looked at her brothers and shook her head.

'I've got to take Daisy to hospital. Is there somebody who could look after you?'

Her old-young face pinched with worry, the child nodded. Her lip wobbled. 'I'll go and get Bertha.' She opened the door, leaving it swinging wide behind her, ran across the landing and began pounding on the door opposite. An ancient, rather overweight woman answered. 'What's wrong with ye, hen? Is yer mammy back yet? Look at the state o yer face.'

'Oor Daisy's taken bad. A lassie wants to take her to the hospital an ma mammy's away with wee Johnny.' The words rushed from her mouth as if she was making an effort not to cry.

Bertha glanced over her shoulder. 'Will ye be alright there, Jock?' she shouted into the flat. 'It's Daisy, she's taken bad. I need to watch the bairns.'

Someone coughed and phlegm rattled in a throat. 'I may be gone by the time ye come back,' came the hoarse reply.

'Ah widna be so lucky, ye auld bugger!' Bertha waddled across the hallway into the kitchen and plonked herself down on one of the chairs. Her body settled around her. 'Jock's lungs are bad. A lifetime doon the mines. Oor laddie works in the docks an he brought us up here to bide with him. I told Myrtle that lassie wasn't well. Ye'd best go to the pub on the corner. They've got a telephone.'

Without waiting to answer, Annie ran all the way to the nearest pub. She walked in through the thick smoky atmosphere and staring eyes of hardened men. The barman eyed her with curiosity.

'Have you a telephone,' she asked. 'I need an ambulance.'

'Sure, darling. In the corner there.' He set down the glass he had been polishing and opened the till, removed a few coppers and handed them to Annie. 'For the phone. We don't charge for an ambulance. Not in these times.'

Johnny died before midnight, Daisy lingered another two days and died in the early hours of the morning. Having refused to go home, Myrtle sat in the corridor staring at the floor and knotting her hands in the material of her coat. 'My bairns are gone,' she whispered when Annie found a minute to sit with her.

The pain of losing a child rose anew in Annie's chest and she cried with her. She cried for Daisy and Johnny, she cried for Sina and Bel, she cried for all the other bairns that had died and would die in the days to come.

She held Myrtle when the sobs changed to a high keening, the sound of someone breaking apart.

'Nurse Reid,' shouted Sister, when she came upon them.

With reluctance, Annie released Myrtle, rose and wiped her eyes.

'My office, now.' Sister jerked her head upwards, indicating that Annie should follow her. 'Pull yourself together, Reid, for heaven's sake. If you fall apart for every child that dies you'll never make the grade.'

'I'm sorry, Sister.' Annie crumpled the wet handkerchief in her hand. 'I knew them and I felt, feel so... useless.'

Sister cleared her throat. 'Your shift ended ages ago. Get to bed and get some rest. You're back on duty in three hours' time and you'll be no use to me if you're half asleep.' For a minute she sounded almost kind.

'I won't be, Thanks, Sister.' She turned towards the corridor where the weeping Myrtle still sat, meaning to say goodbye.

'Where do you think you're going? Get to your room, now.'

'Yes, Sister.' Annie climbed the stairs. What was the use of it all, she thought. She had come here to learn to save lives, but children were still dying; not even the well-trained doctors could save them. She thought of the poverty she had seen in the tenements and wished there was more she could do for the good-hearted Myrtle and others like her. Her family had nothing by the time they left Canada and even less in Raumsey, yet, even though the crops failed, if a family owned or could borrow a gun, a fishing rod, traps and piece of ground to grow vegetables, they would never starve. Tenement dwellers had no such recourse.

Meanwhile, Reggie was helping Tess down from the tram. Together they walked along the river and then turned inland. She looked around at the high buildings to either side that blocked the sun and she breathed in stinking air. From above their heads women conducted conversations with each other through open windows, dirty-faced children played in the streets. 'This is where I was brought up,' he said. 'My mammy worked herself to death trying to keep the place clean. There's only one toilet to a close and it's more often blocked than not. Then all the shit and piss spill onto the stairs. Up here.'

He led her into a narrow lobby where no light penetrated and which was infused by a damp, overpowering stench.

Tess held her nose. 'Is it always like this?'

'Oh aye. The smell even gets into the houses, ye'll see.'

'The folk who live here, do they have jobs?'

'Oh, aye. But the pay'll never be enough to get them anywhere better, especially with ever more mouths to feed and the men liking a drink. It's mostly Irish immigrants and they'll work for less just to have a job and then the priest has to get his cut. Do ye wonder why there is unrest?'

The inequality of this city angered Tess and made her all the more determined to dedicate her life to the cause.

Chapter Thirty

As the months passed, Annie waited for the post, longing, in spite of herself, for the letter that never came. Whenever there was a cry of, 'mail for Reid,' her heart lifted, but her happiness faded when she recognised only her mother's handwriting. Despite his outrage, she had thought Alexander would at least have kept in touch. And to make matters worse, the shoebox she kept under the bed with her previous mail had been confiscated by Sister Beasley. 'You can read your mail in the sitting room, then give it to me. I will not have boxes cluttering up your bedroom.'

Annie wanted to punch her, but she dared not argue.

Occasionally Henry still took her out on the town, often to sip champagne, which she discovered she liked very much. 'Cheer up. Life's about having fun,' he told her and took her to places she had never dreamed about. She looked forward to escaping for a while from both the sickness and poverty she witnessed within the hospital walls and her own self-pity.

One afternoon in a small café, Henry introduced her to some of his friends. Olivia and Cynthia were slim, well-dressed wraiths, who were sisters and shook her hand limply.

'You're a nurse! How exciting,' said Olivia, without enthusiasm.

Cynthia shuddered. 'How brave. I could never clean up someone else's bodily fluids.' She made a grimace.

But it was the young man with them who caught Annie's attention. Tall and slim, his blonde hair fell forward across the bluest eyes Annie had ever seen. He rose, offered Annie his hand and introduced himself. 'Simon, friend of the assembled.'

She was aware of soft, slender fingers, and his touch sent a barely remembered shiver through the length of her body. He applied a bit more pressure than was needed and she fancied she rather enjoyed his touch.

'These two girls go to art school. Cynthia is very good at ceramics. She'll make a name for herself someday,' said Henry.

'Oh, you!' Cynthia batted the air, but her eyes took on an extra sparkle at his words.

'And what do you do?' Annie turned to Olivia.

'Portraits. I'm afraid I'm not very good. I think I'll leave at the end of term. Perhaps I'll try nursing, maybe snare myself a dishy surgeon.' She leaned towards Annie and lowered her voice. 'Perhaps you could arrange an introduction?'

'I'm afraid we're not allowed to socialise with the doctors.' It was true, there were flirtations between many of the young doctors and the nurses, but due to time limitations of their chosen profession, there was seldom anything else. Annie was aware of Simon's eyes burning into her and suffered a heat in her face and neck as she tried to ignore him.

'Henry tells us you come from Canada,' said Cynthia. 'Tell me about the cities. Were you near Toronto?'

At first, Annie did not want to admit that they had eked out a living on a dirt farm. She smiled and said, 'No, we were further west. My grandfather owned a ranch.'

'Oh, how lovely. And did you have a young man there? A handsome cowboy perhaps?' Her eyes slid to her friend and a sly look passed between them.

217

Filled with a sudden desire to get out of here, get away from their judgemental attitudes, away from the eyes of the young man opposite her, Annie gave a narrow smile.

'Yes I did. But he wasn't a '*handsome cowboy.*' His name was Muraco and he was a native, an Indian.'

'Oh.' Cynthia's eyes grew round and she coloured. 'Aren't they... savages?'

'There are some who would call them that.' Annie almost laughed. These girls with their fine education had never known a day's want in their lives. They would marry well and be mistresses in a fine home, but she doubted if their world would ever expand further. She was glad that she had experienced so much more in her life than they ever would and it made her feel somehow superior.

She glanced quickly at Simon and caught an amused gleam in his eye.

'Aren't they dangerous? Don't they scalp people?' Olivia looked horrified.

Annie could not control her laughter. 'You've been reading too many outdated rubbishy novels,' she spluttered at last.

'Oh,' Olivia's face grew scarlet, her mouth pursed as if in fury.

Cynthia quickly recovered her composure. With a look of ice at Annie, she laid a hand on Henry's arm. 'I would love to go to Canada one day.'

'Then you must, Cynthia dear.' Henry rose from his seat. 'Excuse me, chaps, I really must be getting Annie back. My mother is expecting us for tea. Come along, Annie.'

As she left she could sense cold eyes boring into her back, imagine the girls whispering to each other. She could imagine too, Simon's appreciative stare.

'So that was Cynthia,' said Annie, once they were outside. 'I don't think she likes me much.'

'She's jealous. She can see that I like you. Both our families want us to get together and that's what she wants too. It's just not what I want.' He laughed out loud. 'I loved the way you put her in her place, though. A Red Indian for a boyfriend. Fancy telling her that!'

'It's the truth,' said Annie quietly. 'But I was very young then, idealistic.'

Henry gave her a shocked look. 'Really? You don't mean it?'

'Actually I do.'

'There's so much I don't know about you, Annie.' He fell into silence.

'Who is Simon?' she asked.

'His father is Laird of some estate in the Highlands. He helps run it. They own a town house in central Glasgow, where he spends a lot of his time, basically doing nothing.' Henry paused and cleared his throat. 'Stay away from him. I saw the way he looked at you. I think he likes you.'

'What's wrong with that?'

'He uses girls and tosses them aside.'

'Why, Henry, I think you're jealous!'

'I admit it. Simon's my friend. We went through university together and caught the end of the war in the same regiment. But I'm not lying about the kind of man he is.'

Annie settled back in her seat. She didn't care what kind of man Simon was. He was handsome and charming and interested in her and, right now, that was the boost to her confidence she needed. Alexander had been gone almost two years, with not as much as one letter and she was young and healthy and tired of waiting.

Chapter Thirty-One

Two days later, when her shift ended, Annie made her way from the ward, planning to spend the night in study.

The night nurse passed her by the ward door. 'There's a young man waiting for you outside,' she said.

Her thoughts immediately flew to Henry and with it a knot of worry. Henry never called during her working week; if he was here there must be something wrong. It was therefore with a mixture of surprise and relief when she saw Simon leaning against the bonnet of a sports car. In spite of herself, her heart gave a lurch.

He straightened up when he saw her, a wide grin on his face. 'Annie,' he said, 'At last. I thought you were never going to come through that door.'

'My shift's just ended. What are you doing here?'

'I have come to whisk you away for a luxurious meal washed down by the finest champagne.'

Annie shook her head and gave an embarrassed laugh. 'I'm on the way to the food hall and then a night of study. I've exams soon.'

'Is the food excellent in the food hall?'

Annie thought of the pale sausages and soggy mashed potato which seemed to be cook's favourite recipe. She looked up into the twinkling blue eyes, the lop-sided smile and very much wanted to spend some time in his company. The thought of a decent meal was not exactly off-putting either. 'I have to be back before ten o'clock or I'll be locked out.'

'I promise to have you back by then.'

She moistened her lips. 'Alright then.'

220

Her heart soared and she ran up the stairs as if her feet had wings. From her chest of drawers, she took out the blouse and skirt that Margaret had bought for her and quickly changed, brushed her hair out so that it fell loose about her shoulders and applied a touch of lipstick. 'It'll have to do,' she told her reflection, pinched her cheeks to make them pink and ran down the stairs half expecting to find him gone.

His eyes swept the length of her as she came towards him and he let out a low whistle. Opening the car door, he bent forward indicating that she should enter.

He took her to Grosvenor Café where she was served by waiters in black suits, white shirts and bow ties and who called her madam. After the second glass of champagne she relaxed and giggled at the everything he said.

'How long are you staying in Glasgow?' she asked.

'Until the beginning of the grouse season,' he told her. 'Have you ever tasted grouse?'

'I don't think so.'

He threw back his head and laughed. 'You don't know?'

'We hunted for food. I never learned the names of all the birds we ate.'

'Oh, Annie, you are a rare gem.' His eyes rested on her making her feel simultaneously nervous and very special. He was funny and handsome and attentive and she enjoyed herself very much in his company. True to his word, he had her back outside the nurse's home by ten to ten.

Turning to face her, he said, 'You are a very beautiful girl. I have been honoured tonight to have your company.' He exited the car and moved around to open the door for her. For a moment they stood face to face and she could feel his breath on her skin.

221

'I...I enjoyed myself. Thank you very much for taking me.' She lifted her head, expecting him to kiss her, hoping he would, but placing a hand on either side of her face he bent forward and pressed his pursed lips against her forehead. 'Goodnight, little lady,' he said and stroked her cheek once. 'I do hope we can do this again. When's your next day off?'

'Henry usually collects me...' she began.

'Of course, Henry. Rather a comic figure isn't he? I'll deal with him.'

'He's a good friend,' she said, stung by the remark.

'I'm sure he is. Your day off, when?'

She told him. He lifted her hand and kissed her fingers. 'Till then.'

Too excited to sleep that night, she lay awake, staring into the dark for a long time. When she closed her eyes it was Simon's arms she imagined around her. Alexander still intruded into her thoughts, but he had diminished, further away somehow.

On her day off she waited with more enthusiasm than she had for a long time. When Simon's car came around the corner, her heart jumped. He left the car and in two long strides stood before her.

'You look amazing.' His eyes drank her in, making her skin prickle. 'I'm taking you somewhere special today. Come along, fair lady.' He took her hand, gave it a little squeeze and led her to the car where he helped her inside. If she were not feeling so lonely and abandoned by Alexander, would she be having these feelings, she wondered. Probably not. But she *was* feeling lonely and abandoned and, worse still, angry.

He drove her along the old Luss road where a golf course stretched to either side. From here the views of Loch Lomond, Ben Lomond and the mountains beyond were stunning and reminiscent of Canada. Her hair blew back in the wind and she lifted her head, enjoying the fresh breeze cooling her skin and snatching her breath. Here she was, being driven along beautiful countryside by a rich, handsome, well-educated young man who was interested in her. Wasn't this what she had dreamed about as she read her magazines back on Raumsey?

Simon parked the car and they drank tea in pleasant little tearooms. They then walked along the shore holding hands. In the shelter of the trees he kissed her, a long demanding kiss. 'Annie,' he whispered, still pressing her against him. 'I want to make love to you. I've wanted that from the first moment I saw you.'

If he wasn't holding her up, her legs would have buckled at that moment. She gave a little gasp. Alexander had never behaved like this.

'Not here,' he said. 'Come back with me to my house. We'll be alone. We'll send out for dinner and you don't have to leave until your next shift. When is that?'

'Tomorrow morning.' He released her and, grasping her hand, led her to the car.

'Simon, stop.' She pulled his hand from his. 'I'm not …like that.'

'Of course you're not. How insensitive of me. But come back with me, have a meal. I promise you don't have to do anything you don't want to.'

She nodded and a smile lit up his face.

His flat was spacious with high ceilings and tastefully furnished in golds and pale blues and heavy oak furniture. Once inside the door, she suddenly felt shy. They dined together on roast meat and drank wine in the dining room. The wine made her drowsy and more than a little light-headed. When he put his arms around her she relaxed against him dreading the thought of leaving and returning to the nurses' home.

'Stay with me tonight,' he whispered into her hair.

'I mustn't.' But her refusal was weak. Alexander had rejected her and even after all this time it still stung. Somewhere in the back of her mind she wanted to strike back, hurt him, although he would never know. She had heard the other nurses talking, listened to some bawdy remarks, knew several were no paragons of virtue, yet they were good, caring people. Living each day with death, made her long for life and all it had to offer. What had she proposed that was so wrong?

'I can't risk having a bairn.' At that moment she wanted him as badly as it seemed he wanted her. She was more than ready to embark on a physical relationship, but, not knowing what beliefs he held, she would not mention Marie Stopes or contraception.

'You won't. I don't want to be caught out like that either.'

'How can you be sure?'

'I have some things in my drawer. From a catalogue. Trust me, there won't be a baby. I rather think my parents would disown me if I fathered an illegitimate child. I told you I will take care of you.'

Annie felt an instant's hurt. Why was he already prepared?

'What's wrong?' he asked as she stiffened in his arms.

'You presumed I would come back with you, or is it that you often take girls back with you?'

'I presumed nothing. But I did hope.'

'I'm sorry, no. Please take me home.'

He gave a deep sigh. 'That's not the only reason I want to be with you and if you're not ready, I'll wait.'

She looked up at the burning blue of his eyes now watching her and full of questions. 'Please say you'll come out with me again.'

Her body still tingled at his touch. For so long she had kept herself pure for little more than an impossible dream. How foolish could she be?

'Of course I'll come out with you again.' She deserved this, she deserved so much more.

When they parted that night, her thoughts were in confusion. Her upbringing had always taught her that sex before marriage was wrong. Her grandmother's voice appeared in her head. She and Isa had been disagreeing over her dad's unreliability and that was no unusual thing.

'He was never up to much. You should have come with us in the first place,' said her grandmother. 'You could have had the bairn here and maybe met someone better. You were only sixteen. You broke our hearts.'

'I'm fed up with you throwing that in my face,' Isa had replied. 'I love Davie with all his faults and wouldn't have it any other way.'

So her mother had been pregnant before she married. What a hypocrite. And what of her own situation? How could she keep herself for marriage when marriage meant giving up the job she loved so much? Did all professional women throw themselves into their vocation and forget worldly lives? It wasn't fair. Tess had admitted that she did not live like a nun and Tess was one of the best people she knew.

The following month, after they had had dinner in his townhouse, Simon drew her into his arms and kissed her passionately. When they finally drew apart, he gazed down into her eyes. 'I love you, Annie. I've loved you from the very first time we met.'

'I think I love you too,' she whispered. At this moment she believed she did. She wanted him because he lifted her spirits and made her feel like a desirable woman and what was more, her body longed for

225

comfort, the kind Alexander refused to give her. *Well, damn him*, she said inside her head. *He had his chance.*

Simon grabbed her hand and led her towards a door opening off the living area. Still she hesitated, but the champagne had filled her head with bubbles and, giggling, she stumbled against him.

'Is it still no?' he said. 'Look, I'd marry you in a minute, but I understand how much your career means to you and I'm prepared to wait. But I crave for you every minute we're not together. You will marry me one day, won't you?'

Marry him? Have all this luxury and an estate in the Highlands too?

'Only if I can still be a midwife in the Highlands.'

'But of course.'

Her head spun and she laughed when he picked her up and carried her into the next room.

In the centre was a four poster bed covered with a quilt in the same golds and blues as the walls and curtains. 'Don't say no,' he whispered, as she lowered her head and almost tumbled after it.

He put a finger under her chin, raised her face and his mouth closed over hers. His tongue gently probed at first and then the kiss grew deeper, more demanding.

She tightened her arms around his neck as he laid her on the bed. First he slipped her blouse from her shoulders, his lips on hers all the time. Then he moved to her neck as his fingers undid the buttons of her bodice. He slipped his hand inside making her jump a little as his fingers kneaded her breast. He kissed her neck, her throat. Once she was naked, he held wide his arms. 'Now your turn.'

Guessing what he meant, she unbuttoned his shirt, loosened his trousers and gasped at the springing maleness. He slipped the trousers off, led her to the bed where he eased her down, then turned and began to

226

fumble in the drawer of the bedside cabinet. She closed her eyes, assuming he was doing whatever it was that would prevent a bairn. Suddenly he was rolling on top of her. Grasping both her hands, he held them above her head as she cried out with both pain and ecstasy. It was over too quickly. He rolled away and lit a cigarette and she was left feeling strangely empty.

After that, every day off was spent with Simon and ended up in his spacious flat. Before long, her whole being was consumed by the thought of him, his lean, firm body, the way his eyes devoured her, his obvious desire for her. It was as if he could never get enough of her.

On the one occasion when she met up with Henry, he looked at her with reproach. 'What are you doing, Annie? I've warned you about Simon.'

'This is different. We're in love. Why can't you be happy for me?'

He ignored the question. 'Mother's wondering why you don't come any more. I think she misses you.'

'Tell her I'm sorry. I will try to come soon, promise. It's, well, I don't get that much time off and Simon and I, well, we want to be together.'

Henry shook his head. 'Don't say I didn't warn you, my lovely. I'll still be here when it all goes terribly wrong.'

'It won't.' she gave a little laugh, but the laugh didn't come from her heart. 'It won't,' she repeated to herself.

Chapter Thirty-Two

Despite living barely above starvation, Alexander had found his relations well enough. His cousin Marco was making a name for himself, Maria worked in a laundry in town, she said, and Sergio worked with his father from dawn to dusk in their small cobblers shop. His grandparents were both deceased, worn down by eking out a living from unforgiving soil. When the rains had not come and the crops failed for a second year, the family came to the city in search of a better life. His grandfather had been lucky to find employment in a baker's shop and his grandmother scrubbed floors for the more affluent, but they lived in a slum and barely survived. His Aunt Consuela, married Perez, a shoe-maker's apprentice. Her sister, Alexander's mother, danced for a few pesetas a night in a small taberna, where his father frequented on his visit to Spain. They fell in love and he brought her back to Scotland.

Alexander shared a cheap apartment in the Arab district of Barcelona with another teacher, Alonzo Martinez, a friend of Maria's. Both were keen supporters of Los Solitaros, the avengers, a party of anarchists.

Alexander did not agree with their politics and their discussions often carried on well into the night. Alonzo and Maria never confided in him as to the extent of their activities and he had not asked. However, Alonzo often paced the floor railing against King Alfonzo and the noblemen of the country. 'Even those in steady employment find making a decent wage almost impossible,' he ranted, 'While the country is ruled by those who enjoy more wealth than you can ever imagine, those who waste more food in a week than the poor eat in a year.'

'I understand and I sympathise, but I cannot get involved in your fight. No good can come of placing bombs and striking. Surely if you destroy the prosperity, it filters down to the workers.' Alexander could see why the pot of discontent was simmering to the boil, but he truly believed that violence was not the answer. He, too, had seen the luxurious palaces of the Spanish nobility, he, too, had despaired at the injustice of it all, but he had no wish to become enmeshed. Although Spanish blood ran in his veins, he could see no good coming out of this escalating violence. His heart was back in Scotland and this was not his fight. Once more he thought of Annie, of her tears the day they parted and wondered what she was doing now.

'I want to show you something. Come with me,' said Alonzo.

Together they rode in Alonzo's battered car up Montjuic as far as they could drive. The hillside was crossed by winding paths and covered by thick forests. Alonzo pulled the car up in an area full of thickets among which several corpselike figures dressed in rags, wandered aimlessly.

'From here we walk.' Alonzo grabbed a carbide lamp and led him up a winding path into the thick foliage. The trail skirted one of the sheerest escarpments in the area. Alonzo lit the lamp and slid through a cleft in the sheer cliff face. 'Here is a labyrinth of passageways carved out of rock by miners many years ago,' he explained.

Alexander followed and gagged at the foul smell. Although the air was polluted, there was a draught which made it easy to breathe. The flickering light showed up an array of refuse and rubbish, boards and barrels, drums and sheets of metal. Amid reptiles, rats and bats were old men wrapped in rags, women with deformed faces and groups of half-clothed children moving about in the shadows between torches secured to the walls. When they became aware of the two strangers, they clutched at their legs and begged for money.

'The Powder Keg caves,' said Alonzo. 'There are many other caverns, such as those at La Escada. They are all home to the hordes of starving who have come to the city but cannot find work or a place to live. Many are cripples or diseased. There are also caves higher up, more difficult to access where all sorts of criminals live where they are safe from bourgeois law.'

In silence, Alexander followed his friend back to the car. In this city of electric lights, modern railway systems, amazing architecture, it was unbelievable that such poverty could exist.

'I never imagined anything so terrible,' he said, when they took their seats in the car.

'So you are not a totally lost cause. And I have not yet taken you to one of the many settlements on the outskirts of the city. The destitute build shelters out of whatever debris they can find. They have no running water or sanitation. More than forty thousand people live that way.'

Alexander thought of his own grandparents and for the first time he became aware of how much they must have endured. 'The government needs to become aware,' he said. 'Use the press, lawyers, negotiation. You'll never convince me that your way will lead to anything more than more bloodshed.'

Alonzo shook his head and laughed. 'You are such an innocent. Do you think we haven't tried?'

230

Alexander walked to the small, dusty window and stared up beyond the buildings to the clear blue sky, the image of the wasted figures from the cave engraved on his mind. 'There must be a better way,' he whispered and thought of his aunt's words.

'Life is better,' his Aunt Consuela told him when he first arrived, 'since General Primo de Riviera declared his coup, he has restored order. That dreadful general strike brought us beyond starvation. God bless him.' And she had made the sign of the cross on her chest.

Chapter Thirty-Three

It was late afternoon and Alexander suffered the heat of a Spanish July. He had been here almost three years and the time was fast approaching when he had to return to Scotland. Now, in one of the few trips with the family, he could barely understand the cheering of the crowd or the pride that his Aunt Consuela, the driving force behind her family, had in her eldest son, Marco. Alexander only attended today to please her and because his cousin was gaining celebrity status. He could see nothing heroic in a man who rode into the ring to kill an animal which had already been tortured and weakened by the loss of blood. It seemed the matador only entered to complete the final act.

'Your cousin, isn't he splendid!' Consuela elbowed Alexander, her face flushed. 'His name one day will be known in the whole of Spain.' His aunt was a raw-boned woman with big hands and feet and leathery skin that bore sad testament to a hard life. She had a fierce pride in her sons and suffered despair over her daughter.

Alexander agreed, if only to please his aunt. Marco's success in the bullring brought in much needed revenue to the family coffers. Now he rode round the ring holding up the grizzly proof of his victory, the severed ear of the bull.

As they left the shade of the arena amid the surging crowd, Alexander was stopped by a small boy dressed in rags, holding out his grubby hand. *'Por favor, Signor,'* he said, his voice tremulous and high. Alexander rifled in his pocket for a few pesetas. He felt he'd seen the child before, the haunted brown eyes, the dirt-streaked face, or perhaps every urchin had meld into a blur of similarity. The boy grasped the coins. '*Gracias, Signor.*

A sudden explosion from behind them sent a pall of smoke into the air. The force of the blast knocked Alexander off his feet to land face down on the dusty street. Glass showered down around him and the world went black. When he next opened his eyes, it was to see the bloodied face of the child, eyes open and lifeless, his hand extended, his body at an odd angle, the coins scattered in the dirt.

Alexander rose to his knees reached over and closed the boy's eyes, made the sign of the cross, then looked frantically round for the rest of his family. People were everywhere, screaming, crying and running, some injured, lying in the road. Maria was already on her feet. His aunt was shouting for her husband. His twelve year old cousin, Sergio, sat a little way off holding his head, blood seeping from between his fingers. Perez was nowhere to be seen.

Consuela seemed to notice Sergio for the first time and sank to her knees beside him.

Alexander staggered to his feet. Maria grabbed his arm. 'We must find Papa. He cannot abide the bombs.'

Alexander was well aware of his uncle's anxieties, a legacy of the Moroccan war.

They found him slumped in a doorway, shivering, his hands on his head, eyes wild with terror. Maria sat down on the hot street beside him and held him in her arms while he sobbed.

During their many conversations, Alexander had learned that she had been nine years old when her father came back from the war, but she remembered it well.

'Barcelona is a violent city. She is like a pot about to boil. My family all work, yet without my wages, they would not survive I think,' Maria had told him after the first of the many incidents of violence he had witnessed.

The bombs were almost a daily occurrence in the city now and Alexander was glad that his departure was imminent. He took a seat at Perez's other side.

Maria's eyes met his over her father's head 'We are so tired of this life. Go now, tell the others where we are.'

'It's Los Solidarios,' Consuela said as they trailed back to their home, a two roomed flat above the cobbler's shop. Alexander and Pablo supported Sergio between them and Consuela constantly wailed as she washed the blood from her youngest child's face. Thankfully buses were operating that day, driven by right-wing youths who refused to allow the strike to affect the running of the city.

Once in the relative cool of the flat, they laid Sergio on the couch. The blood had congealed around his face and head and stained Alexander's shirt.

He thought again of the urchin he'd left lying in the street. He thought of the mother who might, even now, be searching among the dead for her son.

'They think they will make things better by killing innocent people. Damn them.' Consuela turned to glare at her daughter. 'Is this what you support? The animals who nearly killed your brother?'

'I'm truly sorry this happened, but in a war against injustice there will be casualties. They were robbing a bank. Innocent people were not meant to be hurt.'

'And that makes it right?' She looked at Alexander, fury burning in her eyes. 'You see? You see what a mother has to bear? This daughter supports the anarchists. Supports those who set off bombs every day, cause strikes, robberies. Things are better with Marco's success and I just want to live in peace. And she,'

Consuela pointed at Maria, 'has to fall in love with someone who will bring death to our door.'

Maria lifted her head so that her small chin pointed upwards, her eyes equally charged with fire. 'It is a good thing, you think, that my father whose health is not good toils for ten hours a day to sell his produce for half their worth? That we all toil for ten hours a day, even Sergio who should be in school?'

'We eat, we have a roof above our heads.' Her mother once more turned to tend her injured son. 'We should be thankful. We should feel safe to walk through the beautiful streets, be able to take a bus, but you see, they are on strike again. How would we have got home today if it wasn't for those who support the government? Pah,' she shouted waving her hands. 'This girl reads too much and all the wrong books.'

Maria shook her head. 'It is up to us, the young, to make things better.Mama wants to leave things as they are, but unless we fight nothing will ever change.'

Alexander had heard the same words many times. He also suspected that the food Maria brought home was not paid for by her wages in a laundry. 'How are you Sergio?' he asked.

The boy lifted his head and gave a small smile. 'It's only a flesh wound. Do not worry.'

'Worry? How can we not worry? Is it ever like this in Scotland, Alexander?' shouted Perez, a wizen, spare man who normally said very little.

'Britain has its poor too.'

Consuela wrung her hands. 'With my family grown, we hoped our lives would be better.' A tear ran from the corner of an eye and found its way down the one of the premature lines that creased her face.

Alexander was well aware of the problems facing the country. The violence in the city was escalating and he, too, worried about Maria's safety. He had no doubt that she was deeply involved in some very dangerous work.

Still badly shaken, Alexander had no wish to leave his family yet.

'You will eat now,' said Consuela, and although no one had an appetite, they dined on sausage, cheese and dry bread washed down by water.

There was a sudden sound of running feet followed by a loud banging on the door. Maria pulled the door open and a young man Alexander seen once with Alonzo staggered in. He leaned against the wall regaining his breath before he spoke. 'They got him, Maria, Alonzo's dead.'

Maria gave a cry and covered her mouth with her hands. Silent tears welled up and spilled down her cheeks.

'They know he had a female accomplice. They're looking for you.' He turned and looked at Alexander. 'And you.'

'I'm a British citizen. I have nothing to do with it.'

'They won't believe you. You shared his home. Within days, or even hours, a patrol is bound to show up at your apartment.'

'Will they come here?' cried Consuela.

'They don't know who Maria is yet. But it's only a matter of time.'

'Alexander, you have to leave. Please take Maria with you. She has put us all in danger. Leave before it's too late.'

'I want to take you all with me. It's safer in Britain.'

'Ah, that will not be possible. What could we do with no jobs and no language? And what money do we have? But do not tell my sister about the danger here.'

Alexander turned to Maria. 'Will you come?' He had asked her this before and she had always declined.

236

This time she let out a long wail. 'Without Alonzo, what is my life worth? I'd rather stay here and fight to the death, but I will not put my family in any more danger. I'll go, Mama, but only for your sake.'

'I will arrange a passport for you, quickly,' said the strange man.

'I've already got one, Lascalle, and some money. Alonzo and I were prepared in case we had to leave the country in a hurry.'

'So much the better,' said Lascalle. 'Come with me now. I have a cart outside.'

'My clothes, my things…' began Alexander.

'I have already been to your apartment. Your money and your passport and a few more papers and some clothes I threw into a bag. They are in the cart already. There is no time for more. Who knows when they might close the roads from Barcelona?'

Maria already had a bag packed for just this emergency. In spite of the warmth of the night, she shivered against Alexander.

'How did you really make your money?' he asked, as they jolted along the road in the donkey cart.

'I danced for the nobility. I spied for the Socialists. I will surely be put to death if they discover who I am.'

Alexander wondered whether dancing was all she did and suddenly he did not want to know.

Maria moved against him. Her breath shuddered. 'You have told me of your lady friend, Alexander. Do you know what pain it is to lose the one you love?'

He thought about Annie. 'It hurt to leave her, but without death, there is hope. We believe different things. I think I've lost her anyway.'

'Do not let her go. Alonzo and I, we did not agree on many things, but I would give my life if I could see him one more time.'

237

Alexander covered her hand with his. He could well imagine how he would feel if Annie's life was in danger and losing her to a violent death was unthinkable.

'What was so bad that you cannot put it right? What did you disagree about?' asked Maria.

'She wanted us to live like man and wife without the sanctity of marriage. It's against God's laws.' Faced with Maria's dark, swollen eyes in the streetlights, his reasons sounded weak. He had come to understand that faced with death and violence the primeval instinct for every aspect of life became more insistent. Perhaps it was the inborn desire to procreate, or to lose oneself in a few moments of total forgetfulness that raised the sexual need in a man. And that need had caused Annie to become a nightly feature in his fantasies. Annie, who had to deal with death every day. Her words, her offer, his refusal. It spun in his head so that neither his nightly prayers nor weekly confessions gave him any peace.

Maria gave an unhappy hoot. 'What god would allow this suffering? Should I have remained a virgin, for what? To have him torn from me in the most brutal manner and never known his love? What is wrong with love when all this killing goes on around us? If I could have one more night in his arms I would surrender my very soul. I have no regrets about giving him my body.'

The walls in the flat were not thick and Alexander was well aware of his cousin's nightly activities. It had initially shocked him, but Maria reminded him so much of Annie. She made her own rules, caring little for the opinions of others. She seldom attended mass and he doubted whether she ever entered the confessional.

'I loved him and I feel no guilt. If man is made in God's image, then God must have such desires too, no? If you love that girl go to her and never let her go. If only I had the same option.'

As he held her, Alexander's own heart ached. 'It's maybe already too late,' he said. 'Annie never replied to my letters.' He had written to her the first week he arrived, even then regretting that they had not parted on good terms. In the small chance that she had not received the letters, he wrote again, several times. He wrote another last night, telling her that he was coming home soon and to contact him via his parents' address if she wanted to see him. He had meant to post it today, but because of the bomb, he forgot all about it. Now he thought it better to deliver the letter by hand. At least he would then be sure she actually got it. Who knew what was happening in this country? With *Los Solidarios* gaining sympathy from abroad, perhaps the government saw every letter as a coded message. He rubbed his eyes. Maybe it was the heat of the sun or the simmering atmosphere of fear and hate he could feel all around him, but he was becoming paranoid.

Maria shook her head. 'Ah, my cousin, the cold of Scotland has replaced your hot Spanish blood.'

'Maybe not completely,' he said, longing for his uncomplicated life in a small country school, but at the same time wondering whether he could ever settle back into it.

Today was just the last in a long line of incidents he had seen since coming to Spain, incidents that made the sin of Annie's proposal seem trivial. He thought of the emaciated people living in caves or at the waterfront or sheltering in sheds built from debris, producing child after child to die of starvation or disease before their first birthday. For some time now he had been doubting his own faith. Surely these children would have been better to have never been born.

Lascalle pulled the donkey to a stop at the harbour, in the shadow of a warehouse.

239

'Wait here,' he said, swung down and disappeared. He returned after a few minutes. 'Good. It seems they do not yet know your identity. I have bought you tickets to Marseille on a ship due to sail within the hour. Once you are there, you will be safe.'

Chapter Thirty-Four

Finally in Glasgow, Alexander helped Maria onto the platform. 'We've got a few hours before the train north,' he said.

'And we will go and see Annie? I too would like to meet this lady you are so fond of.'

'Yes. Of course you must. I think you two would be friends.' Now they were so near, his heart raced. Mentally he rehearsed what he would say, how he would apologise. He knew how he must look, eyes red-rimmed with lack of sleep, unshaven, hair too long and untidy, already showing signs of grey, face lean and hollow-cheeked, body spare and hard with poor diet, clothes crumpled and ill-fitting, but there was no opportunity to wash and change.

They didn't go to the hospital itself, but instead to the nurses' home. If she was on duty he would wait, even if it meant booking a room for the night and travelling to Aberdeen in the morning, where he meant to stay with his parents and rest up until he found another teaching position. He could only hope Annie was still here, that nothing had happened that diverted her from her vocation. He fingered the letter in his pocket.

A young nurse passed them and went towards the door.

'Excuse me.' Alexander stepped before her. 'Do you know Annie Reid?'

'Aye. I do. We share a room. But she's gone for the night with her young man.' The nurse's eyes looked heavy and her face was flushed.

241

Alexander started as if a stake had been driven into his heart. 'So...so she has a young man?'

'Aye, posh fellow. Comes and collects her most nights.'

'I've not got long. Will you give her this, please?' He handed her the letter. 'Tell her...tell her Alexander was here and he would like her to get in touch.'

The nurse took the envelope. 'Aye, I'll tell her.'

'Are you all right?' he asked. The girl looked as if she might collapse at any minute.

'Aye, but I need to go, I'm...I'm dead beat.' She disappeared into the dark hallway of the house.

Alexander stood for a minute. Annie had a young man. Someone posh. With a sigh he returned to the waiting Maria.

On the way north, Alexander lapsed into his own thoughts. Of course there had been every chance Annie had carried on with her life. She had been so young, too young after all, to know her own mind. If she wanted to see him, she now had his parents' address. She would write. Please, God, let her write. Even if she'd forgotten him, he wanted to see her face, tell her he was sorry he'd been so hasty, wish her happiness in her life.

Maria fell asleep with her head on his shoulder. Poor Maria. She was exhausted. He had to get her to his parents as soon as possible and offload the responsibility. His mother's welcoming arms and chicken soup would go a long way in comforting the girl. If it had not been for Maria, he would have remained in Glasgow anyway and heard the truth from Annie's own lips.

As the train carried him ever further away, Annie walked up the stairs in the nurse's home, planning to study for an hour before retiring for the night. She opened the door of her room and started. Bernie lay curled on her bed, her face white and screwed up in pain.

'Bernie,' cried Annie. 'What's the matter, are you ill?'

'No,' Bernie opened her eyes. 'I'll...I'll .. be fine by morning.'

'You don't look fine. Do you need a doctor?' Annie pulled back the covers and let out a little cry.

A red stain was spreading over the bed around Bernie.

'You're bleeding.'

'A bad monthly, that's all.' Bernie struggled to sit up. Her strength failed her and she sank back down.

'That's more than a monthly. What have you done?'

'You've got to help me. If they find out I'll lose my job. Please Annie, don't tell. I've...I've had an abortion.'

'What? Where?'

'A man a friend knows about.'

'Oh, Bernie. You've seen what happens to girls who get the sepsis. How could you?'

'The man used to be a doctor, a real doctor, and was struck off for helping women. I thought it would be alright, but it hurt like hell.'

'How can we hide this? If you don't turn up for your shift Matron will be called and she's bound to have a doctor look at you.'

'You're right, Annie. I'll need to go to work. I have to.'

'You're in no fit state.'

'I'll be fine in the morning. A good night's sleep. I promise I'll tell Sister I don't feel well. If she sends me to a doctor, I'll tell him it's just a bad monthly.'

Annie piled the sheets up ready to take down to the laundry room. She doubted Bernie would get away with that.

'Where's Tess?'

'In the night nurse's rooms. She's on shifts.'

'Does she know?'

Bernie nodded miserably. 'I made her promise too.'

Annie felt a surge of panic. She doubted whether Bernie was so ill when she last saw Tess and she didn't want to cope with this alone.

'I'll be fine,' said Bernie, 'just let me sleep.'

Annie filled a pitcher of water and set it by her bedside. 'Have a good night,' she said before preparing for bed herself. But she didn't sleep. All night she listened to Bernie's ragged breathing, worried she had done the wrong thing by not getting help.

Next morning Bernie lay on the bed, still and white. Drops of blood had leaked from the sheets and puddled on the floor.

'Bernie,' she shouted, 'Bernie, can you hear me?' Bernie gave a low moan. Annie felt for the girl's pulse and they were fluttering and weak. 'I'm sorry, I've got to get help.'

'No.' But the moan was feeble.

Annie ran down the stairs and alerted the Sister.

'Did you know about this?' Matron's face was red with anger.

Annie stared at the floor. 'No, Matron. The first I knew of it was yesterday morning.'

She raised her eyes and realised her mistake. The admission would cost her her job and chance to be a nurse.

'Yesterday morning? And you didn't think to report it?'

'She…she said it was a bad monthly, she could cope.'

'You have to tell me you did not know about the abortion.' Matron was staring into her eyes as if willing her to say the right words.

Annie wet her lips and mentally crossed her fingers. Turning her eyes down, she said, 'I did not know it was an abortion.'

Matron drew in some air. 'I sincerely hope you didn't. I would hate to think that your carelessness may have cost your friend her life and yourself your career.' She turned to Tess. 'And what about you?'

Tess snorted and jutted out a defiant chin. 'Yes, I did know. And I knew what would happen if she was found out. For pity's sake, her father goes straight to the pub as soon as he gets his pay and the priest has to have his share of what little is left. Apart from the family ending up in the workhouse, you know the stigma attached to having a bastard bairn especially in the Catholic community. She knew the risks, what nurse doesn't, but she was desperate. If she survives this, please let her stay.' She leaned over towards Matron. 'You could cover this up. You're in a position to actually help. Have you no compassion?'

Matron's face grew red. 'I have compassion, but I cannot cover this up, as you put it. We cannot condone nurses behaving in this way, it's preposterous. She knew the risks when she let a man have his way with her.'

'For pity's sake, Matron, I'm pleading….'

'Enough!'

Tess stepped back, her eyes blazing. 'I suppose I'll be dismissed too.'

'Of course. Do you realise the seriousness of your actions? Your misguided loyalty has severe consequences, let alone your insubordination.' Matron's face had turned almost purple. Then she seemed to calm

245

down. She pressed a hand against her forehead. 'I must say I am deeply disappointed. You showed such promise. But the decision won't be mine alone. The case will be heard before the hospital board at the end of the month. Until then I have no other choice than to suspend you.'

'May I see her?'

'Once you are officially dismissed, you may see her as a regular visitor. If she's still here and alive that is.'

'Thank you, Matron.' Tess's voice was sharp. She spun on her heel and marched from the room. Matron sank onto her chair, looked up at Annie and shook her head. 'The foolish, foolish girl. If sepsis sets in, I'm afraid there's little hope.' She flapped her hand. 'You may go.'

In their room, Annie found Tess packing her kist. 'Don't be too hasty, maybe they'll let you stay,' she said.

'They could beg me on their bended knee and I wouldn't stay. It's awful the way some people are forced to live, what they're forced to do just to survive. I've been thinking about quitting nursing anyway.'

'What?' Annie raised her eyes. 'I thought you loved it.' Annie had envied Tess. She seldom studied, yet sailed through her exams passing out higher than any of the others.

'Truth is, I've not been seeing Reggie – well I have, but not in the way you think. I've been attending meetings. Have ye heard of the Red Clydesiders?'

'I don't know...'

'Reggie was one of them and they're still struggling against injustice. You saw it with Bernie, but she's not the only one. Poverty is rife in the slums and the women have the worst of it. Imagine doing the best to keep a single-end clean when rats and bugs infest the place. One lavatory up a close for several families and these

246

are always blocking. They have bairn after bairn that they can't afford. Me and several others are trying to educate the women in birth control, but it's no easy, especially among the Catholics who don't believe in it. They're ruled by the church and they'd rather die than go against the priest. There's a politician, Mary Barbour, she's our champion. She'll help wherever she can. She's gathering support for the Glasgow Women's Welfare Clinic. She's even got a building in the centre. That's what I want to do. Maybe, with my nursing experience, we can at least help those willing to accept it. There's a lot of work to do and I want to be part of it.'

'They'll give you a job?'

'I don't know how much they pay, but I don't care. All I need is a place to sleep and enough to eat. I mean to make a difference, Annie.'

'And Reggie?'

'He sees the real me. Looks don't come into it. We both share a dream and that's more important than anything else.'

'Henry's a socialist.'

'Huh, Henry! He plays at it. He hasn't a clue about the reality. If Daddy stops his cash flow, you'd soon see how committed he is.'

Annie stung at the harsh words, but she couldn't deny them. 'I'm going to miss you, Tess. But I admire your bravery.'

'This is reality, Annie. Maybe someday, you'll join us.'

Annie shrugged. 'I really want to become a registered nurse, then I'll decide what to do next.'

Chapter Thirty-Five.

When her shift ended that night, Simon picked her up as usual. 'What's the matter?' he asked.

She told him about Bernie.

'You're a sweet girl, Annie, but I think you get too involved with your work. You need to leave it behind.'

'It's not just work, she's a friend.'

He ran his hand across her shoulders caressing her neck as he did so. 'Forget her. I've chosen the ideal restaurant for us tonight.'

Annie didn't speak much as they drove through the streets. She didn't notice where they went, or the building they entered. Simon helped her off with her coat and pulled out her chair for her. 'I've managed to get some champagne for later,' said Simon as they took their seats in a cosy nook.

'Couldn't we do something else tonight?' It was always the same. Food and back to the hotel. Sex was the last thing on her mind right now and it worried her that they seldom talked the way she wanted to; he was in too much of a hurry to get her into bed. Then he would fall asleep, while she lay awake, longing for a different kind of intimacy, one where souls bonded. Simon never wanted to discuss important things, he didn't seem to care about what was going on in the world. There was not the depth there had been in Alexander and even, to a much lesser degree, in Henry. It had been Simon's eyes, his smile, the way he ran his hand along her arm, making her skin tingle, that got her, but would that be enough to sustain a lifetime? Did he even want a lifetime? For the first time she regretted having allowed him to make love to her at all.

'Your friend?'

Annie nodded.

'Forget her.' His voice sounded unusually sharp.

'I can't forget her. I'm worried sick. I should have ignored her and gone for help right away. What if I really cause her death?'

Simon's steely eyes hardened. He withdrew his hand. 'Why do you expect *me* to care about a girl from the slums?'

Annie gasped. His face seemed to change before her eyes. Anger made him ugly. She stood up. 'I'm not all that hungry. I think I'll just go home, do some studying.'

'I've ordered, Annie. Do you want me to look like a fool?' His hand shot out and he grabbed her wrist so tightly it hurt.

'I don't care what you look like,' she snapped. She had not seen this side of him before and a frisson of fear raced through her. She dropped back into her chair. When the food came she tried to eat but everything tasted like cardboard. Finally she pushed her plate away. 'I wonder what happens to all the wasted food,' she said, thinking again about Bernie, a desperate girl who risked her life rather than lose her job, a desperate girl whose family would starve without her wage.

'You don't have to worry about that.' There was an irritation in his voice. He waved to the waiter for the bill.

Out on the pavement, he took her arm. Gone was his earlier charm as he steered her towards his car.

She jerked herself free. 'I want to go back to the nurses' home.'

'Don't be ridiculous. Come on, I know you've had a bad day, but I'll soon make you forget everything.'

249

'I do not want to sleep with you tonight. Take me home.' She tried to pull away, but his grip was steel.

'Why are you behaving like this? I don't understand you sometimes, Annie.'

'That's the problem. You don't understand me at all.'

Simon ran his fingers through his hair. His voice suddenly dropped and returned to its smooth velvet tones. 'Look, I've decided on something that might cheer you up.' He traced his finger down the side of her face, cupped her face and kissed her again, long and demanding, creating a fire that raged through her body in spite of her anger. 'Marry me now, soon. I want to be with you every minute, every day.'

Annie scanned his face for signs of affection, but saw only lust. 'I won't give up the nursing.' She spoke when they broke apart. 'I can't live like your mother or other women in her position. I enjoy my work, enjoy the company.'

'You're turning me down?'

'Not exactly. Couldn't we go on as we are at least till I finish my training? I haven't even met your family.'

A shadow crossed Simon's eyes. 'Something that must be remedied very soon. I'm going to tell my parents about us tonight, and tomorrow, I'll take you to meet them.'

'What will they think of me?'

'Oh they'll object, but in time they'll come to love you as much as I do.' He slipped his arm around her shoulders and cupped a breast with his other hand. His breath was hot against her cheek. 'Come on now, back with me.'

She climbed into the car in silence, not at all convinced that she was doing the right thing.

Annie had no wish to meet his family. She imagined that they would not approve of her. She thought she loved Simon, but was no longer sure. She never thought

250

beyond their next meeting, the next time he held her in his arms. And she was content the way things were for now. Other times she felt she was hanging onto him by a thread, a thread that could snap at any moment. But he had said he wanted to marry her. He had really said it!

'Alright now?'

'Yes, yes, I'm alright.' Her brain swam with confusion.

His love-making did not affect her like it usually did. With her mind still on Bernie, she remained stiff and unresponsive. When he was finished he rolled from her. 'Come on, Annie, forget this silliness now.'

'It is not silliness. Don't you feel anything that my friend could die?

'Why should I care? I don't know her.' His face was white, angry now. He jumped from the bed and began to pull on his clothes. 'Let's go. Get in the car, I'll take you back if that's what you want.'

Annie shook her head. Tears weren't far off. 'I think I'd rather walk, thank you.'

'You're mad, it's miles. And it's after ten.'

She knew he was right. The smog was thick, cold and cloying and if she was caught sneaking in late, on top of what happened to Bernie, she could wave goodbye to her career. 'It's not what I want.'

'Then what do you want, for heaven's sake?'

She ignored him and walked to the window where she stared out into the dimly-lit streets. He made a disgusted noise and climbed back into bed. 'Sit there all night if you want to,' he said.

She ignored him. When the first light of dawn appeared on the horizon, she tiptoed downstairs, out of the door and made her way through the grainy streets until she caught an early tram.

251

Chapter Thirty-six

By good fortune, Bernie did not contract sepsis. Annie used a lot of her time off sitting by the girl's bed as her strength gradually grew. The day she was released, Annie came to the door with her.

'Don't worry,' Annie tried to reassure her. 'You'll soon get a job. You're a grand wee worker. You just take care and get your strength back. I'll come and visit on my next day off.'

'But,' she lifted a tear-stained face, 'I'll never have another bairn. I'm that cut up inside.'

'It's hard, I know, but you might get a job working with bairns. There's plenty that need help.'

Bernie's mother arrived in a black car driven by a straight-faced priest with hard eyes. Bernie looked questioningly at the car and then her mother. The woman's face was white and dull, life leaching from her pores. She scowled at Annie, as if she were the cause of all Bernie's troubles, a very different woman than when Annie had met her previously.

'Mammy,' said Bernie. 'Where are we going.'

'Oh, Bernadette, yer daddy'll no have ye in the house. Ye're to go back to Ireland.'

'But, now? Am I no to go home first, see the weans?' Her mother shook her head.

'But, where will I stay – with Auntie Clodagh?'

'Father Flannigan's got ye a job in a laundry. Ye'll be sleeping there too.'

'How often will I get home?'

Her mother shook her head again. 'I told ye, yer da'll no let ye in. Ye've shamed us, so ye have.'

'Mammy, I don't want to go. I'll get another job, maybe in the Singer factory or on the trams...don't make me go.' Terrified eyes met Annie's. Eyes that pleaded for her to intervene.

Annie bit her lip to stop the tremble; she could not understand a father throwing his own daughter out. Once more she felt totally useless. 'Working in a laundry mightn't be so bad,' she said lightly. 'I'll write and we'll meet up again. Your dad's bound to forgive you in time.' If he loved her, how could he fail to, Annie thought.

Bernie suddenly turned around. 'Wait, Annie, there's something I forgot to tell you...'

'What's that?' Annie walked towards her, but Bernie's mother had forced her into the car. She struggled to get out of her mother's grip.

The priest grabbed Annie's arm and pushed her away. 'Haven't you caused enough trouble? You'll never see Bernadette again.'

'A man came to see you...' Bernie's voice muffled as the car door slammed. She was desperately shouting something as the car took off. Annie managed to read her lips as she mouthed the words 'letter for you.' And then she was too far away.

With a heart as cold as the Glasgow air, Annie watched as the car disappeared in the gathering fog.

What had Bernie been trying to tell her? A man came with a letter for her. At least she thought that was what she'd had been trying to say. What man? What letter? Had she said something completely different? Annie turned away sadly. If it was important, Bernie would probably write to her once she was settled, let her know.

As the days passed, Annie's own worries grew. Her monthly period had not come. She couldn't be pregnant, they had always been careful. Then she remembered that last night, Simon's anger and his hurry, and she was suddenly not so sure. She wished Tess was here so that she could ask her what could have gone wrong.

She wasn't sure what she felt for Simon any more. Did they actually love each other? He didn't seem very loving apart from when he wanted her physically. But he had asked her to marry him and they had been happy in the beginning. All couples fall out from time to time, everything would be alright, she reasoned. They would discuss it when he came for her on her next day off. The day he was taking her to meet his parents. In any case, it could be a false alarm, she had been that worried about Bernie.

Three weeks later, Annie stood waiting at the door of the nurse's home. By now she had begun to feel sick although she had not actually vomited.

Where was he? She shivered in the cold, damp air under the wintry sky. Eventually, the cold drove her indoors. Worry rose and twisted and the feeling of dread that had plagued her this last six weeks intensified. Consoling herself with the idea that he had not abandoned her, she decided that he must have had an accident. Then the thought of him lying in a hospital bed seriously injured and unable to get word to her took hold. She had to know. There was a telephone in reception. Nurses were not supposed to use it except in cases of emergency, but wasn't this an emergency? Without an explanation, she would explode. Thankfully, the receptionist was someone she knew and liked. 'Go ahead,' she said, 'I'll keep an eye out for the sentries!'

Her hand shook as she waited for the telephonist to connect her to his town home.

A few minutes later she hung up the receiver.

'Everything alright?' asked the receptionist.

Annie shook her head. 'No answer.'

Clutching her handbag, Annie fled to the outside. He could be anywhere. Unable to settle she took a bus up town and walked the short distance to his door. She saw it from a few feet away. A For Sale sign. She knocked at the door anyway and heard the echoing emptiness within. Now she had no way of getting in touch with him. Pulling herself together she counted the pennies in her purse and returned to the hospital.

'Can I use the phone again, Violet?'

Her next phone call was to the Charleston house.

Pleased to hear Myrtle's voice, she asked after the woman's health, then for Henry.

'Annie. I'm delighted to hear from you. Is everything alright?' he said.

She forced lightness into her words. 'I haven't seen Simon for a while,' she explained. 'His house is for sale. I have to speak to him urgently. How can I get in touch with him?'

'You mean he's dumped you. I told you what he was like.'

'No, he asked me to marry him. He was going to take me to meet his parents this month, but then we had a row and he didn't show up. Henry, what's going on?'

There was a silence for a beat. 'Oh, Annie, you are such an innocent. He would say anything to have his way with you.'

'It's not like that. He was going to take me to meet his parents.'

Henry cleared his throat. 'I haven't seen him either. But I have heard rumours. His father gambled heavily on the stock exchange. He's made some very heavy losses. The whole family are lying low. Lots of families have been ruined by this crash. We've lost a lot ourselves, but my father was wise enough not to invest too much.'

'I knew something had to be wrong. Can you get in touch? Can you phone him – give me his number?' She imagined him being devastated, rushing home to support his family and she experienced a measure of relief. Of course he wouldn't have abandoned her.

She wanted to go to him, tell him that it didn't matter if he was poor, that she would still marry him.

'You mustn't phone him on the estate. That would be rather foolish. I'll get in touch. He'll come and see you, I promise.'

'Please do. I really need to speak to him.'

'Don't worry, Annie,' said Henry, his voice angry. 'I'll make sure of it. He's a coward, you know. If he wants to finish it he'll avoid telling you to your face.'

'He won't want to finish it. He must feel ashamed, not worthy of me. That'll be it.'

Oh, poor Simon, she thought. *I really don't care, I really don't. It'll be hard with the bairn coming, but we can still be happy. I'll show you how.*

'I'll make sure he comes.' Henry's voice was low, not like Henry at all..

He came two weeks later. She found him waiting for her when her shift ended.

'Simon, I knew you'd come.' she gave a little cry and ran towards him, then stopped. There was no welcoming smile, no hands reaching out to take hers.

'Simon, what's wrong?'

'Why do you have to see me so urgently?'

'I wanted to tell you that I will marry you.' She waited for what seemed an age for his response.

'Annie, there's something...' His voice was hesitant. 'You were right. I should not expect you to leave your training until it's over.'

'Henry told me about the money, but it doesn't matter. It's you I want.'

'I can't marry you, especially now.'

'What do you mean, especially now?'

'I have to marry money. I'm sorry Annie, I really am.'

'But you can get a job. It won't be so bad...' she said.

'You don't understand. I'm not going to see my inheritance go down the toilet, not when there's a little heiress who will have me in a shot. It is you I love, Annie. We could still meet, go on as we were. If there's any way I can keep the town house we could still meet there regularly.'

'You...you want me to live as your mistress?'

'Keep your voice down.' He glanced up the street. 'There's no other way.'

'Is she bonny—your new fiancée?'

'God, no. she has a face like a goat. It's the way it is for people like us. We marry who we have to.'

'And have affairs on the side? Is that a normal way to live?' asked Annie.

'It's not uncommon.'

'Well I will not live like that. You could get a job...maybe Henry could find something in the bank.' When she saw the horror in his eyes, she realised that her suggestion was as abhorrent to him as his was to her.

'I've offered you a life most girls in your position would jump at. Why do you even want to continue nursing? I could set you up in luxury once I get all this sorted.'

'Under no circumstances.'

'Then this is goodbye. But remember, I did love you at the time, dearly.'

257

'If you loved me the way I want to be loved, nothing would stand in our way.' As she said the words she realised that her love for him was not that strong either. Heat yes, when they were gripped by desire, but if it weren't for her imminent child, the affair would have simply been something to chalk up to experience. Why, oh why had she ever gone to his bed? But now she had to think of the baby's future.

'I'm pregnant.'

His eyes opened wide with horror. 'What? How? You can't be. I made sure…'

'I don't know how. But I've not been with anyone else, I swear.'

He swallowed visibly. 'I don't believe that. It can't be mine. Let's face it, you jumped into bed with *me* easily enough.'

'What? You think…' She swung her hand back and struck him as hard as she could.

'It is your child.'

His eyes gleamed with fury, he rubbed his hand down his face where she had struck him. 'I'm just glad I found out in time what kind of whore you are. Don't dare try to pin this on me. You won't get one penny, you hear?'

She stared at him in horror. Saw the cruelty in his steely eyes. Had he always felt that way? Had he seen her as a fast woman all along? Had he only said the things he did to keep her in his bed?

A cold anger slowly replaced the fire in her blood.

'Goodbye, Simon. You will never set eyes this bairn.' With icy resolution and no idea what she was going to do next, she marched away from him into the drizzly grey streets.

She glanced back once, but his car was pulling away, without, it seemed, a backward glance. Setting her hand on her stomach, she whispered, 'It's just you and me now, darling.' Fear of the future had already wrapped its shadowy cloak around her. Where could she go? She would have to leave the nursing as soon as her condition began to show. She thought of Alexander. Even if he did come back now he was lost to her as surely as if he had died. And she did not want to return to Raumsey a failure and a disgrace. Although she knew her mother and the reverend would not judge her, others would.

She needed to pour her troubles out to someone and there was only one person she could turn to now. She went into reception and telephoned Henry.

Chapter Thirty-Seven

He stood before her in Kelvingrove Park. A moon had risen over the river and a chill wind rustled the empty branches above them. She pulled her coat tighter round the neck and felt the cold of the frozen ground seep through her shoes.

'Why are you helping me like this?'

'You should know why.' Henry took a step towards her, his eyes never leaving her face. She moved backwards a little. He held her gaze, as if daring her to drop her eyes.

'Henry, no. I told you...'

'You told me about a blaggard who said he loved you and left you pregnant. You told me about a Spaniard who went back to his country and forgot about you. Surely you still don't have any loyalty to either? Look, I'm offering you a way out of this. I can give you a good life, and my parents do like you. They'll come to accept that we're together in the end.'

'And you can bring up Simon's bairn?'

'We can find a way round that.' He wet his lips. 'I'll tell my parents the child is mine. They'll be far from happy, but they'll rush the wedding through, you'll see.'

'But you, can you accept it?'

He took another step towards her. 'To have you as my wife, Annie Reid, I would sell my soul.'

She put out a hand, warding him off. 'Don't...I don't know if I can do that.' Her voice was higher pitched than usual.

He continued to gaze at her, then he dropped his head and stared at his feet. The image of a little boy lost was never more obvious. 'Isn't there any chance at all?' he asked. 'What else can you do?'

'I like you a lot. It's just not ...' how could she word this? How could she tell him she cared deeply for him, but she wanted something else – the excitement two other men had stirred within her. 'It's just that...'

'So you'll go back to the island?'

'I'll buy a wedding band, say I'm a widow.'

'I know you, Annie. You'll never settle for that. Marry me, we'll hire a nanny and you can immerse yourself in charity work.'

She considered that for a moment. Maybe she could work with Tess. She could still use the skills she had already gained and help the cause of women's rights. But somewhere deep inside, she still nurtured a vague hope that Alexander would return, that his love for her would overcome his prejudices. Somewhere in her heart she still believed in the future she once dreamed about. Not in a grand mansion, but with a reasonable income and the ability to help the less fortunate with Alexander by her side. At the same time she knew it was an impossible dream. Her own actions had sealed her fate.

Yet, how could she marry a man she did not love? Would it be fair on him? Would they grow to resent each other over the years? Could she live a lie?

'Thank you so much, Henry. Give me time to think about it.' She set her hand on her stomach knowing she had very little time to think about it.

Chapter Thirty-Eight

Alexander re-read the letter asking him to come back to the island. His replacement, a young woman, had decided she wanted marriage after all and had handed in her resignation.

You were so good with the children, William Dick had written, *They still ask for you. Remember Bobby Gordon? He's getting set to go to university. He told me that it was your influence that encouraged him to turn his back on the fishing.*

Alexander smiled to himself. Bobby Gordon. A third son who would have no claim to his father's land and whose only other choice was the navy or the herring fishing. But Bobby had little love for the sea, a rare thing in an island lad. However, he was good at his lessons, so good he was away ahead of the others, grew bored and was constantly getting into mischief.

University eh? Good lad, Alexander thought. But much as he'd enjoyed working on the island, he had never planned to return. He had relations in America, cousins who, like him, were becoming increasingly worried about the situation in Spain and he longed to meet up with them, share his experiences, trade thoughts and ideas. Getting enough money together wasn't easy and, although he had secured a position in a local school and remained at home with his parents, saving enough would take some time.

As she often did, Annie intruded into his thoughts and he wondered what she was doing now. She had not replied to his letters and her silence told him all he needed to know. Yet he would have loved to see her face one more time, if just to wish her well.

No, he decided, he could make no decisions about his future without at least speaking to her, hear from her own lips that there was no hope for them. The school was closed for half term and the best thing he could do was see her again, put that ghost to rest. He made a spur of the moment decision, went to the station and boarded a train for Glasgow.

He picked up a newspaper from the stall at the station. During the journey he mentally rehearsed what he would say when he saw her again. He settled back and shook open the newspaper.

Suddenly there it was, screaming at him. The engagement announcement of Anne Reid to Henry Charleston.

Disappointment crushed him, not so much for himself, as he fancied he had lost her anyway, but in Annie. She had such high aspirations and now she had thrown it all away for a different life. What a fool he'd been, constantly pining for a girl who would never be his. He caught the next train back to Aberdeen.

Chapter Thirty-Nine

Annie stepped from the tram and made her way to the Women's Welfare Clinic in the centre of Glasgow. Once she found the right address she looked up at the high imposing building. The door opened and a furtive looking woman in shabby clothes and a tired face came out. She nodded at Annie. 'On ye go, hen,' she said, holding the door open. Annie made her way inside a large dim room with a wooden floor, wood panelling on the walls and tall, narrow windows. She took her seat on a bench that ran the entire length of the wall, beside a lassie who looked no more than sixteen or seventeen. Another three older women came in behind her.

Thank God this place exists, thought Annie. These women didn't look as if they could afford a decent stitch to put on their back, let alone another bairn. The lassie beside her lifted her head and tired eyes met Annie's. She gave a small smile of acknowledgement. 'Yer first time here, hen?' she said.

Annie nodded. The woman leant towards her and lowered her voice. 'Get the Dutch Cap. My man'll no use the other, but he has to have his rights, he says. Ken what I mean? Ah've just had one wean and couldn't cope with any more the noo. I hope I can afford to keep coming here.'

'Yes. This place is a godsend.'

When it was her turn she walked in.

'Annie! Good to see you.' Tess rose from behind the desk and came forward to clasp her hands. 'Don't say the Spaniard came good in the end.'

'No, Tess.' And she let loose the tears she had held in for so long.

'Oh, love.' Tess led her to a chair and knelt beside her. 'Look, I'm finished here in a couple of hours. Come back and share my sandwiches. We'll have more time to talk then. Nothing's so bad that we can't fix it.'

Feeling as if a load had been at least shifted from her shoulders, Annie dried her eyes. 'I'd like that. It's so good to see you, Tess.'

Annie passed the time exploring the streets. She came to a fair-sized area where several traders parked their barrows daily and the spreading market enthralled her. The pushcarts boasted a wealth of goods, second-hand clothes, books, jewellery, sweetmeats, cooking utensils and brasses, and all at the most reasonable prices she had seen in Glasgow. From a baker's barrow, she bought two small cakes to share with Tess.

Back in the centre, Tess listened to Annie's story.

'So those are my choices.' Annie finished talking. 'How did I get in the family way, Tess?'

'Nothing's one hundred percent. We have women come back from time to time asking the same question. We do our best to support them. There are never guarantees.'

'I'll have to leave the hospital. Would there be any chance of me working here?'

'We could use you in the clinic, but the pay is minimal.'

'Do you still use your nursing skills?'

'Unpaid. I go into the places that are too poor to pay for a doctor. I do my best. There's a lot of areas where we could use your help. Is Henry still a Socialist?'

'I don't think he bothers much with politics any more. He's making a fair wage with his father and he can give me a decent life. But oh, Tess, I dreamed of so much more.'

265

'I always thought his heart was never in it. I hate to see you throw away your life on a man you don't love, but for selfish reasons I hope you do marry him; you'd have time and freedom to join us. Help the cause.'

'The cause?'

'The suffragette movement.'

'You mean they're still active? But I thought women already had the vote.'

Tess made a pah sound. 'Only for some. The National Union of Women's Suffrage Societies continue to lobby discreetly. And we won't stop until *all* women have the vote. Not only that, we want to do away with the marriage bar and gain equal rights to men. Come with me to the meeting tonight. Millicent Garrett-Fawcett's coming to talk with us. She's an inspiration, I believe.' Tess's voice rose, clear and expressive, a far cry from the island lassie who'd first come to Glasgow. Annie thought she would make a grand speaker herself.

'I've never heard of her, but yes, alright, I'd love to.'

'Good. Join us, Annie. There's so much to do. Now come home with me until it's time to go. It's just a single end, but all I need is a place to lay my head.'

With Tess at her side, Annie edged into a packed hall and found a seat on a long bench. Millicent Garrett-Fawcett was a very old lady, petite and slightly built, her voice was not strong, but her talk was a revelation and not without moments of humour as she spoke about her fifty years of struggle for women's rights. By the time it was over, Annie was as enthusiastic as Tess and her friends.

She couldn't wait to tell Henry on their next meeting. Expecting him to be supportive, she was shocked by his reaction.

'You won't have to work. You'll have enough to do with household duties.'

'I can't believe this. I thought you'd be on our side. Where's all your socialistic values?'

'My wife getting involved with a lot of rebellious women has nothing to do with my Socialist sympathies. Annie, I'm offering you the life of a lady.'

She studied the ring on her finger. 'I'm going to get involved. If you can't accept that then we don't have a life together.' Deep inside she hoped he *would* turn her down. She knew then that she could never love him the way she should.

'Annie, these women are campaigning against prostitutes being medically examined for syphilis. They pass it on to the men they sleep with. They, in turn, can pass it on to their wives who are innocent. How can you think that's right?'

For a moment Annie could not speak. Then, with her blood so hot that she felt her body could not contain it, she spluttered. 'Then test the bloody men!'

'That'll never happen and you know it.'

'It's not just prostitutes, it's anyone the police think might be a prostitute. And they can be prosecuted while the men get off scot free. It's probably them who give the diseases to the girls in the first place.'

'Look, Annie, my love, you can't change the way things are. I've learnt that, in the long run, it's best not to try. You'll just break your own sweet heart. I don't mind you helping at the clinic for nothing, but I cannot allow you to get involved with these women. What's more, it took a great deal for my parents to accept our engagement. I haven't even told them about the child. You know I don't care what they think about me, but I won't have them turn against you.'

'You cannot *allow* me? Listen to yourself, Henry. What's happened to you? You've changed so much since we first met.'

267

'It's true I would do anything to annoy my parents once, but if we're to marry, we'll need their support. I want a better wage and a place of our own to live.'

'And we can't stand on our own two feet?'

'I've annoyed my father for too long. He was ready to dismiss me a short time ago and what else can I do? Especially with a wife and child.'

Annie stared at him. She no longer recognised the man before her. 'This is a mistake. I think the old saying, love who you will, but marry your own kind, is true in this case.'

'You can learn to be a lady. What options do you have?'

'Not many, but I know I can't marry you.' She twisted off his ring and handed it back to him. 'Tell your parents I'm sorry.'

Incredulity spread across his face. 'No, Annie, we can compromise. You can't leave me. I know I'm a bit of a fool, just give me a chance.' Grabbing her hand he tried to replace the ring. 'For heaven's sake, girl, think of what you're giving up.'

She jerked her hand away. 'We think differently and we always will.' In that moment she saw his future; he would work in the bank and vote Conservative and put down the politics of his idealistic youth as a passing phase.

'If I have to, I'll go home to bring up my child. But if I stay here, I'll fight for the rights of women.'

'Annie...'

She could swear she saw the tears rise in his eyes.

'You've been a dear friend, Henry. I wish it could have been different, but I think in the end, this is for the best.'

She made her way back to the hospital, her heart simultaneously lighter and heavier. Lighter because she had freed herself from being shackled to a man she did not love, heavier because she hadn't a clue what she was going to do now.

The longing to see her mother had never been stronger. She wanted to sit in the manse kitchen and listen to the sheep and the gulls and the sea, the tick of the fat clock on the mantel, the purr of a contented cat, and the settling of a fire. She longed to hear again the soft island lilt in the voices of the people she met and she knew it was time to go home. By good fortune her body was still neat and, in spite of the discomfort, she wrapped bandages tightly around her stomach to hold her in further.

In another six weeks, she would sit her final exams, and she was confident she could keep her secret until then. If she passed, she would return home a registered nurse. Whether the residents of Raumsey saw her as a fallen woman or not, whether they gossiped about her till their tongues fell out, whether they would ever accept her as one of their own, with the nearest doctor so inaccessible, they sorely needed her expertise.

Chapter Forty

With her recently acquired Nursing Certificate firmly clutched in the hand, Annie knocked on Matron's door.

'Enter,' came the booming voice from within.

'Could I have a word with you, please?' she said.

'Take a seat,' commanded Matron.

Once Annie was sitting, the Matron stood up and came around the desk. 'We will be very sorry to lose you, Nurse Reid.'

Annie opened her mouth but no sound came forth. She had not yet told Matron the purpose of her visit.

'Do you think I haven't noticed? You've hidden your condition well and any other Matron might have dismissed you before now. It is only because of your skill and dedication that I have allowed you to sit your final exams. As I predicted, you passed with flying colours. But you must know that you cannot remain an employee of this hospital. I trust you will marry soon, unless of course, you are married already and kept it secret.'

As Annie began to speak, Matron held up her hand. 'No, you do not have to tell me. Please work your shifts till the end of the week, then leave as soon as possible.'

Annie hesitated. 'Thank you, Matron.' She turned to go. As she reached the door, Matron spoke again.

'Nurse Reid?'

'Yes, Matron.'

'Good luck.'

'Th…thank you, Matron.'

Bemused, Annie trailed up the stairs. She would miss the hospital, the nurses she had grown so fond of, even the patients with their ever changing variety of conditions. She would even miss Glasgow with the trams and the shops and the cafés and the streaming population. But oh, how excited she was about seeing her own folk again.

As the bus rattled along the familiar narrow roads through the flat countryside north of the mountains, memories of the day she first came to Raumsey seeped into her consciousness. The thatched cottages, the sheep and cattle in the fields, crofters with their horse-drawn carts along the road. Then they crested Warth Hill, and the fields of Canisbay lay before them and beyond that, the Pentland Firth and the islands of the north.

'We're nearly home,' Annie whispered, and rubbed her stomach. In these last few days, making sure her baby was born on Raumsey had become very important.

She exited the bus and stood on the shore at Huna breathing in the salt air and listening to the familiar sounds of sea, gulls and wind. White clouds bubbled along the horizon in a sky of harsh blue and feathery greys. In the firth, the familiar yole bobbed towards her. The crossing should be calm today, thankfully.

Since the tide was well out, she picked her way down the lifeboat slip and waited on the concrete base. Owld Sanny sat at the helm, his pipe in his mouth, a week's stubble on his chin, his cheesecutter cap pulled low on his brow. She wondered how old he was. He had seemed ancient to her when she first came to the island and, it appeared, he hadn't changed a bit in the intervening years. His head dipped in welcome and she replied with a smile.

'Annie Reid.' Magnus, the only other member of the crew, threw a rope onto the slipway and leapt after it. At first glance, she was startled at how handsome he had become. He had broadened out since she'd last seen him

271

and the tragic, distant look she remembered had gone from his eyes.

After securing the rope, he took her arm and helped her aboard the boat. His hands, firm and confident, supported her on the unsteady deck and down to where she could sit on a clean, overturned fish box.

'I'll get yer case.' In spite of his limp, he negotiated the rungs of the slip with the ease of a man used to balancing on precarious surfaces and retrieved her luggage from where she had left it beside the lifeboat shed.

'How are you, Magnus?' she asked, when he settled the case in the yole and they cast off.

'I'm doing well. My father died two years since and I own the boat and croft. All Tess wants of it is a bed and a hot meal when she comes to visit.'

'And Nick?' She marvelled at how that name still soured her mouth.

'Scartongarth is thriving, but he never had another bairn. He's drinking a lot and I've heard tell their marriage is far from happy.'

The news pleased her. 'And you?' she asked. 'Have you got a lass?'

Magnus shook his head. 'There's no a lass I've felt enough for.'

She didn't understand why that news should also please her.

It was not until she stepped from the boat, that she felt complete, like her old self, as if she'd breathed something out of the air. Isa and Donald stood, hand in hand, waiting to greet her and in turn they enveloped her in a brief hug.

'Are you too disappointed in me, Mam?' she asked when Isa released her.

'I'm disappointed, yes, but for you, not because of you. But, my, it's grand to have you home.'

The lump that had risen in Annie's throat as Raumsey drew ever nearer, now threatened to cut off her air. She longed to hug her mother again, to breathe in the familiar scent of the lavender water Isa had taken to wearing since moving to the manse, but excess shows of emotion had never been the island way. The old conventions still moved within Isa and in spite of the glistening in her eyes, she held herself stiffly.

Donald took Annie's case. 'We don't judge you, Annie, we never will.'

'Maybe I'll see you later?' she shouted to Magnus who was mooring the boat.

'Aye, no doubt ye will.' He lifted a hand in a salute, a broad grin spreading across his face.

As they walked up the hill, she asked, 'Have you ever heard word of Alexander?'

'Yes,' said Donald. 'I'm sorry Annie, but William Dick received a wedding invitation last week. Seems Alexander is marrying a girl he brought back from Spain.'

His words had the effect of a hammer blow to the stomach. The last shred of hope dashed itself at her feet and, as her head wished him well, her heart split in two. What did she expect? He was marrying a good Catholic girl, in a Catholic chapel and they would live good Catholic lives. *Love who you will but marry your own kind.* 'Whe…when?'

'Six weeks from today.'

Islanders smiled at her on the road, others took in her obvious condition and exchanged knowing looks. No doubt they would gossip about her later, but for now they greeted her warmly. The high-pitched peep of an oystercatcher sounded from somewhere nearby, a flock of ever-present sheep scattered before them. But Annie

273

only saw the ghost of the young schoolteacher walk down the road towards her, wearing a wide smile of greeting. Their eyes met and she knew everything would be fine.

'We've made your old room all ready for you. Donald made a crib for the bairn and all.' Isa's word cut through her dream.

'Oh, yes. Thanks, Mam. That's grand.' Why had she clung to the impossible hope that somehow, she might find him here, returned and once more working in the school?

After a tea of fish stew and oven scones spread with home-made rhubarb jam, the tiredness of the journey overtook her. 'I think I'll go up, Mam. It's been a long day.'

Alone in her old room, she lay in bed, staring at the ceiling and listening to the music of the island. Here she would stay awhile to regain her soul and contemplate the rest of her life. Her child was the most important thing now, but she could still help Tess by writing letters to members of Parliament and to sympathetic businessmen to appeal for donations. Letters to which she had little hope of ever getting a reply.

The first twinges of labour began a week later in the middle of the night. The birth was easier than she had feared and, before dawn, Alexina helped her birth an angry baby boy who was born screaming at the world while fog horns droned and a fine drizzle misted the realm outside her window. She named him David Donald Reid and from the beginning, he became affectionately known as Deedee.

At the start of the pregnancy, she had toyed with the idea of leaving the baby with her mother and returning to help Tess at the clinic, but as she gazed into the tiny red face, felt the body squirm against her, she knew that

she could no more leave this child than she could have
left Sina all those years ago.

Chapter Forty-One

Annie was outside emptying the burnt-out contents of yesterday's fire on the ash-heap. The familiar figure of Young Tom the Post, the new lad, rode his bicycle up the road and stopped at the gate. 'Something for ye, Annie,' he shouted and waved a large brown envelope. She walked towards him and took envelope from his hand. On the outside was her name, but addressed to the hospital. That had been scored out and her island address written above. With a curious frown, she carried it back to the kitchen before opening it. Inside she found a letter and a smaller envelope.

Dear Miss Reid,
I am sorry to say that Bernadette was involved in a fatal accident in the laundry where she worked. They passed her effects back to me. In them was a letter addressed to you at the hospital. I thought you should have it.

Mrs Finnegan, (Bernadette's mother.)

Picking up the other letter and recognising the handwriting, she tore it open.

Darling Annie,
Since I've been away I've thought about you constantly. When you didn't reply to my letters I assumed you wanted nothing more to do with me, but I have to try one more time. The situation here in Spain is

not good, but I have seen many things that have opened my eyes.

Although the way we perceive the world is different, I think we can come to a compromise, for I realise now that there is no one else I will ever love the way I've loved you. You may have found someone else by now and if that is so, I will not interfere, but I pray with all my heart this hasn't happened. I pray that I will have a chance to explain my feelings and that we will be wed one day. I will be home soon and if you still want me, write to me at my parent's home. If I do not hear from you, I will understand.

All my love forever,
Alexander.

It was followed by an Aberdeenshire address.

Bernie's frantic face at the car window when they drove her away flashed through her mind. The way she mouthed the words 'a man came…letter.' The letter was dated a year ago.

Alexander had been at the hospital looking for her. She put her hand to her head and moaned. It was too late now. Much, much too late. The thought of him walking down the aisle with someone else because he thought she didn't want him was almost too much to bear. And what did he mean, My letters? *He wrote to me before*, she wanted to scream. That Sister Ogre, if she got her hands on the mail, she would not have passed it on. That would be just like the spiteful cow.

The room grew darker as if a heavy cloud hid the day outside. The wind had picked up and a splattering of rain struck the window, reflecting Annie's mood back at her.

Isa came into the kitchen, carrying a basket of eggs which she set on the dresser. She pulled off her shawl

277

and draped it over a chair back. Drops of water sparkled on her hair. 'Got caught in that shower.' She turned to look at her daughter. 'Annie, what is it?'

Annie sniffed and wiped her eyes. 'It's not important.' If only she'd received one letter, especially this one, her life would have been so very different.

'Annie?' Isa took a seat at the table.

Wordlessly, Annie handed her the letter with the devastating words screaming from the pages. 'It's too late now. It's all too late. I hope he's happy, I really do.'

Deedee started to cry from where he had been sleeping in his basket. Eager to get away from her mother's sympathetic face, Annie rose, picked up her baby and went upstairs, leaving Isa holding the page that had turned Annie's already fragile world upside down.

Chapter Forty-Two

'What is it, dear?' Maria came up behind Alexander, slipped her arms around his neck and laid her cheek against his hair.

He rubbed her arm. 'Just word from William Dick.'

'Is he coming to the wedding?'

'Yes, yes, he is.'

'Then why the worried look?'

'It's nothing.'

'I have grown to know you so well. There is something on your mind and we promised each other honesty, did we not?'

'It's Annie. She's back on the island. Seems she didn't get my letters, so who knows whether she wanted to keep in touch or not? Anyway, it's irrelevant. She has a child and,' he grabbed her hand, 'Maria, I would never break my promise to you.'

'But you do not love me?'

'Of course I love you, you silly girl. Annie's my past.'

Maria studied his face. 'But hearing this news has made you sad, no?'

'Hearing that she never received my letters? It's upsetting, but I doubt if it would have made any difference. She has a child, so she must have loved another. She's my past, believe me.'

Maria took a deep breath. 'You have been honest with me, so I will be with you. I've been thinking about this. Marrying you would be a mistake. Scotland is your home, but it can never be mine.'

'What are you saying?

'You are willing to marry me so I can legally stay here, but in the end, I do want to return to Spain.'

'No, you can't. It'll not be safe. We've spoken about this.'

She walked to the window and looked over the green fields. 'I've grown to love Scotland and your family, but Spain is my home and the unrest is growing stronger. You said yourself that there is bound to be a revolution.' She turned and stared at him, saw the warring emotions in his eyes and knew she was making the right decision. 'I want to see my family, I want to fight against the fascists, I want to honour the memory of the only man I'll ever love. Please, Alexander, set me free from my promise to be your wife.'

'Maria, you can't go back. Please reconsider.'

'The authorities will not be looking for me after all this time. Dear Alexander, I will never forget you, but I cannot go through with this marriage. Please forgive me. I must go now and explain to your parents.' Unable to say more, she hurried through the door.

She did not go straight to find his parents, but instead went to her room, ran her fingers over the wedding gown once worn by Alexander's mother and was meant to be hers. She twisted the ring from her finger and pressed the metal against her lips. 'I have set you free, my love,' she whispered, as she wiped the tears from her cheek.

Chapter Forty-Three

Magnus came striding up the path with his lopsided gait. He dropped onto the stone seat beside her and picked up the baby, a tender smile on his face. 'Hi peedy manny.'

Deedee was eight weeks old and he smiled, his small fat fingers waving in the air.

'He's a grand wee lad,' said Magnus, a wistfulness in his voice. 'His dad is missing out on so much.'

Annie looked up and saw genuine warmth in his eyes. 'Maybe I'll tell you about it someday,' she said. Since she'd been home she had grown very fond of Magnus, and looked forward to his visits. They had grown close, and she had the feeling that if she gave him any encouragement they could become much more than friends. That he was already attached to Deedee was obvious.

He averted his eyes and tickled the baby's tummy. 'Do ye still think of Alexander?'

'Yes, I do,' she answered honestly. 'But he'll be married and settled by now.' Still, she often wondered where he was and whether he was happy.

Alexander didn't quite know whether Scotland was his home any more. Since returning from Spain his interest in the situation had increased. It wasn't just Spain. Fascism seemed to be growing everywhere and Europe was simmering to the boil. If there was a revolution, he knew he would not be at peace unless he returned to support his family.

In his heart and mind, emotions warred with each other. He would miss Maria, but he had never forgotten Annie. He knew he had to see her again and if the flame still burned, there was no bridge they could not cross together.

It was a mild day when the wind was gentle and the sea lay somnolent in the firth. Annie had taken the spinning wheel and wooden chair from the kitchen and sat with her face turned up to a sun that glanced between feathery clouds.

Uncut corn waved before her, glistening like a golden ocean, the corn stalks moving as one, each shape bending obediently in unison in the soft breeze. The whispering that ran among them was indiscernible from the sound of rolling waves in the sleepy firth.

A dark shape seemed to rise above the ripe corn like a great bird. She shielded her eyes and the shape came towards her taking on human form. A man's form. She stood up, her spindle falling from her grasp.

The man stopped a little way from her. 'Annie.'

Her mouth was already dry. Had been since she recognised the long stride of the man she had carried in her heart for so long. 'Alexander, what are you doing here?' Her eyes roamed beyond him. 'Is your wife with you?'

'I have no wife.'

'But you were getting wed.'

'That was when I thought you wanted no more of me.'

'How did you know I was here?'

'William Dick. Reverend Charleston told him about the letter. Told him about you, your situation, everything.'

'He'd no right...'

'I'm glad he did.' His hands dangled loosely by his sides. His eyes searched her face, but there was a guardedness to them, as if he were seeking something he couldn't quite reach.

'But the girl from Spain...?'

'When I got word from William, I had to see you. I'm not in love with Maria, nor she with me. I wanted to help her to stay in Scotland, but we both have a past we cannot forget. We were second best for each other and we both understand that.'

This was what she had wanted, dreamed about, longed for, but now that dream had become a reality there was an awkwardness between them. A space much wider than the few feet separating them.

'You know I've got a son?'

'Yes. He should have been mine.'

Where was the ease they had once enjoyed? Had she expected it to come rushing back, as if it had been yesterday when they'd said goodbye? The truth was, she had. 'I feel so ashamed of what I did. I was hurt and I reacted badly. I didn't think you'd ever forgive me.'

'If God can forgive, then why should I be a lesser man?'

'What are you saying?'

'I don't rightly know. I had to see you, find out if you still wanted me, find out if there was any chance for us.'

'Could you love another man's child?'

'I was once willing to take on Sina, remember?'

Annie nodded, but she knew by the hesitation in his voice, barely discernible, that her infidelity made this situation different. She knew, too, by the defensiveness in his eyes, that she was as much a stranger to him as he was to her.

'I thought of coming back to work on the island. Here our religious differences made little difference once. I would do it in a heartbeat, but...' He stopped, his eyes still claiming hers.

'But?' she asked.

'Things are getting worse in Spain and I must admit my loyalties are torn. I fear there'll be a revolution and I think I must go back and fight for what is right. I meant to ask you to wait for me.' He stopped and looked at her as if waiting for a response.

'You *meant* to?'

'I realise now that it wouldn't be fair on you.'

'And Maria, will she stay in Scotland?'

'No. Maria will go back with or without me. In her heart she is a strong revolutionary. I think I always knew it.'

In that instant, Annie understood what she had to do. 'Then that's where your future lies. Not here, not with me. You would grow to resent me, I think.'

'Is this island enough for you?'

'Maybe, and then again, maybe not for ever. But if I can fight injustice in the future, it will be in Scotland. The islands are ignored by the government, something I almost forgot. But for now my child is my main concern. I want him to grow up as carefree as the children of the islands.'

Their eyes continued to hold each other's for a long time, and the chasms of religion, loyalties, beliefs, and race, conspired to build no bridges.

'I'm glad I saw you again, Annie,' he said at last. 'Believe me, you'll always have a piece of my heart.'

'I'm glad, too.' She felt she was already mourning the death of the dream she had lived with for so long. Then she released the tension she had been holding, and smiled. 'Come away in. My mam'll have the kettle on. They'll be right pleased to see you again.'

Epilogue

Annie and Magnus sat by the shore in the soft gloaming. Beside them on the grass lay a new bicycle, bought to help her get to her patients more quickly. As the first state-paid, district nurse of Raumsey, she had argued that she needed transport.

Over the hill, someone was playing a mouth organ and the music drifted in the breeze and mingled with the barks of the seals.

'Do you still love Alexander?' Magnus asked, as he batted away the midges clustering round any bit of exposed skin.

Annie shook her head. 'I suppose there will be a part of me that always will, but our lives are too far apart. I was in love with a dream, a memory. We're not the same folk we were back then. I'm glad I saw him, though. I feel like I've buried a ghost. But he left months ago. Why are you bringing it up now?'

'I had to be sure.'

She turned to look at him and his face was so close to hers that their breath mingled and he smelt of the mint leaves he'd been chewing earlier. Magnus was a good, honest man whom she cared for deeply and, suddenly, in that moment, she wanted to kiss him more than anything.

When he didn't move towards her, she leaned closer until their lips touched. His body trembled against hers and his arm came up around her shoulder. The kiss was light and soft and reticent. Finally they drew apart, and he laughed.

'I didn't expect that,' he said.

'Neither did I.' She laid her head on his shoulder. They remained like that, wrapped in a comfortable

285

silence. Finally, she lifted her head and looked into his eyes. 'There's one thing more I have to do.'

'What's that?'

'Get Scartongarth back.'

Magnus said nothing, but she heard his sigh and decided not to mention it again. At least, not yet.

They held each other as the day bled into night and the full moon, casting a silvery path over the ocean, grew more pronounced.

'If we could walk on that road,' said Magnus, his arm tightening. 'Where do you think it would lead?'

'To the land where dreams come true,' she whispered, enjoying the pressure of his body, the sensation of his breath against her hair. She turned up her face to his, inviting his kiss once more and this time there was no more holding back. The kiss deepened and became more demanding, until nothing and no one else mattered.

Finally, Annie broke free and laughed.

'What's so funny?' asked Magnus.

'All these years I've been chasing a dream. Who could have guessed that my destiny was here among my own folk, waiting for me on this island.'

He cupped her face in his hand, turning her towards him. 'But will it be enough for you? Will I be enough for you?'

She looked at him, really looked at him, at his honest, weather-beaten face, at the eyes so full of depth and love. 'I have a strong feeling it will be.' She leaned towards him and kissed him again

.

About the author

Catherine Byrne always wanted to be a writer. She began at the age of eight by drawing comic strips with added dialogue and later, as a teenager, graduated to poetry. Her professional life however, took a very different path. She first studied glass engraving with Caithness Glass where she worked for fourteen years. During that time she also worked as a foster parent. After the birth of her youngest child she changed direction, studying and becoming a chiropodist with her own private practice. At the same time she did all the administration work for her husband's two businesses, and this continued until the death of her husband in 2005. However she still maintained her love of writing, and has had several short stories published in women's magazines. Her main ambition was to write novels and she has now retired in order to write full time.

Born and brought up until the age of nine on the Island of Stroma, she heard many stories from her grandparents about the island life of a different generation. Her family moved to the mainland at a time when the island was being depopulated, although it took another ten years before the last family left.
 An interest in geology, history and her strong ties to island life have influenced her choice of genre for her novels.

Since first attending the AGM of the Scottish Association of Writers in 1999, she has won several prizes, commendations and has been short-listed both for short stories and chapters of her novel. In 2009, she won second prize in the general novel category for 'Follow The Dove' and has since written three more novels in the series, *The Broken Horizon, The Road to Nowhere and Isa's Daughter*. She has attended an Arvon Foundation course and a Hi-Arts writing program, receiving positive feedback on her work from both.

Catherine Byrne lives in Wick, Caithness.